Harrods
COOKERY BOOK

MARILYN ASLANI

**ARBOR
HOUSE**
NEW YORK

Published in the United States of America by Arbor House Publishing Company
and in Canada by Fitzhenry & Whiteside Ltd.
by arrangement with Ebury Press, London

Additional contributions by:
Pat Alburey, Mary Cadogan, Sue Peart, Jane Suthering and Hilary Walden

Edited by Laurine Croasdale, Beverly LeBlanc, Susan Friedland
Art Director Frank Phillips
Designer Mike Leaman
Photography by Paul Kemp
Stylist Mary Jane Kemp
Cookery by Susanna Tee, Maxine Clark, Janet Smith

Library of Congress Cataloging in Publication Data

Aslani, Marilyn.
    Harrods cookery book.

    Includes index.
    1. Cookery, British.   2. Cookery, French.   3. Harrods
Ltd.   I. Harrods Ltd.   II. Title.
TC717.A85   1985   641.5   85-7474
ISBN 0-87795-736-3

Computerset by MFK Typesetting Ltd, Saffron Walden, Essex

Printed and bound in Italy by New Interlitho, S.p.a., Milan

CONTENTS

INTRODUCTION

The Harrods tradition of selling the finest food began 136 years ago, when Henry Charles Harrod bought a small grocery business from his friend Philip Burden in the then less than fashionable Knightsbridge area. Now a tourist landmark, Harrods stands on 4½ acres of the choicest property in London.

Its slogan – Enter a Different World – could hardly be more appropriate, for Harrods is more of a small town than a department store. Twelve entrances offer access to 230 selling departments where more than 4,000 members of staff attend to the various needs of their customers. On any one day, up to 30,000 customers will enter this different world, a further 19,000 will dial the Harrods telephone number and hundreds of thousands of pounds' worth of transactions will be made.

Although it may not strictly be true, the saying still goes that you can buy anything at Harrods from a pin to an elephant. Because of its origins as a grocers, Harrods has remained true to that tradition and the Food Halls continue to attract tourists world-wide.

Situated in the very heart of the store, the Food Halls occupy a large central section of the shop floor. The grandeur of the Edwardian mosaic tiles and original plaster ceilings blend with the marble floors to offset the variety of produce so skillfully displayed. A stroll through the several, linked rooms could reveal politicians, celebrities and even the odd VIP browsing through the merchandise; local, regular customers dashing in to stock up on everyday groceries; keen cooks and gourmets searching out a rare and elusive ingredient; and visitors who have come simply to marvel at the displays.

The Harrods tradition of personal service lives on alongside the ringing of the checkout registers. You can still place an order for almost anything, and your order will be taken with the same efficiency whether you are sending a couple of cases of champagne to the Far East – or asking for one soft bread roll to be delivered to Kensington.

What is now a unique and flourishing business started in a very small way. Henry Charles Harrod first went into business as a wholesale grocer and tea dealer in 1835 in Stepney, East London. His business grew rapidly, and when one of his customers, Philip

Above: In 1911 building work was completed and Harrods now occupied its present-day site.

Left: This photograph, taken in 1889, shows extensions from 87–105 Brompton Road.

Previous page: 1936 Christmas display of poultry and fish.

Burden, apparently ran into financial difficulties, Harrod took over his grocery shop in Brompton Road, and moved into living quarters above.

Knightsbridge at that time was just becoming fashionable, and business prospered. In 1861, Harrod's son, Charles Digby, joined the business and expanded it further by improving the service and putting regular advertisements in the newspapers.

Seven years later, in 1868, the family was forced to leave their home above the shop in order to provide more space. A new shop front was fitted and a two-story extension was built in the garden.

By all accounts, Charles Digby Harrod was an extremely hard-working and ambitious man, and he expected similar dedication from his staff, stressing that they should always arrive at work with a clean face. However, he was not without his compassionate side, and if he saw a regular customer in financial embarrassment, Charles Digby was known to waive the bill entirely, murmuring to his salesman, "See that he has what he needs and send the bill to me."

And so the business grew, and with it its reputation for excellence and customer service. In 1877 the leases of 101 and 103 Brompton Road were acquired, and a sign saying "Harrod's Stores" was erected above the store front. Additions to the range of merchandise were made, and with the help of a cousin, William Kibble, fresh vegetables, fruit and provisions were brought in daily from Covent Garden market.

One freezing night in early December 1883, when building work on the expansions was almost complete, tragedy struck. A fire broke out, and in a few short hours, a lifetime's work was reduced to ashes. The *Chelsea Herald* of Saturday, 8th December 1883, reported the incident in ghoulish detail:

Harrod's stores are now a heap of ruins. The alarm was raised shortly before midnight, and at half past one in the morning, the fire was at its height. From the raised pavement on the west side of Brompton Road a considerable crowd watched the scene of splendidly terrible character. Only the skeleton of the three large shops and the stores at the back remained, but the fire raged in a seething mass, shooting high up in the air from the inner portion, whilst the flames clung tenaciously to the window frames, mouldings and other woodwork, thus outlining the structure as if by an intentional illumination.

Even in what must have been his blackest hour, for Charles Digby Harrod the customer still came first. Shortly after the inferno, his customers received a letter thus:

Harrod's Stores,
101/103/105 Brompton Road
7th December 1883

Madam,

I greatly regret to inform you that, in consequence of the above premises being burnt down, your order will be delayed in the execution a day or two. I hope, in the course of Tuesday or Wednesday next, to be able to forward it.

In the meantime may I ask you for your kind indulgence.

Your obedient servant,

C. D. Harrod.

PS All communications to be addressed to 78 Brompton Road.

While rebuilding on a grander scale began on the original site immediately, Charles Digby rented premises across the street, and, with the help of an acquaintance, Edgar Cohen, succeeded in fulfilling all the Christmas orders.

Nine months later, in 1884, the newly built store was opened. Once again, the *Chelsea Herald* was quick to chronicle the event:

Stretching for a long way into the distance is the tea and grocery counter, where pyramids of tea and sugar, mountains of coffee are mixed up with tins of biscuits, breeches' paste, blancmange, glycerine, lobsters, plate powder, sugar candy, boot top powder, wax vestas, salt, prawns, phosphor paste, oysters, milk, knife polish, house flannel, dog biscuits, mustard, and a thousand and one other articles.

Next on the right comes the fruit and flower department and here is to be a collection that will hold its own against any Covent Garden shop.

Beyond this is a stall where poultry and game are to be on view, and we are informed that arrangements have been made for a constant and daily supply direct from the country, and to complete this side of the place, there is a long counter where cheeses and general provisions are to be found.

Customers remained loyal to Harrod, and shortly after reopening, the first credit accounts were opened by a few selected patrons, including Oscar Wilde, Lily Langtry and Ellen Terry. A staff of 200 were employed at this time, and the shop day began at 7 a.m. and ended at 9 p.m., except on Fridays and Saturdays, when the store remained open until 10 and 11 p.m. respectively.

Notwithstanding the earlier setbacks, expansion continued apace. In 1891 counters for fish and cooked meat were added to the food department, and in 1897 a French confectionery counter was opened. This counter proved so popular that Harrod's catalogue in 1902 included the following statement: "The directors beg to call special attention to their 'own make' cooking and eating chocolates. These are all made on the premises on French principles, by French workmen, from the finest materials obtainable, and absolute purity and perfect cleanliness are guaranteed. Part of the machinery used in manufacture may be seen in the Department." An impressive list of chocolates followed, including 17 different brands of plain and milk chocolates from 5¢ to $1.00 per pound.

Henry Charles Harrod lived to see the success his son achieved before he died in 1885. His father's death, combined with the strain of rebuilding the store, may have influenced Charles Digby's decision to sell, and in November 1889 Harrod's Store was floated as a public company. Charles Digby remained in charge for a further 18 months, until Richard Burbridge was appointed General Manager.

At the time, the store stretched from 87 to 105 Brompton Road and, as a result of Richard Burbidge's foresight and enthusiasm, the building was finally completed in 1911 and Harrods now occupied the full island site that it stands on today. A new store front had been built and a terracotta facade was supplied by Royal Doulton.

Within the store, redecorating was also taking place. Two new Halls – for the flowers, fruit and vegetables, provisions, grocery and bakery departments – were opened, decorated with green and brown tiles by Malkin, and large dome-topped mirrors. For the Meat Hall, tiles were commissioned for the walls from Royal Doulton. Appropriately for a room that should house meat, fish, poultry and game, W. J. Neatby – Royal Doulton's head of architecture from 1890 to 1907 – used Parian ware tiles in a design entitled "Scenes from the Hunt," consisting of 20 medallions depicting farming and hunting, set in an overall pattern of birds, fishes and trees.

The Food Halls continued to prosper, despite two World Wars, rationing and staff shortages. Few changes were made until the early 1970's when two refits resulted in 50 percent more space, giving the Food Halls a total 45,000 square feet. On 4th October, 1983, Her Royal Highness The Princess Anne officially opened the newly extended Food Halls.

And so, to this day, the Food Halls have retained their unique atmosphere. To wander through them is a feast for all the senses. In the Fruit and Vegetable Hall you can breathe in the delicate fragrance of mangoes and pineapples, admire the ripe melons displayed alongside wild strawberries, kumquats and shiny hot-house grapes. In this room the seasons merge, bringing ugli fruit, apricots and passion fruit to cheer in the dead of winter.

Then there is the charcuterie counter, decked with hundreds of sausages and salamis; the salad bar and

Above: *Clever, eye-catching displays such as the All England Egg Week, photographed in the post-war era, have remained one of the Food Hall's most popular atttractions.*

pasta shop which sells over 500 pounds of pasta every week; the Dairy, where over 500 different types of cheese rest on cool marble slabs. In the Bakery, you can now choose from over 170 different varieties of bread, with even the more unusual organic loaf selling at a rate of 200 loaves per day.

The new Pantry, on the lower ground floor, stocks a huge range of teas, including no less than 24 flavors of fruit tea, including mango and kiwi. The rich aroma of coffee permeates the room, as a choice of 17 blends are ground to customers' requirements.

In the Confectionery, glass counters containing regiments of hand-made chocolates are handled by white-gloved assistants, who wrap the confectionery in decorated presentation boxes. With over 100 different types to choose from, it's hardly surprising that 130 tons of chocolate are sold each year.

In the Meat Hall, 30 butchers stand behind marble counters, ready to advise and cut prime joints of meat. Renowned for its fresh seafood display, the fish department is the most photographed in the building. As in the meat and poultry departments, a fresh display is dressed daily at around 7.30 a.m., upon the buyer's return from Billingsgate Fish Market.

Even for those who are not connoisseurs, the wine department is a must to visit. This is the department which, in 1977, had on display what is believed to be the largest bottle of port in the world; a bottle of 1963 vintage port which will not be ready for drinking until 2020. Called Nebuchadnessar, it contained the equivalent of 48 bottles of port, and would have retailed at that time at $15,000.

Like a huge bustling market under one roof, Harrods Food Halls account for a high percent of the store's transactions, with a turnover which runs into tens of millions of pounds.

And yet, after a century of continued success, Henry Charles and Charles Digby Harrod's original aspirations of excellence in both quality and service are undiminished. The store's exacting high standards are maintained with the same precision now as they were 100 years ago. This is one reason why Harrods is proud to have been appointed purveyor of provisions and household goods to Her Majesty the Queen. It is testimony to the hard work and vision of Henry Charles Harrod, his son Charles Digby and the Burbidge family, that Harrods is what it is today: the store with a difference.

THE MEAT HALL

MEAT

MEAT

In this most famous and splendid of the Food Halls, 30 butchers stand ready to prepare the superb cuts of meat brought in daily from Smithfield Market. Tender and succulent, the quality never wavers, and is perfect for traditional dishes like Steak and Kidney Pie or something with a slightly more exotic flavor, such as Lamb Kabobs Marinated in Yogurt and Onion.

STEAK AND KIDNEY PUDDING

There are many variations of this classic British pudding. In this recipe, which has a straightforward method, the suetcrust pastry absorbs the meat juices and is quite delicious.

Serves 4–6

INGREDIENTS

¾ quantity suetcrust pastry dough
(see page 249)
1 lb beef shin, trimmed weight, cut
into 1-inch cubes
½ lb beef kidney, trimmed weight,
coarsely chopped
½ cup finely chopped onion
1 teaspoon unbleached flour
salt and pepper
2 cups chilled beef stock
(see page 246)

Divide the dough into thirds and reserve one-third. Roll out the dough on a lightly floured surface into a 14-inch circle. Lightly grease a 1½-quart pudding bowl or mold and line with the dough. Fold the circle in half, then in half again, place it in the bowl, open out and press the dough into the shape of the bowl. The dough should overlap the edge a little. Roll out the remaining dough into an 8-inch circle and reserve.

Mix the beef, kidney and onion with the flour and season. Place this mixture in the lined pudding bowl. Pour the chilled stock over the meat.

Moisten the edge of the dough with a little cold water and place the circle of dough on top of the pudding. Gently press the lining and the top layer of dough together and leave it overlapping the bowl by about ½ inch. Cover the top of the bowl with a pleated circle of greased wax paper or aluminum foil and secure with string.

Immerse the pudding in a saucepan with enough boiling water to come two-thirds up the side of the bowl. Steam for 20 minutes, reduce the heat and steam gently for another 3½–4 hours. Serve from the bowl wrapped in a white starched napkin.

STEAK AND OYSTER PIE

STEAK AND OYSTER PIE

During the last century oysters were cheap and plentiful and were often used in pies to pad out the more expensive ingredients. Canned oysters may be used if fresh are unavailable.

Serves 4

Preheat the oven to 375°.

Carefully pry open the oysters and remove from the shells, reserving the liquid. Season the flour with salt and pepper and cayenne pepper and use to coat the steak.

Melt the butter and sauté the onion until soft. Remove from the heat.

Roll out two-thirds of the dough on a lightly floured surface to ⅛-inch thick and use to line a 2-quart deep pie dish. Place a pie funnel in the middle.

Place half of the steak in the pie dish with half the onion. Arrange the oysters on top and sprinkle the liquid over. Cover with the remaining onion and steak, then add the stock. Brush edges of the pie with the beaten egg. Roll out the remaining dough and cover the pie. Press gently to seal, then trim and crimp the edges. Reroll the trimmings and cut into decorative shapes. Brush the pie with beaten egg, position the shapes and brush these with beaten egg. Make a small hole around the pie funnel. Bake 1½ hours. Serve hot.

INGREDIENTS
6 fresh oysters
2½ tablespoons unbleached flour
salt and pepper
pinch of cayenne pepper
1½ lb sirloin, trimmed and cut into ¼-inch thick strips
2 tablespoons butter
½ cup finely chopped onion
1 quantity puff pastry dough (see page 248)
1 cup beef stock (see page 246)
1 egg, lightly beaten

CROWN ROAST OF LAMB
WITH TARRAGON

CROWN ROAST OF LAMB WITH TARRAGON

*A crown roast is always impressive-looking, as well as delicious. It is best to order
the prepared roast as far as in advance as possible. To make your own crown,
however, use half a rib, trimmed 1–2 inches from the end.*

Serves 6

INGREDIENTS

4 lb lamb crown roast, containing
    18 ribs
4 tablespoons butter
1 shallot, sliced
6 tablespoons dry white wine
2 fresh tarragon sprigs
1 tablespoon unbleached flour
1¼ cups beef stock (see page 246)
salt and pepper
1 bunch watercress, to garnish

Preheat the oven to 400°.

Wrap the exposed end of each of the ribs with aluminum foil to prevent the
tips from burning during roasting.

Place the butter, shallot, wine and tarragon into the roasting tin and roast for
50 minutes. Baste the meat frequently. Return to the oven for 10 minutes, then
transfer to a warmed serving dish to rest in a warm place.

Pour off all but 1 tablespoon of the fat from the pan. Stir in the flour, then the
stock and bring to the boil. Simmer for 3 minutes and adjust the seasoning.

Remove the aluminum foil from the bones and place a paper frill on each. Fill
the crown with watercress and serve hot with the gravy.

16

ROAST BEEF WITH SMOKED OYSTER STUFFING

*This smoked oyster stuffing is extremely quick and easy to prepare. Its
splendid rich flavor really complements a good piece of beef.*

Serves 4–6

Preheat the oven to 425°

In a saucepan, melt the butter and sauté the shallots until soft. Remove the shallots with a slotted spoon and add them to the oysters. Reserve the butter. Season with black pepper only, because the oysters are already quite salty. Carefully spoon the stuffing into the meat's pocket. Tie the steak with string in several places to retain the shape. Place the meat on a rack in a roasting pan. Brush with the olive oil and reserved melted butter

Roast for 20 minutes. Reduce the temperature to 325° and roast for an additional 15 minutes per 1 lb for rare meat or 20 minutes per 1 lb for medium rare. Cover with aluminum foil and leave to rest in a warm place for 10 minutes before carving.

To make the sauce, put all the ingredients into a bowl and mix thoroughly. Serve with the pan juices and horseradish and green peppercorn sauce.
Note
This sauce is also delicious with cold beef or smoked trout.

INGREDIENTS
2 tablespoons butter
¼ cup finely chopped shallots
2 oz canned smoked oysters,
    drained and roughly chopped
    (⅓ cup)
pepper
3 lb eye roast, butterflied
1 tablespoon olive oil
Horseradish and Green
    Peppercorn Sauce
1 cup sour cream or crème fraîche
1 tablespoon freshly grated
    horseradish
2 teaspoon green peppercorns,
    crushed
1 tablespoon lemon juice
salt

SIRLOIN WITH HERB STUFFING

*Finely chopped mushrooms, celery and fresh herbs are combined for this stuffing.
Quick and easy to prepare, this dish is ideal to make when there is a
shortage of time.*

Serves 4

Melt the butter in a skillet and sauté the shallot until soft. Add the mushrooms and celery stalk and sauté for 5 minutes. Transfer the vegetables to a bowl and add the bread crumbs, pepper, herbs, celery leaves, brandy and cream. Mix together well.

To make the pocket for the stuffing, place the steak on a board with the fat away from you. Insert a sharp knife about 1-inch in from one end of the steak and slice horizontally to within 1-inch of the other end of the steak.

Place the stuffing into the pocket, then sew up with thick kitchen thread or string. Place the meat in an ungreased cast-iron skillet and brown for 2 minutes on each side. Reduce the heat and cook for 4 minutes on each side. The meat will be browned outside but pink and juicy inside.

Place the steak on a serving plate, remove the thread and carve into thick slices across the grain. Serve hot.

INGREDIENTS
2 tablespoons butter
¼ cup finely chopped shallots
½ cup finely chopped mushrooms
1 small celery stalk, plus leaves,
    finely chopped separately
1 cup fresh bread crumbs
pepper
½ teaspoon finely chopped fresh
    thyme or a pinch dried
1 tablespoon chopped parsley
1 tablespoon brandy
2 tablespoons light cream
2 lb sirloin, about 1¾-inches thick

ROAST BEEF AND YORKSHIRE PUDDING

*Yorkshire pudding was originally cooked under the roast to catch the juices
as the meat cooked and was then served as a first course with thick gravy.
Mustard and horseradish sauce are the traditional accompaniments for roast beef.*

Serves 4–6

INGREDIENTS
4½ lb standing rib roast
lard or beef dripping
pepper
Yorkshire pudding
¾ cup unbleached flour
pinch of salt
½ cup milk, at room temperature
½ cup water, at room temperature
1 egg, at room temperature
*1 tablespoon melted fat, taken from
    the roasting pan*
Gravy
2 teaspoons unbleached flour
1¼ cups beef stock (see page 246)
salt and pepper

To make the Yorkshire pudding, sift the flour and salt into a bowl. Mix the milk, water and egg together and gradually beat into the flour and continue mixing until the batter is smooth and lump free. Leave to stand for 30–40 minutes.

Preheat the oven to 425°.

Place the beef on a rack in a roasting pan, smear with lard and season with pepper. Cook the beef for 20 minutes. Reduce the temperature to 375° and continue to roast for 15 minutes per 1 lb for rare meat, 20 minutes per 1 lb for medium and 25 minutes per 1 lb for well done. When the meat is cooked, transfer it to a warmed serving plate and let it rest for 20 minutes before carving. Increase the oven temperature to 425°.

While the meat is resting, put the fat from the beef into a 9-inch square and 2-inch deep baking pan. Place the pan in the oven to melt the fat (it must be very hot before the batter is poured in), then beat the batter and immediately pour it into the hot pan. Bake in the center of the oven, or on the top shelf for 35 minutes. Do not open the oven door during the first 20 minutes of the cooking time. Cut into portions and serve with the roast beef.

To make the gravy, the meat juices alone may be used. For a thicker gravy, skim some of the fat from the surface and place the pan over moderate heat. Sprinkle 2 teaspoons of flour into the pan and stir it into the pan juices, scraping up the brown sediment. Cook over high heat, stirring constantly, until the flour has browned slightly. (When the meat is carved, any juices from the meat can be added to the gravy.) Add up to 1¼ cups of beef stock to the pan and stir well. Bring to the boil and simmer for 2–3 minutes, then season to taste. Pour into a sauce boat and keep hot.

For individual Yorkshire puddings, pour the batter into 10–12 muffin tins and bake as above for 15–20 minutes.

FILLET OF BEEF WITH FOIE GRAS

Use only the finest fillet of beef for this impressive dish. Because of the richness of the pâté de foie gras only a small amount is needed. Serve with steamed broccoli and new potatoes.

Serves 4

INGREDIENTS

3 tablespoons chilled butter

1 tablespoon olive oil

20 oz fillet of beef, cut into 4 tournedos

salt and pepper

2 tablespoons finely chopped shallot

½ cup port

½ cup Madeira

1 tablespoon canned or bottled truffles, drained and finely sliced, with the juices reserved

⅔ cup beef stock (see page 246)

2 tablespoons diced pâté de foie gras (1 oz)

Melt 1 tablespoon of the butter with the oil in a large skillet and sauté the tournedos for 2–5 minutes on each side, depending on whether you like them rare or well done. Season, remove from the skillet and keep hot.

Sauté the shallot in the fat in the skillet until soft, then add the port, Madeira and truffle juices. Boil rapidly until reduced by half. Stir in the beef stock and boil rapidly until reduced slightly. Add the truffles and pâté de foie gras and simmer very gently for 2 minutes. Adjust the seasoning. Remove from the heat and stir in the remaining butter, a little at a time. Serve at once with the steaks.

BEEF WELLINGTON

This classic dish is said to have been a favorite of the Duke of Wellington.

Serves 4

INGREDIENTS

2 lb fillet of beef

2 teaspoons brandy

pepper

6 tablespoons butter

½ cup finely chopped onion

1½ cups finely chopped mushrooms

1 quantity puff pastry dough (see page 248)

¼ lb smooth chicken, duck or goose liver pâté

1 egg, lightly beaten

Sauce

2 tablespoons butter

2 tablespoons finely chopped onion

½ cup finely chopped mushrooms

1 tablespoon unbleached flour

1¼ cups beef stock (see page 246)

⅔ cup dry red wine

salt and pepper

Preheat the oven to 400°.

Trim the fat from the beef and brush with brandy, then season with pepper. Melt the butter in a skillet, add the beef and brown for 2 minutes, turning to seal all over. Remove the beef from the pan and roast for 15 minutes.

Meanwhile, sauté the onion in the fat in the skillet for 10 minutes. Add the mushrooms and sauté for 4–5 minutes or until most of the moisture has evaporated. Season, then remove from the skillet and cool. Remove the meat from the oven and cool completely. Reheat the oven to 400°.

Roll out the dough to a large rectangle. Mix the pâté with 2 tablespoons of the onion and mushroom mixture and spread it over the top of the beef. Place the meat, pâté-side down, on the center of the dough. Cover the meat with the remaining mushroom mixture. Brush the edges of the dough with the beaten egg and wrap the fillet in the dough. Press the edges to seal and place, seam side down, on a cookie sheet.

Reroll the dough trimmings and cut into decorative leaves and a flower. Brush the dough with the egg. Place the leaves and flower onto the dough and brush with beaten egg. Bake for 20 minutes or until the pastry is golden brown. Transfer to a warmed serving dish.

Meanwhile, to make the sauce, melt the butter and sauté the onion for 5 minutes, then add the mushrooms and cook for 3 minutes more. Stir in the flour and cook for 1 minute. Gradually stir in the stock and red wine, bring to the boil, then simmer 10 minutes. Strain the sauce, if preferred, and serve with the beef.

BRAISED BEEF ROLLS

These thin slices of bottom round are rolled around a herb and green olive stuffing to make a delicious casserole.

Serves 4

Flatten the beef slices with a meat mallet or rolling pin. Set aside and make the stuffing.

Mix the pork with the bread crumbs. Melt the butter in a skillet and sauté the onion until soft. Allow to cool slightly, then add to the pork mixture with the parsley, olives, marjoram and lemon zest. Season to taste and bind with the egg.

Spread the stuffing over the beef slices and roll up, starting from one short edge. Tie with kitchen string in two or three places.

Heat the oil and half of the butter in a flameproof casserole. Sauté the rolls for 2 minutes or until browned all over. Remove from the casserole. Add the onion, celery and carrots and sauté for 5 minutes. Return the beef rolls to the pan, add the stock and bring to the boil. Reduce the heat, cover and simmer for 1½ hours. Remove the beef rolls from the casserole and remove the string. Keep hot.

Pour the wine into the casserole. Knead the remaining butter with the flour, then stir into the liquid, a little at a time. Simmer, stirring, for 5 minutes. Return the beef rolls to the casserole to reheat. Transfer with the vegetables and pan juices to a warmed serving dish. Serve hot, sprinkled with chopped parsley.

INGREDIENTS
4 slices beef bottom round, about
    ¼ lb each
1 tablespoon vegetable oil
2 tablespoons butter
½ cup finely chopped onion
¼ cup finely chopped celery
1 cup finely chopped carrots
1¼ cups beef stock (see page 246)
2 tablespoons dry white wine
1 tablespoon unbleached flour
1 tablespoon chopped parsley, to
    garnish
Stuffing
¼ lb lean ground pork
1 cup fresh bread crumbs
2 tablespoons butter
2 tablespoons finely chopped onion
2 tablespoons finely chopped
    parsley
6 pitted Spanish olives, finely
    chopped
½ teaspoon dried marjoram
finely grated zest of 1 lemon
salt and pepper
1 egg, lightly beaten

VEAL CHOPS WITH PORT AND MUSHROOM SAUCE

The veal chops in this dish are beautifully complemented by a creamy mushroom sauce, the taste of which is heightened by a touch of port.

Serves 4

Melt the butter in a large skillet and sauté the chops for 10 minutes on each side. Season with black pepper. Place the chops in a serving dish and keep hot.

Add the mushrooms to the pan juices and cook for 2 minutes. Stir in the port, stock and cream, then bring to the boil. Boil until the sauce has reduced and thickened. Adjust the seasoning and spoon the mushrooms and sauce over the chops. Sprinkle with the chopped parsley and serve.

INGREDIENTS
4 tablespoons butter
4 veal shoulder chops, about ½ lb
    each
pepper
1½ cups sliced mushrooms
2 tablespoons port
½ cup chicken stock (see page 247)
½ cup heavy cream
1 tablespoon chopped parsley

BEEF TENDERLOIN WITH ANCHOVY SAUCE

A beef tenderloin is always popular. The anchovy extract in this sauce
provides a sharp taste to off-set the richness of the beef.

Serves 4

INGREDIENTS

2½ lb beef tenderloin
pepper
2 tablespoons olive oil
3 slices bacon, halved
10 tablespoons butter, melted
3 tablespoons dry white wine
¼ cup finely chopped shallots
1 bay leaf
Sauce
4 egg yolks
2½ tablespoons dry white wine
2 tablespoons chilled butter
1 tablespoon anchovy extract

Preheat the oven to 425°.

Trim the beef and tie with kitchen string in about four places, to keep the shape. Season with pepper.

Heat the olive oil in a large skillet and sauté the meat, turning, until browned all over. Transfer to a small roasting pan. Cover with the bacon and pour the melted butter and white wine over. Add the shallots and bay leaf. Roast for 10 minutes. Baste, then reduce the temperature to 375° and cook for 15–20 minutes more, if you like the meat rare, or up to 30–35 minutes for well done.

Meanwhile, to prepare the sauce, place the egg yolks in a bowl and beat until thickened. Beat in 1½ tablespoons of the wine and half the butter. Place in the top of a double boiler over simmering water and cook, stirring constantly, for 10–15 minutes or until thickened. Beat in the remaining butter, a little at a time. Cover and keep warm.

Transfer the meat to a warmed serving plate. Remove the string and the bacon and leave to rest in a warm place for 10 minutes before carving.

Scrape any sediment from the bottom of the roasting pan and strain the juices. Stir in the remaning wine and the anchovy extract, then gradually beat into the sauce. Carve the meat into slices and serve with the sauce.

LAMB CASSEROLE WITH CARAWAY SEED DUMPLINGS

This is a filling casserole, ideal for serving on a chilly winter evening.
The flavorful dumplings make the casserole into a complete meal.

Serves 4

INGREDIENTS

3 lb loin lamb chops, trimmed
4 tablespoons seasoned flour
1 cup finely chopped onions
1½ cups diced carrots
salt and pepper
5 cups hot chicken stock (see page
 247)
1 tablespoon chopped parsley
Caraway seed dumplings
¾ cup unbleached flour
¼ teaspoon baking powder
½ cup shredded beef suet
large pinch of salt
½ teaspoon caraway seeds
about 5 tablespoons cold water

Preheat the oven to 350°.

Coat the chops in the seasoned flour.

Place half the onions and carrots in the base of a casserole. Place the meat on top, then put the remaining vegetables on top. Season, then pour the stock over. Cover and cook the casserole for 2½ hours.

To make the dumplings, mix the flour, baking powder, suet, salt and caraway seeds together in a bowl. Add sufficient water to make a firm, stiff dough. Divide the mixture into 8 equal portions and shape into balls.

Add the dumplings to the casserole and cook for 30 minutes. Sprinkle with chopped parsley and serve.

ROAST LAMB WITH CHERRY PILAF

ROAST LAMB WITH
CHERRY PILAF

A half leg or whole shoulder of lamb may be used for this recipe.
The lamb is accompanied by deep pink rice which has been tinted by the cherry juices.

Serves 4

Preheat the oven to 350°.

Place the lamb on a rack in a roasting pan. Spread half the butter all over and season. Roast for 20 minutes per 1 lb, plus 20 minutes.

Meanwhile, to make the cherry pilaf, place the cherries and sugar in a saucepan. Cook over gentle heat, stirring, until the sugar dissolves. Cover and simmer for 10 minutes, then drain and reserve the juice. Cook the rice in a large pan of boiling salted water for 5 minutes. Drain and rinse under cold running water. Drain well.

Spread the remaining butter over the bottom of a heavy-bottomed saucepan and sprinkle the oil over. Spread one-third of the rice over the bottom of the pan and top with one-third of the cherries. Do not allow either the rice or the cherries to touch the sides of the pan from now on. Continue to make layers, building them up into a pyramid, ending with a layer of rice. Spoon the cherry juice evenly over the rice. Wrap the saucepan lid in a clean dish towel. Cover and cook over gentle heat for 25 minutes.

About 20 minutes before the lamb is cooked, brush it with the red currant jelly and stir the port into the cooking juices. When cooked, transfer it to a warmed serving plate and rest in a warm place for 10 minutes.

Plunge the bottom of the pan with the cooked rice in cold water for 30 seconds. Spoon the rice onto a serving plate, leaving the bottom layer behind. If this crust is not too dark, it may be served with the rice, but the sugar in the syrup tends to burn this layer slightly. Keep hot.

Skim the pan juices, strain and serve with the meat and the rice.

INGREDIENTS

3 lb half leg or shoulder of lamb
4 tablespoons butter
salt and pepper
3 tablespoons red currant jelly
6 tablespoons port
Cherry pilaf
¾ lb fresh Bing cherries, pitted
    weight
½ cup sugar
2 cups basmati rice, rinsed and
    drained
1 tablespoon peanut oil

23

LAMB KABOBS MARINATED IN YOGURT AND ONION

Marinating the lamb in yogurt breaks down the tough fibers in the meat, making it as tender as butter. Serve in warm pita bread with shredded lettuce and sliced tomatoes and cucumbers instead of rice, if preferred.

Serves 4

INGREDIENTS

1 lb leg of lamb, boned weight, in
  1 piece
½ cup grated onion
1¼ cups plain yogurt
salt and pepper
Rice
1 cup long-grain rice
4 tablespoons butter
4 egg yolks

Trim any fat off the meat, then cut it in half horizontally. Cut the 2 pieces into 3-inch strips across the grain. Place in a shallow container with the onion, yogurt and pepper. Cover with plastic wrap and marinate in the refrigerator for at least 12 hours and at most 2 days.

Thread the meat onto skewers. Cook under a hot broiler for about 15 minutes, turning frequently. Season with salt. Meanwhile, cook the rice in boiling salted water for 15 minutes or until tender. Spoon the rice onto individual serving plates. Each guest should mix the rice with butter and a raw egg yolk, then top with a kabob. Serve hot.

LAMB KABOBS MARINATED IN YOGURT AND ONION

PORK TENDERLOIN WITH TRUFFLES AND THYME

This dish combines the flavors of fresh thyme and truffles, one of the world's most sought-after delicacies. By using bottled truffle trimmings, you can enjoy the taste without the vast expense.

Serves 4

Make a couple of incisions down the eye of the meat to form a shallow pocket. Drain the juices from the truffles and reserve. Mix the truffles, garlic, thyme, butter and seasoning together and place in the incision in the pork. Secure at 1-inch intervals with string, cover and chill for 24 hours.

Preheat the oven to 375°.

Place the meat in a roasting pan and season. Roast for 1½ hours. It is cooked, if the juices run clear when a skewer or fork is inserted into the center.

Remove the pork from the roasting pan, pour off the excess fat and stir in the flour. Cook, stirring, for 1 minute. Stir in the wine and cook over moderately high heat for 1 minute. Stir in the truffle juices and stock and simmer for 5 minutes. Season to taste. Slice the pork, pour a little of the sauce over and serve the remaining sauce separately.

INGREDIENTS

3 lb pork loin tenderloin
¼ cup truffle trimmings
1 garlic clove, crushed
½ teaspoon dried chopped fresh thyme or ¼ teaspoon dried
2 tablespoons butter
salt and pepper
1 tablespoon unbleached flour
¼ cup dry white wine
1¼ cups chicken stock (see page 247)

PORK TENDERLOIN WITH TRUFFLES AND THYME

BAKED HAM GLAZED WITH HONEY, ORANGE AND GINGER

This is an excellent way of cooking ham, as it absorbs the flavor of the glaze, and remains succulent and tender.

Serves 8

Soak the ham in sufficient cold water to cover for 3 hours, then discard the water.

Place the ham, onion stuck with cloves, bay leaf, peppercorns and 1 cup of the white wine in a large saucepan. Add sufficient cold water to cover. Bring to the boil, cover the pan and boil gently for 1 hour.

Preheat the oven to 400°.

Meanwhile, to make the glaze, place the brown sugar, 2 tablespoons of the orange juice, honey, ginger and mustard in a bowl and mix well.

Drain the ham and discard the vegetables. (Reserve the stock for soup if it is not too salty.) Remove the skin from the ham, score the fat into a diamond pattern, and stud with cloves. Place the ham in a baking dish and pour the remaining wine and orange juice into the dish.

Cover the ham with one-third of the glaze. Bake for 45 minutes. Baste the ham with the cooking juices and glaze 3–4 times during cooking. Discard the juices and serve the ham hot or chilled, garnished with orange slices and chicory.

INGREDIENTS
4 lb smoked ham
1 onion stuck with 3 cloves
1 bay leaf
6 peppercorns
1¼ cups dry white wine
3 tablespoons dark brown sugar
½ cup orange juice
1 tablespoon honey
½ teaspoon ground ginger
1 tablespoon Dijon mustard
whole cloves for studding
orange slices and chicory, to garnish

LAMB WITH GARLIC POTATOES

This dish has the most wonderful aroma and is easy to cook. The meat is placed directly onto the oven rack to roast, enabling the garlic-flavored juices to seep down into the dish of potatoes underneath.

Serves 4

Preheat the oven to 375°.

Grease a large, shallow baking dish. Crush 2 garlic cloves and layer with the potatoes and seasoning. Dot with the butter, reserving 1 tablespoon. Cut the remaining garlic into slivers. Pierce the meat with a sharp knife in several places and insert the garlic slivers. Push the sprig of rosemary into the center of the lamb. Rub the remaining butter over the meat and season well.

Place the meat directly onto the oven rack with the dish of potatoes on the shelf below. The juices will drip down onto the potatoes as the meat cooks. Roast for 1½ hours. Serve with the potatoes and a green vegetable or salad.

INGREDIENTS
3 large garlic cloves
2½ lb potatoes, peeled and thinly sliced
salt and pepper
5 tablespoons butter
3 lb half leg of lamb
large fresh rosemary sprig

LAMB STUFFED WITH ROQUEFORT CHEESE AND MINT

*A boned shoulder of lamb is easy to carve and produces neat slices of
meat and stuffing.*

Serves 6

INGREDIENTS

3 lb shoulder of lamb, boned
*6 oz Roquefort cheese, crumbled
   (1 cup)*
2 sprigs fresh mint, finely chopped
26- × 3-inch strip of pork fat
2 tablespoons butter
3 tablespoons mint jelly
⅔ cup port
⅔ cup beef stock (see page 246)
salt and pepper

Preheat the oven to 350°.

Lay the lamb skin-side down on a flat surface. Score a cross, about 3-inches wide, in the center of the meat. Mix the cheese with the mint and place it in the center of the meat. Pull the edges of the meat up and around the filling to make a neat roll. Wrap the strip of pork fat around the meat, overlapping the ends, to cover completely. Tie tightly with string in 8 even wedge-shaped sections.

Weigh and smear the joint all over with butter. Place in a roasting pan. Roast, allowing 25 minutes per 1 lb plus 25 minutes. The lamb is cooked when a skewer or fork is inserted into the thickest part and the juices run clear.

About 15–20 minutes before the end of the cooking time, remove the string and the fat. Brush the lamb with the mint jelly. Stir the port into the pan and return the roast to the oven, basting several times. Transfer to a warmed serving plate and leave in a warm place to rest for 15 minutes.

Stir the pan juices and stir in the stock. Simmer, stirring frequently, over moderately high heat, for 10 minutes, until slightly reduced. Adjust the seasoning and serve with the meat.

PORK ROASTED IN HONEY, SOY SAUCE AND SHERRY

*Marinating pork in this way makes it deliciously sweet and tender.
Cook directly on the oven rack with a tray of water placed underneath
to catch the drips. This not only prevents burning, but keeps the pork
moist during cooking. Hoisin sauce and miso paste are available from
specialty stores or gourmet delicatessens.*

Serves 6

INGREDIENTS

3 lb boned half leg of pork
pepper
Marinade
¾ cup honey
3 tablespoons medium-dry sherry
6 tablespoons light soy sauce
3 tablespoons hoisin sauce
3 tablespoons miso paste

Remove the rind from the pork but leave on as much fat as possible. Lay the meat out flat and cut into 4 equal strips. Slash diagonally 3 or 4 times. Season with pepper.

To make the marinade, mix 6 tablespoons of the honey with the remaining ingredients in a shallow container. Place the meat in the marinade, cover with plastic wrap and marinate in the refrigerator overnight.

Preheat the oven to 375°.

Place a tray filled with about 1-inch water in the oven. Remove the meat from the marinade and place it directly onto the oven rack with the tray underneath. Roast for 30 minutes.

Remove each piece of meat, one by one, then dip it into the marinade and return to the oven. Roast for a further 15 minutes, dip in the marinade and return to the oven. Repeat once more. Cook for a further 10 minutes. Remove the meat from the oven and immediately brush it with the remaining honey. Serve hot or cold.

LOIN OF VEAL WITH TURMERIC AND LEMONS

The addition of turmeric gives the meat a delicate golden tinge.
Lamb is also very successful cooked this way. If liked, during the last
30 minutes of the cooking time, arrange new potatoes, carrots and
pearl onions around the meat and cook them in the pan juices.

Serves 6

Heat the oil in a large flameproof casserole and brown the meat all over to seal. Stir in the turmeric and seasoning and sauté for 1 minute. Pour over the lemon juice and water and bring to the boil. Reduce the heat, cover and simmer very gently for 2–2½ hours or until tender. Add more water if the mixture gets too dry.

To serve, slice the meat and serve with the pan juices.

INGREDIENTS
2 tablespoons peanut oil
3 lb veal rump roast, boned and rolled
1 teaspoon ground turmeric
salt and pepper
juice of 1 lemon
6 tablespoons water

NOISETTES D'AGNEAU CHASSEUR

This is a delicious combination of tender lamb with lightly sautéed mushrooms,
shallots and white wine. Accompany with a red or white Burgundy.

Serves 4

Melt the butter with the oil in a large skillet and sauté the lamb for 2–5 minutes on each side, depending on whether you like it rare or well done. Remove from the skillet and keep hot.

Pour off all but about 2 tablespoons of the fat from the skillet. Sauté the shallots and garlic until soft. Add the mushrooms and sauté for 3 minutes. Stir in the brandy and wine and cook over high heat for 1 minute.

Mix the stock, arrowroot and tomato paste together and stir into the skillet with the tomatoes and tarragon. Simmer gently for 10 minutes.

Adjust the seasoning and stir in the parsley. Serve at once with the lamb.

INGREDIENTS
3 tablespoons butter
1 tablespoon olive oil
12 boneless double loin lamb chops, about 1-inch thick
¼ cup finely chopped shallots
1 garlic clove, crushed
1 cup thinly sliced mushrooms
1 tablespoon brandy
⅔ cup dry white wine
⅔ cup chicken stock (see page 247)
1 teaspoon arrowroot
1 teaspoon tomato paste
4 tomatoes, peeled, seeded and chopped
1½ teaspoons chopped fresh tarragon or basil or ¾ teaspoon dried
salt and pepper
1 tablespoon chopped parsley

PORK CHOPS WITH ARTICHOKE HEARTS

*These thick pork chops from the loin are simmered in a wine and
tomato sauce, delicately flavored with marjoram, and garnished with
whole artichoke hearts.*

Serves 4

INGREDIENTS

2 tablespoons butter

2 tablespoons olive oil

1 slice bacon, finely chopped

¼ cup finely chopped shallots

1 large garlic clove, crushed

4 pork loin chops, about ½ lb each

¼ teaspoon dried marjoram

1¼ cups dry white wine

salt and pepper

1½ teaspoons tomato paste

¼ cup water

14 oz can artichoke hearts, drained

Melt the butter with the oil in a flameproof casserole and sauté the bacon, shallots and garlic for 3 minutes. Add the pork chops, sprinkle with majoram, and sauté for 3 minutes on each side to brown. Pour in the wine and season. Cook, uncovered, for 10 minutes.

Blend the tomato paste with the water and stir into the liquid in the pan. Bring to the boil, reduce the heat, cover and simmer for 30 minutes. Add the artichoke hearts, cover and simmer for a further 10 minutes. Serve hot.

STEAK TARTARE

*Steak Tartare is raw filet mignon which is finely ground and served
with a variety of chopped vegetables. The meat is shaped into
individual mounds and garnished with raw egg yolks in their shells.*

Serves 4

INGREDIENTS

*1 lb lean filet mignon, finely chopped
or ground*

salt and pepper

Worcestershire sauce, to taste

2 tablespoons sunflower seed oil

½ cup finely chopped onion

*1 green pepper, seeded and finely
chopped*

1 tablespoon chopped capers

2 tablespoons finely chopped parsley

4 egg yolks, in their half shells

lettuce leaves, to garnish

mayonnaise, to serve

Mix the ground beef with seasoning, Worcestershire sauce and the oil. Mix thoroughly, then form into 4 mounds. Arrange on individual plates and surround with the onion, green pepper, capers and parsley.

Make a shallow indentation in the center of each mound of ground beef and place an egg yolk in its shell inside. Garnish with lettuce leaves and serve with mayonnaise.

RAISED PORK AND APPLE PIE

*Raised pork pies are a traditional English dish with sage and apple as a
tasty addition. During the 18th century, apples were commonly
used in savory pies.*

Serves 8–10

To make the veal stock, place the veal knuckle, salt, peppercorns and bouquet garni in a large saucepan with enough cold water to cover. Bring to the boil, skim the surface, cover and simmer for 2 hours. Strain through a piece of cheesecloth, then skim off the fat when cool.

Sift the flour and salt into a mixing bowl. Bring the shortening and water to the boil, remove from heat and quickly stir it into the flour to form a dough. Cool slightly, then knead the dough until smooth. Cut off one-third of the dough and place it under an upturned bowl until required.

Flour the inside of an 8-inch springform pan or pâté mold. Roll out the dough and line the bottom and sides of the pan. Preheat the oven to 375°.

Mix the bacon, pork, seasoning and sage together and add 2 tablespoons of the veal stock to moisten. Press half the mixture into the pastry shell. Cover with apple slices and press the remaining mixture over the top.

Roll out the remaining dough to cover the pie. Brush the edges of the pie with water, place the lid in position and press the edges together to seal. Mark around the edge of the pie with a fork and make a hole in the center. Brush with the beaten egg. Reroll the trimmings and cut them into leaves. Arrange on top of the pie and brush with the egg. Place on a cookie sheet.

Bake for 1 hour. Reduce the temperature to 350° and bake for a further 1–1¼ hours. Remove the outside of the pan and brush the sides of the pie with beaten egg, then return to the oven for about 10 minutes until golden. Carefully pour the veal stock through the hole in the center of the pie and leave for 2–3 hours until the stock has set to a jelly. Remove from the bottom of the pan.

INGREDIENTS
3 cups unbleached flour
¼ teaspoon salt
½ cup shortening or 4 tablespoons
  butter
¾ cup cold water
8 bacon slices, diced
1½ lb lean pork, cut into ½-inch
  cubes
salt and pepper
2 teaspoons chopped fresh sage or
  1 teaspoon dried
1 large tart apple, peeled, cored and
  thinly sliced
beaten egg, to glaze
Veal stock
1 veal knuckle, chopped
salt
6 black peppercorns
bouquet garni

VEAL IN PASTRY

This cut of meat is extremely tender. The veal is spread with chicken liver pâté,
pistachio nuts and ham, then rolled and encased in puff pastry.

Serves 4

INGREDIENTS

2 tablespoons butter

1 lb boned and rolled veal roast

salt and pepper

¼ lb smooth chicken liver pâté

2 tablespoons shelled, skinned and
*   roughly chopped pistachio nuts*

4 large slices prosciutto or
*   Westphalian ham*

½ quantity puff pastry (see
*   page 248)*

1 egg, beaten

Sauce

⅔ cup dry white wine

⅔ cup chicken stock (see page 247)

½ cup sliced mushrooms

1 tablespoon red currant jelly

Preheat the oven to 375°.

Melt the butter in a roasting pan, add the veal and turn until it is well coated with the butter. Roast for 20 minutes. Remove from the pan and leave until cold. Reserve the meat juices in the roasting pan. Increase temperature to 425°.

Season the veal with salt and pepper. Combine the pâté and pistachio nuts and spread over the veal. Completely wrap the veal in the ham.

Roll out the dough on a lightly floured surface to a rectangle large enough to completely encase the meat. Place the meat in the center, wrap the dough around and seal the edges securely by brushing with water and pressing together. Reroll the trimmings and use to garnish. Brush beaten egg over the dough and place, seam side down, on a dampened cookie sheet. Bake for 25 minutes or until crisp and golden. Transfer to a warmed serving dish.

To make the sauce, add the wine, stock and mushroom slices to the juices in the roasting pan and boil rapidly until reduced by half. Stir in the jelly.

VEAL IN PASTRY

PORK LASAGNE

This delicious pasta dish, flavored with marjoram and Italian cheeses,
is best served piping hot with a green side salad.

Serves 6–8

Heat the oil in a skillet and sauté the bacon, onion, and garlic for 5 minutes. Add the pork and cook, stirring, until browned. Stir in the tomato paste, then the wine, water, seasoning, bay leaf and marjoram. Bring to the boil, cover, reduce the heat and simmer for 1 hour.

Place a layer of lasagne in a buttered shallow oblong baking dish. Top with a layer of meat, then some ricotta cheese. Continue in this way, ending with a layer of pasta.

Preheat the oven to 400°.

For the sauce, melt the butter and stir in the flour. Cook, stirring, for 1 minute. Remove from the heat and gradually stir in the milk. Add the bay leaf, salt, pepper and nutmeg. Cook over a gentle heat, stirring constantly, for 5 minutes.

Pour the béchamel sauce over the lasagne. Sprinkle with Parmesan cheese and dot with the butter. Bake for 30–40 minutes or until the topping is golden brown. Serve hot.

INGREDIENTS
2 tablespoons olive oil
4 bacon slices, finely chopped
½ cup finely chopped onion
1 garlic clove, crushed
1 lb lean ground pork
2 tablespoons tomato paste
½ cup dry red wine
1¼ cups water or stock
salt and pepper
1 bay leaf
½ teaspoon dried marjoram
½ lb fresh lasagne
¾ lb ricotta cheese (2 cups)
2 tablespoons finely grated
    Parmesan cheese
2 tablespoons butter
Béchamel sauce
2 tablespoons butter
¼ cup unbleached flour
2 cups milk
1 bay leaf
pinch of grated nutmeg

PAUPIETTES DE VEAU

Paupiettes are thin slices of meat or fish which are stuffed and rolled.
These paupiettes are filled with prosciutto and fresh tarragon and
cooked in a subtle wine sauce.

Serves 4

Place the veal scallops between two sheets of wax paper and flatten with a meat mallet or rolling pin. Lay the scallops flat and cover with the ham, trimming to fit if necessary. Season and place 2 tarragon sprigs on each. Roll up and secure with toothpicks. Coat lightly in seasoned flour.

Melt 2 tablespoons of the butter in a skillet and sauté the shallots and any ham trimmings until the shallot is soft. Add the veal rolls and cook until evenly browned all over. Stir in the wine, tomato paste and stock. Season to taste. Cover the pan tightly and cook over gentle heat for 20 minutes or until tender. Transfer the veal rolls to a warmed serving dish and remove the toothpicks. Keep hot. Boil the pan juices until reduced and thickened. Taste and adjust the seasoning. Stir in the remaining butter, heat until melted, then pour over the veal rolls and serve.

INGREDIENTS
4 veal scallops
1 oz prosciutto, cut into 4 slices
salt and pepper
8 fresh tarragon sprigs
seasoned flour
3 tablespoons butter
⅔ cup finely chopped shallot
⅔ cup dry white wine
2 teaspoons tomato paste
¼ cup veal stock

VEAL MEATBALLS WITH CAPER AND CREAM SAUCE

Serve with buttered noodles and a green vegetable such as snow peas or French-style green beans.

Serves 4

INGREDIENTS

1 lb lean ground veal
½ cup finely chopped onion
1 tablespoon chopped parsley
salt and pepper
pinch of grated nutmeg
1 cup fresh bread crumbs
1 egg, lightly beaten
seasoned flour
4 tablespoons unsalted butter
¼ cup dry white wine
1 tablespoon drained capers
⅔ cup sour cream
chopped parsley, to garnish

Mix the veal, onion, parsley, seasoning, nutmeg and bread crumbs together. Mix in the lightly beaten egg.

Shape the mixture into 16 oval balls and toss in the seasoned flour. Melt the butter in a large skillet and sauté the meatballs for 15 minutes or until evenly browned and cooked through.

Remove from the skillet with a slotted spoon and keep hot while preparing the sauce. Pour off half the fat from the skillet, then add the wine, scraping the bottom to loosen any sediment. Bring to the boil.

Reduce the heat and stir in the capers and sour cream. Heat gently but do not allow the sauce to boil. Taste and adjust the seasoning. Arrange the meatballs on a warmed serving plate, pour the sauce over the top and sprinkle with parsley.

VEAL CHOPS WITH SAGE AND GRUYERE CHEESE

These veal chops are cooked in bread crumbs, seasoned with sage leaves to give a distinctive flavor, then topped with melted cheese.

Serves 4

INGREDIENTS

1½ cups fresh bread crumbs
salt and pepper
5 fresh sage leaves, finely shredded, or 1 teaspoon dried
4 veal shoulder chops, about ½ lb each
1 egg, lightly beaten
8 tablespoons butter
½ cup finely grated Gruyère cheese (3 oz)
4 fresh sage leaves or parsley sprigs to garnish

Mix the bread crumbs with the seasoning and the shredded sage leaves.

Coat the chops first in beaten egg, then in the bread crumbs, pressing them on lightly.

Melt the butter in a large skillet and sauté the chops over moderate heat for 4 minutes on each side or until the coating is crisp and golden brown. Remove the chops from the pan and place them in a flameproof serving dish. Sprinkle the cheese over the chops. Cook under a hot broiler for 2 minutes or until the cheese melts and bubbles.

Place a sage leaf on top of each chop and serve at once.

MEAT PILAF

Saffron threads are the dried stigmas of the crocus flower and there are varying grades of quality. The very best saffron is a burnished orange color, and in some countries, it is more expensive to buy per ounce than gold, because 70,000–80,000 crocus flowers are needed to make 1 lb of saffron.

Serves 6

INGREDIENTS

6 tablespoons butter
¾ cup finely chopped onion
1½ lb beef chuck, trimmed and cut into 1½-inch cubes
5 tablespoons tomato paste
½ teaspoon saffron threads
1 teaspoon hot water
salt and pepper
1½ lb green beans, trimmed and cut into 2-inch pieces
4 cups basmati rice
extra butter and plain yogurt, to serve (optional)

Melt 4 tablespoons of the butter in a skillet and sauté the onion until golden. Add the meat and cook, stirring, for 5 minutes or until browned. Stir in the tomato paste and cook for 2 minutes. Stir in 1 quart cold water, bring to the boil, cover and reduce the heat. Simmer for 2 hours or until the meat is tender and the sauce has reduced and thickened sufficiently to just cover the meat.

Place the saffron threads in a mortar and pound with a pestle until they are ground to a fine powder. Place in a small bowl, add the hot water and leave to infuse for 10 minutes.

Add the saffron and water mixture, seasoning and green beans to the meat and simmer for 10 minutes. Cook the rice in boiling salted water for 5 minutes. Drain immediately, rinse in cold water, then drain thoroughly.

Melt the remaining butter with 6 tablespoons cold water in a large deep saucepan with a tight-fitting lid. Spoon a 2-inch layer of rice over the bottom of the pan. Using a slotted spoon, place some of the meat and bean mixture on top of the rice layer. Do not spread the meat to the edges of the pan. Continue making alternate layers of meat and beans and rice, in a pyramid shape, ending with a layer of rice. Very gently pour the sauce over the top of the rice pyramid. Push the handle of a wooden spoon down through the center of the rice. Wrap the saucepan lid in a dish towel and cover the pan.

Cook over a moderately low heat for 30–35 minutes, stirring occasionally. Plunge the bottom of the pan into cold water to prevent further cooking. Spoon onto a warmed serving dish and serve hot. The crunchy rice at the bottom of the pan should be served on a separate plate.

ROAST PORK WITH BLUE CHEESE SAUCE

In this dish the roast pork flavor is complemented by this surprisingly easy-to-make cheese sauce. English Stilton cheese is used in this recipe, although Roquefort or Danish blue can be substituted. If fresh sage is unavailable, rub dried sage on the roast with the salt.

Serves 4

INGREDIENTS

2 lb pork loin
12 sage leaves
oil
Blue cheese sauce
¼ cup hot water or vegetable water
⅔ cup sour cream
½ cup crumbled Stilton cheese
salt and pepper

Preheat the oven to 350°.

Wipe the meat with damp paper towels. Make small incisions in the meat and insert the sage leaves. Brush the skin with oil.

Roast for 35 minutes per 1 lb plus 35 minutes. Transfer to a warmed serving dish and keep hot while preparing the sauce.

To make the sauce, pour off all but 2 tablespoons of the fat from the roasting pan. Pour the remaining 2 tablespoons and the sediment into a small saucepan with the water. Bring to the boil, stirring. Reduce the heat and stir in the sour cream and Stilton cheese. Stir over gentle heat until the cheese has melted. Do *not* boil. Adjust the seasoning.

Carve the meat into thin slices and serve the sauce separately.

CHARCOAL GRILLED VEAL WITH DIJON BUTTER

The Dijon butter may also be served with steak, pork or lamb chops.

Serves 4

Brush the veal scallops with the oil and season with pepper.

For the Dijon butter, place all the ingredients in a blender or food processor and blend for a few seconds until just mixed. Alternatively, beat the butter by hand until smooth, then beat in the remaining ingredients. Season and chill until firm.

Prepare a charcoal grill. When the coals are ready, lay the scallops on the grill and cook for 2–3 minutes on each side, depending on the heat from the coals.

Remove from the heat and season with salt. Arrange the scallops on a serving plate and garnish with lemon slices and parsley. Place a pat of the Dijon butter on each scallop and serve immediately.

INGREDIENTS
8 thin veal scallops, about ¼ lb each
6 tablespoons olive oil
salt and pepper
Dijon butter
8 tablespoons unsalted butter,
*   softened*
2 tablespoons finely chopped
*   shallot*
1½ tablespoons Dijon mustard
1 tablespoon chopped parsley
Garnish
½ lemon, thinly sliced
4 parsley sprigs

PORK AND BEAN CASSEROLE

If a thicker sauce is preferred, strain the casserole and boil the sauce to reduce to the desired consistency. Return the meat and beans to the sauce and reheat gently.

Serves 4

Rinse the beans and drain. Heat 2 tablespoons of the oil in a large skillet, add the pork and sauté until brown all over.

Transfer to a flameproof casserole. Add the remaining oil to the skillet and sauté the onion until soft. Add to the casserole with the beans, bay leaf, cloves, thyme, stock, lemon juice and tomato paste.

Bring to the boil, cover and simmer for about 2 hours or until the meat and beans are tender, stirring occasionally. Remove the bay leaf and cloves – and thyme, if possible.

Add the tomatoes, season and simmer for 1–2 minutes to heat through. Sprinkle with chopped parsley before serving.

INGREDIENTS
½ lb dried kidney or pinto beans, or
*   black-eyed peas, soaked*
*   overnight and drained*
3 tablespoons vegetable oil
1½ lb pork shoulder, cubed
½ cup chopped onion
1 bay leaf
6 cloves
few fresh thyme sprigs
2 cups chicken stock (see page 247)
3 tablespoons lemon juice
1 tablespoon tomato paste
2 cups peeled, seeded and chopped
*   tomatoes*
salt and pepper
chopped fresh parsley, to garnish

TODAYS MARKET
of
SHELL FISH

Oysters Large / Small	1.00 each / 90p
Crevettes	8.50
Crab Claws	14.25
Lobster Tails	11.50
Cockles	2.60
Winkles	N/A
Escallops	
Mussels	2.51
Lobsters	10.50
Crab	
Crab Meat white/Brown	6.50
Dublin Bay Prawns	
" " Tails	9.5
Crawfish	
Prawns Eng.	
Prawns N.	

FISH

FISH

—◆—

With at least 40 different types of fish on show from Scottish salmon and Cornish sturgeon to jumbo shrimp from the Indian Ocean, it is hardly surprising that visitors flock to look at the renowned display which changes daily. Delicious to eat, tempting to look at, fish makes the ideal appetizer, such as Little Lobster Tail Soufflés, or an impressive main course dinner dish.

SPAGHETTI WITH ANCHOVY AND OREGANO SAUCE

In this tasty dish, the spaghetti is tossed in an anchovy and oregano sauce. Serve with a generous amount of freshly grated Parmesan cheese.

Serves 4

INGREDIENTS

7 tablespoons olive oil

2 garlic cloves, crushed

2 oz can anchovy fillets, drained

1 lb fresh spaghetti

2 teaspoons finely chopped fresh
  oregano or 1 teaspoon dried

salt and pepper

3 tablespoons finely chopped parsley

Parmesan cheese, to serve

Heat the oil in a small saucepan and sauté the garlic until golden. Reduce the heat to very low, stir in the anchovies and cook gently until the anchovies have completely disintegrated.

Meanwhile, cook the spaghetti in plenty of boiling salted water for about 8 minutes or until al dente.

Stir the oregano and pepper into the sauce. Drain the spaghetti well and turn onto a warmed serving dish. Pour the sauce over, sprinkle with the parsley and gently toss together. Serve with plenty of Parmesan cheese.

SHELLFISH SALAD

This salad is very colorful and quick to prepare. If fresh mussels are unobtainable, shrimps or clams can be used instead.

Serves 6

INGREDIENTS

12 fresh mussels

1 lb sea scallops

⅔ cup dry white wine

1 yellow pepper, seeded

12 pitted ripe olives

¼ cup white wine vinegar

1 tablespoon Dijon mustard

1 garlic clove, crushed

salt and pepper

¾ cup sunflower seed oil

Wash the mussels under cold running water and cut off the "beard." Discard any that do not close when the shell is tapped sharply. Steam the mussels for about 3 minutes, or until the shells open.

Poach the scallops in the white wine for 1 minute, then drain. Arrange the mussels and scallops in a large serving bowl. Cut the yellow pepper into fine shreds and add to the bowl with the olives. Pour the vinegar into a screw-top jar and add the mustard, garlic and salt and pepper. Stir well and add the oil. Place the lid on the jar tightly and shake the dressing until thoroughly mixed. Pour the dressing over the salad and toss well.

DEEP-FRIED SHRIMP WITH RADICCHIO SALAD

DEEP-FRIED SHRIMP WITH
RADICCHIO SALAD

*The addition of ale makes this a light batter to coat the shrimp with. If
English ale isn't available, use beer.*

Serves 4

Sift the flour, mustard and salt into a bowl and make a well in the center. Pour in
the oil and light ale, then gradually draw the flour into the liquid. Beat well to
form a smooth batter. Cover with plastic wrap and leave to rest for 30 minutes.

Beat the egg white until stiff, then fold into the batter. Add the shrimp to the
batter in batches and carefully turn them over to coat thoroughly. Remove with
a slotted spoon, allowing the excess batter to drain off.

Heat the oil in a deep-fat fryer to 350°. Place the shrimp in the basket, lower
into the oil and cook for 3 minutes.

Drain the shrimp on paper towels and keep hot. Continue in the same way
until all the shrimp has been cooked.

Arrange the radicchio and fennel on the side of each serving plate. Cut the
strips of green pepper in half and add these to the plates with the walnuts. Mix
the olive oil, vinegar, sugar and seasoning together, then pour over the salads.
Divide the shrimp between the plates and serve.

INGREDIENTS
1 cup unbleached flour
pinch of dry mustard
salt and pepper
2 tablespoons vegetable oil
⅔ cup light ale or beer
1 egg white
¾ lb shelled jumbo shrimp
oil for deep frying
1 small head radicchio
*½ fennel bulb, cut into julienne
    strips*
*½ green pepper, cut into julienne
    strips*
2 tablespoons chopped walnuts
3 tablespoons olive oil
1 tablespoon tarragon vinegar
pinch of sugar

CREAMY CLAM CHOWDER

CREAMY CLAM CHOWDER

*An all-American favorite, this creamy and substantial soup, with
potatoes and salt pork, will satisfy a hearty mealtime appetite.*

Serves 4

INGREDIENTS
16 clams
¼ lb parboiled salt pork, diced
½ cup finely chopped onion
1 tablespoon unbleached flour
½ lb potatoes, peeled and diced
2 cups milk

To shuck the clams, hold each one in your hand, well protected by a thick cloth,
with the hinge facing outward. Insert the point of a sturdy short-bladed knife in
the hinge and give a short quick upward twist. Strain and reserve the clam
liquid. Remove all the clams from their shells and reserve.

Cook the pork in a heavy-bottomed skillet until the fat runs. Reserve the pork
and strain 2 tablespoons of the fat into a saucepan. Add the onion and sauté
until soft and lightly browned. Add the flour and cook, stirring, for 2 minutes.
Add the potatoes and clam liquid, cover and simmer for about 10 minutes or
until the potatoes are almost tender.

Chop the clams, add them to the pan, cover and cook for 8–10 minutes. Stir in
the milk, season and cook for 5 minutes more. Sprinkle with the reserved pork
and serve at once.

MONKFISH TERRINE WITH TOMATO CREAM

Monkfish is often referred to as "poor man's lobster." This appetizer is as impressive looking as it is delicious.

Serves 4

Preheat the oven to 300°.

Remove the stems from the watercress and discard. Place the leaves in a small saucepan with just enough boiling water to cover. Bring back to the boil, then drain and rinse in cold water. Squeeze dry to remove as much liquid as possible. Purée or finely chop the leaves.

Roughly chop the fish and place in a blender or food processor. Purée until smooth, then slowly add the egg whites and cream while the machine is still running, until the mousse mixture is firm.

Add the lime zest and juice and seasoning. Divide the mixture in half and stir the watercess purée into one half.

Lightly grease a 8½- × 4½- × 2¾-inch loaf pan and line the bottom with wax paper. Spread the watercress mousse evenly over the bottom of the pan, arrange the shrimp down the center and top with fish mousse. Level the surface, cover with aluminum foil and place in a roasting pan. Pour in enough boiling water to come half-way up the sides of the loaf pan. Bake for about 45 minutes or until just firm to touch.

To make the tomato cream, mix the puréed tomatoes and lime juice together. Beat the cream until it just holds its shape, then fold in the tomato mixture. Season to taste. Chill until required.

Remove the terrine from the oven and take out of the roasting pan. Leave to cool, then pour off any liquid on the surface.

Unmold onto a plate and remove the lining paper. Cut into 8 slices and arrange 2 slices on 4 individual plates. Serve with a little tomato cream and garnish with watercress.

INGREDIENTS
1 bunch watercress
1 lb chilled boneless monkfish
2 chilled egg whites
1¼ cups chilled heavy cream
grated zest and juice of 1½ limes
salt and pepper
6 shelled shrimp
watercress, to garnish
Tomato cream
2 tomatoes, skinned, seeded and puréed (½ cup)
1 teaspoon lime juice
½ cup heavy cream
salt and pepper

SHRIMP NEWBURG

Serve on a large bread croustade as an appetizer. For a main course, double the quantities and serve on a bed of boiled rice, garnished with fresh watercress.

Serves 4

Preheat the oven to 300°. Place the slices of bread on a cookie sheet.

Melt half the butter and brush over the bread. Bake for 25 minutes.

Meanwhile, melt the remaining butter in a pan and add the Madeira and brandy. Simmer for 5 minutes, then add the shrimp. Season and simmer for 2 minutes, then remove from the heat.

Mix the egg yolks with the cream and stir into the pan. Cook over a gentle heat for 5 minutes, stirring until the sauce thickens. Do not allow the mixture to boil or it will curdle.

Spoon the shrimp and the sauce onto the baked bread and sprinkle with paprika. Serve hot garnished with watercress.

INGREDIENTS
four ¾-inch thick slices white bread, crusts removed
4 tablespoons butter
3 tablespoons Madeira
2 teaspoons brandy
1 lb shelled shrimp
salt and pepper
2 egg yolks
⅔ cup cream
½ teaspoon paprika
watercress, to garnish

SOUSED HERRINGS

These herrings, strongly flavored by the white wine vinegar, make a tasty hors d'oeuvre.

Serves 4

INGREDIENTS

4 herrings, cleaned, and filleted
salt and pepper
1 tablespoon finely chopped parsley
1 tablespoon chopped fresh chives
½ cup onion slices
6 black peppercorns
2 bay leaves, crumbled
4 parsley stalks
1¼ cups white wine vinegar

Preheat the oven to 350°.

Lay the herring fillets out flat, season and sprinkle with parsley and chives. Roll up the herrings from the head to the tail with the herbs on the inside and secure with toothpicks.

Pack into a fairly shallow baking dish. Scatter the onion slices, peppercorns, bay leaves and parsley stalks over. Pour the vinegar over and sufficient water to cover the fish rolls.

Cover with aluminum foil and cook for 45 minutes–1 hour, until the flesh flakes easily. Leave the herring to cool in the liquid, then chill until required.

SEA BASS WITH CUMIN AND ZUCCHINI

Sea bass has very white, delicate flesh and is similar in shape to salmon. It has steely gray scales and a white underside. Large bass have good flavor and are usually poached, as here.

Serves 4

INGREDIENTS

3½ lb sea bass, cleaned
2½ cups water
3 tablespoons olive oil
1 cup finely chopped onion
2 garlic cloves, crushed
1 teaspoon ground cumin
large pinch of cayenne
1 tablespoon tomato paste
14 oz can tomatoes, coarsely chopped
2 tablespoons finely chopped parsley
1 lb potatoes, peeled and cut into
  bite-sized chunks
salt and pepper
1 lb zucchini, thickly sliced

Cut the heads and tails off the fish and cut the bodies in half lengthwise. Place them, with the heads and tails, into a large saucepan. Add the water, bring to the boil, cover and simmer gently for 20 minutes.

Meanwhile, heat the oil in a skillet and sauté the onion and garlic until soft. Stir in the cumin and cayenne, then the tomato paste. Stir for 1 minute before stirring in the tomatoes. Add the parsley, then set aside.

Remove the fish from the pan and discard the heads and tails. Skin the fish and remove any bones. Reserve the flesh. Strain the liquid and add it to the tomatoes. Bring to the boil, then add the potatoes and salt. Simmer, covered for 15 minutes. Stir in the zucchini and cook for a further 15 minutes, adding more water, if necessary. Add the fish to the pan and simmer for 5 minutes. Adjust the seasoning and serve hot with crusty bread.

DEVILED WHITEBAIT WITH DEEP-FRIED PARSLEY

DEVILED WHITEBAIT WITH DEEP-FRIED PARSLEY

If whitebait are unavailable, use sprats.

Serves 4

Sift the flour, curry powder, ginger, cayenne pepper and salt together into a large plastic bag. Put a quarter of the whitebait into the bag and shake well to coat. Lift out and shake in a sieve to remove excess flour. Repeat with the remaining whitebait.

Heat the oil in a deep-fat fryer to 375°. Put a single layer of whitebait into the frying basket and fry for 2–3 minutes, shaking the basket occasionally, until the whitebait make a rustling sound as they are shaken. Tip out onto a warmed plate lined with paper towels. Fry the remaining in the same way. Reduce the temperature to about 365°. Deep-fry the parsley for a few seconds, until it stops sizzling. Drain on paper towels, then sprinkle with sea salt.

Divide the whitebait between four individual warmed plates. Scatter over the parsley sprigs and garnish with the lemon wedges.

INGREDIENTS
½ cup unbleached flour
¼ teaspoon curry powder
¼ teaspoon ground ginger
¼ teaspoon cayenne pepper
salt
1¼ lb whitebait, fresh or frozen
oil for deep-frying
large bunch parsley sprigs
sea salt
2 lemons, cut into wedges

SMOKED SALMON PATE WITH MELBA TOAST

*This delicious pâté is quick to make, using a food processor or blender.
Smoked salmon trimmings may be used, which are far more
economical than slices.*

Serves 8

Put the butter in a small saucepan and heat gently until melted. Leave to cool slightly for 5 minutes. Place the salmon in a blender or food processor. With the machine running, pour in the melted butter and mix until the salmon is a smooth paste. Remove the mixture from the bowl, season to taste, then stir in the lemon juice and cream.

Spoon the pâté into a serving dish and garnish with the smoked salmon and cucumber slices. Cover and chill for 30 minutes before serving.

To make the melba toast, toast the bread slices. Using a serrated knife, cut off the crusts and slide the knife between the toasted edges to split the bread. Cut each piece into two triangles, then toast the untoasted side under the broiler until golden and the edges curl.

Serve the pâté with the melba toast.

INGREDIENTS
8 tablespoons butter
½ lb smoked salmon
salt and pepper
1 tablespoon lemon juice
*⅔ cup heavy cream, lightly
    whipped*
*extra smoked salmon and
    cucumber, to garnish*
8 thin slices white bread

POTTED SALMON

Serve this recipe with thin slices of brown bread and butter and lemon.

Serves 4–6

Preheat the oven to 325°.

Put the salmon into a shallow baking dish and pour the wine over. Season and add the bay leaf and nutmeg. Cover tightly and cook for 45 minutes–1 hour or until the flesh flakes easily.

Leave the salmon to cool in the liquid. Remove with a slotted spoon and drain well. Flake the salmon, then purée in a blender or food processor with half of the butter. Pack firmly into 2 pots, cover and chill for at least 1 hour.

Meanwhile, melt the remaining butter in a small heavy-bottomed saucepan over gentle heat until it stops foaming. Remove from the heat and stand until all the sediment has sunk to the bottom. Carefully pour off the clear liquid and pour it over the surface of the salmon mixture. Leave in a cool place to set, then cover and chill until required.

INGREDIENTS
1¼ lb tail cut of salmon
7 tablespoons dry white wine
salt and pepper
1 bay leaf
pinch of grated nutmeg
½ lb butter, softened

LITTLE LOBSTER TAIL SOUFFLES

*These individual soufflés can be served as a light, appetizing first
course or as a luncheon dish served with a crisp green salad. If
available, langoustine tails are an excellent substitute.*

Serves 6

INGREDIENTS

3 tablespoons toasted bread crumbs
½ lb lobster tail meat
1¼ cups fish stock (see page 246)
1 tablespoon butter
1 tablespoon chopped shallot
¼ cup unbleached flour
2 egg yolks
pinch of cayenne pepper
pinch of grated nutmeg
3 egg whites
pinch of salt
whole lobster tails or langoustines,
    to garnish (optional)

Preheat the oven to 350° and preheat a cookie sheet.

Grease 6 individual ¾-cup ramekins and coat the insides with toasted bread crumbs. Chill.

Poach the lobster tails in the fish stock for about 2 minutes. Drain and roughly chop the meat. Reserve the stock.

Melt the butter and sauté the shallots until soft. Stir in the flour and cook for 1 minute, then remove from the heat and gradually stir in the reserved fish stock. Cook, stirring, until the sauce has thickened. Simmer for 1 minute, then remove from the heat and beat in the egg yolks. Stir in the lobster meat and season well.

Beat the egg whites with the salt until stiff, then fold them into the sauce. Spoon into the prepared ramekins.

Arrange on the preheated cookie sheet and bake for about 20 minutes or until risen and golden. Serve immediately, garnished if desired.

TAGLIATELLE WITH CRAB AND ASPARAGUS CREAM SAUCE

The quick-and-easy recipe turns tagliatelle into a special meal.
The sauce is also delicious served with other pasta shapes.

Serves 4

Steam the asparagus until just tender, then drain and rinse under cold running water. Roughly flake the crabmeat.

Melt the butter and sauté the shallots until soft, then stir in the ham. Add the asparagus, crabmeat, half the cream and seasoning. Simmer gently over moderate heat, carefully stirring until the sauce has thickened slightly. Reduce the heat and simmer gently while cooking the pasta.

Cook the pasta in plenty of boiling salted water until al dente. Drain, well, then return to the pan with the remaining cream and half the Parmesan cheese. Toss over a low heat until well mixed.

Transfer to a warmed serving dish and make a hollow in the center of the pasta. Pour the crab and asparagus sauce in the center and sprinkle with the remaining Parmesan cheese. Serve at once.

INGREDIENTS
½ lb fresh asparagus, trimmed and
    cut into 1-inch pieces
6 oz crabmeat (1 cup)
6 tablespoons butter
6 tablespoons finely chopped
    shallots
1 thin ham slice, finely chopped
1 cup heavy cream
salt and pepper
¾ lb fresh tagliatelle
    (see page 251)
2 tablespoons finely grated
    Parmesan cheese

SCALLOP PILAF

Golden saffron powder subtly flavors this delicious pilaf of fresh
scallops and julienne vegetables.

Serves 4

Melt 4 tablespoons of the butter in a large saucepan and sauté the shallots until soft. Add the rice and cook, stirring, until transparent. Add the saffron and ⅔ cup of the white wine, then bring to the boil. Stir in 1¼ cups of the stock and simmer gently for about 15 minutes, adding a little more stock if necessary, or until all the liquid has been absorbed and the rice is tender.

Cut each scallop in half horizontally. About 5 minutes before the rice is cooked, melt the remaining butter in a skillet and stir-fry the leek and fennel for 3 minutes or until just tender. Remove from the pan and keep hot. Add the scallops and sauté quickly on both sides until just opaque.

Season generously. Pour over the remaining white wine and simmer gently for 2 minutes. Stir in the Parmesan cheese and adjust the seasoning.

Pile the rice into a serving dish. Top with the leek, fennel and scallop mixture and garnish with the fennel leaves. Serve at once.

INGREDIENTS
7 tablespoons butter
6 tablespoons finely chopped
    shallots
1 cup arborio rice
¼ teaspoon saffron powder
1 cup dry white wine
about 2 cups fish stock
    (see page 246)
salt and pepper
16 sea scallops
4 oz leek, cut into julienne strips
    (½ cup)
4 oz fennel, cut into julienne strips
    (½ cup)
2 tablespoons freshly grated
    Parmesan cheese
fennel leaves, to garnish

LITTLE LOBSTER TAIL SOUFFLES

STUFFED SEA BASS BRAISED IN WHITE WINE

*This sea bass is a hearty and satisfying meal, attractively garnished
with fresh fennel leaves and served with a thick creamy sauce.*

Serves 4

INGREDIENTS

*2 fennel bulbs, trimmed and thinly
    sliced*
⅔ cup water
1 sea bass, about 2 lb, cleaned
1 cup fresh bread crumbs
2 tablespoons milk
6 tablespoons butter
¼ cup finely chopped shallots
2 tablespoons finely chopped parsley
1 teaspoon finely grated lemon zest
2 egg yolks
salt and pepper
⅔ cup full-bodied dry white wine
2 tablespoons dry white vermouth
¼ cup heavy cream
fennel leaves, to garnish

Cook the fennel in the water in a covered pan for 10 minutes.

Meanwhile, cut the fins and gills from the fish. To remove the bones, place the underside downward with the sides of the fish spread slightly outward on the work surface. Press firmly along the backbone with the thumbs. Turn the fish over, cut through the backbone at the head and tail, then carefully lift the backbone out. Remove any extra bones.

To make the stuffing, soak the bread crumbs in the milk, then squeeze dry. Melt 2 tablespoons of the butter and sauté the shallots until soft. Stir into the bread crumbs with the parsley, lemon zest, egg yolks and seasoning. Spoon the stuffing into the cavity in the fish and sew up with fine string or secure with wooden cocktail sticks.

Preheat the oven to 325°. Place the fish in a shallow, buttered baking dish and pour the wine and vermouth over. Drain the fennel and add to the dish. Dice the remaining butter, sprinkle over the fish and season. Cover with buttered aluminum foil and cook for 30–40 minutes or until the flesh flakes easily.

Carefully transfer the fish to a warmed serving plate. Remove the fennel from the cooking liquid and place on the dish with the fish. Cover and keep hot.

Strain the cooking liquid into a saucepan and boil until reduced to a light, syrupy consistency. Stir in the cream and continue to boil until slightly thickened. Adjust the seasoning. Remove the string or cocktail sticks from the fish and spoon the sauce over. Garnish with fennel leaves and serve at once.

PLAKI

*This dish is popular in Greece and throughout the Middle East. Many
varieties of fish are suitable for cooking this way and may be left whole
or sliced into steaks. Whole sea bass is an ideal choice, but halibut, cod
or haddock are all good alternatives.*

Serves 4

INGREDIENTS

*2 lb fish, left whole or cut into thick
    steaks*
juice of 1 lemon
¼ cup olive oil
2 large onions, thinly sliced
3 garlic cloves, finely chopped
*14 oz can tomatoes, drained and
    finely chopped*
¾ cup dry white wine
*1 tablespoon chopped fresh oregano
    or ½ tablespoon dried*
1 bay leaf
salt and pepper
5 tablespoons chopped parsley
parsley and lemon slices, to garnish

Preheat the oven to 350°.

Place the fish in a baking dish and pour the lemon juice over. If using a whole fish, pour some of the juice inside.

Heat the oil in a skillet and sauté the onions and garlic until golden. Add the tomatoes, breaking them up with a fork, and cook for a further 5 minutes. Add the wine, oregano, bay leaf and seasoning. Bring to the boil, remove from the heat and add the parsley, then cool for 5 minutes.

Pour the sauce over the fish and bake uncovered for 40 minutes. Serve garnished with parsley and lemon slices, accompanied by hot crusty bread.

STUFFED SEA BASS BRAISED IN WHITE WINE

STIR-FRIED SHRIMP

The quick cooking by stir-frying preserves the crunchiness of all the ingredients. Serve with a chilled, dry white wine.

Serves 4

INGREDIENTS

1 lb shelled and deveined shrimp
½ teaspoon salt
¼ cup peanut oil
2 large scallions, white part finely sliced and green part cut into ½-inch slices
2 large garlic cloves, finely chopped
1 teaspoon finely chopped fresh ginger root
½ lb tomatoes, peeled, seeded and finely chopped
2 tablespoons light soy sauce
½ teaspoon sugar
½ teaspoon potato flour
1 tablespoon medium-dry sherry or rice wine
½ lb snow peas
few drops sesame oil

Place the shrimps in a dish and sprinkle with half of the salt.

Heat a wok until it is very hot, then add the oil. Add the shrimps and stir-fry for 1 minute. Remove from the wok with a slotted spoon and reserve. Add the white scallion parts, garlic and ginger to the wok and stir-fry for a few seconds. Add the tomatoes, the remaining salt, soy sauce and sugar. Stir, cover the wok with a lid and reduce the heat. Cook for 3 minutes.

Mix the potato flour to a paste with the sherry, then add to the wok with the green scallion parts and snow peas. Stir-fry for 2 minutes, add the shrimps and stir-fry for 1 minute more. Sprinkle with sesame oil and serve immediately.

BAKED TROUT WITH HAZELNUTS AND DILL

This is a delicious way to cook trout. The fish are baked in wine and seasoned with dill, served with hazelnuts and butter.

Serves 4

INGREDIENTS

4 trout, about ¾ lb each, cleaned
2 tablespoons plus 2 teaspoons lemon juice
salt and pepper
4 fresh dill sprigs
½ cup dry white wine
2 tablespoons chopped shallot
3 oz hazelnuts (½ cup)
4 tablespoons butter
lemon wedges and parsley sprigs, to garnish

Preheat the oven to 350°.

Cut the fins from the fish, then sprinkle 2 tablespoons of the lemon juice over the skin and the cavities. Season inside and out and put a dill sprig in each cavity. Place the trout in a baking dish large enough to hold them tightly in one layer. Pour the wine over and add the shallot. Cover the dish with greased wax paper, then bake for 20–25 minutes or until the flesh flakes easily.

Meanwhile, place the hazelnuts under a moderately hot broiler for about 5 minutes or until the skins dry and flake. Rub off the skins and chop. Melt the butter, add the hazelnuts and cook over moderately high heat, stirring frequently, until golden brown. Add the remaining lemon juice and seasoning.

Carefully transfer the trout to warmed serving plates. Boil the cooking juices rapidly until reduced to about 3 tablespoons. Spoon the juices over the fish, then spoon the hazelnuts and butter over them. Serve at once.

INDIVIDUAL MUSSEL SOUFFLES

These soufflés make a very elegant beginning to a dinner party meant to impress.
To save time, cook the mussels and mix with the sauce in advance.

Serves 4

Preheat the oven to 350° and preheat a cookie sheet.

Grease 4 individual 1-cup ramekin dishes and coat the sides with Parmesan cheese. Chill.

Scrub the mussels well and remove the beards. Discard any which are open. Place the mussels in a saucepan with the wine. Cover and cook over high heat for 5–7 minutes, until all the shells have opened. Discard any with closed shells.

Drain the mussels and return the cooking liquid to the pan. Add the garlic, shallot and herbs, and boil rapidly until reduced to ⅔ cup. Strain through a piece of cheesecloth and reserve.

Remove the mussels from their shells. Combine the cornstarch, water and egg yolks, then add to the reduced liquid in a small saucepan. Cook gently, stirring, until thick. Stir in half the butter, then add the lemon juice and pepper to taste.

Beat the egg whites until stiff, then fold into the sauce mixture until evenly combined. Spoon half the mixture into the prepared ramekin dishes. Sprinkle the mussels on top and finish with the remaining soufflé mixture.

Place the ramekins on the preheated cookie sheet and bake for about 20 minutes, until risen and golden. Serve immediately.

INGREDIENTS
2 tablespoons grated Parmesan cheese
1½ lb fresh mussels
⅔ cup dry white wine
1 garlic clove, chopped
2 tablespoons chopped shallot
fresh thyme sprig
fresh parsley sprig
1 bay leaf
2 teaspoons cornstarch
1 tablespoon water
2 egg yolks
2 tablespoons butter
1 tablespoon lemon juice
pepper
3 egg whites

THON A LA PROVENÇALE

Tuna fish is found in the warmer parts of the Atlantic and Mediterranean seas.
The flesh is firm and is eaten fresh, salted, smoked or canned in oil or brine.

Serves 4

Place the tuna steak in a shallow dish and lay the anchovies on top. Mix ¼ cup olive oil, lemon juice and pepper together and pour it over the fish. Leave to marinate for 1 hour.

Melt 2 tablespoons of the butter in a flameproof casserole and sauté the onion until golden. Add the garlic and sauté for a further 2 minutes, then add the tomatoes and the bouquet garni and cook for 5 minutes.

Preheat the oven to 350°

Drain the fish. Heat the remaining ½ tablespoon olive oil and sauté the fish for 1 minute on each side. Add the fish to the casserole and pour the white wine over. Bring to the boil, then cover and cook for 40 minutes, basting frequently.

Remove the fish from the casserole and discard any skin and bones. Remove the bouquet garni.

Knead the remaining butter with the flour. Gradually stir in the flour a little at a time over gentle heat, then cook until the sauce is thick.

Pour the sauce over the fish and serve.

INGREDIENTS
2 lb whole tuna steak
6 anchovy fillets, soaked in cold water for 10 minutes, then drained
¼ cup plus ½ tablespoon olive oil
¼ cup lemon juice
pepper
3 tablespoons butter
½ cup chopped onion
1 garlic clove, crushed
1 lb tomatoes, peeled and finely chopped
bouquet garni
¾ cup dry white wine
1 tablespoon unbleached flour
few capers (optional)

SALMON TROUT STEAKS WITH WATERCRESS SAUCE

This recipe may also be made with fresh salmon. Reserve some of the large watercress leaves, dip them in a little oil and arrange around the border of each plate as a garnish.

Serves 4

INGREDIENTS

1¼ cups dry white wine

2½ cups water

bouquet garni

6 peppercorns and salt

½ cup sliced onion

½ cup sliced carrot

2 tablespoons heavy cream

12 tablespoons butter, diced

2 bunches watercress, 4 small sprigs and some large leaves reserved for garnish

4 salmon trout steaks or salmon steaks

2 teaspoons lemon juice

½ lemon, thinly sliced, to garnish

Bring the wine, water, bouquet garni, seasoning, onion and carrot to the boil in a large shallow pan. Simmer for 20 minutes or until the vegetables are tender.

Strain 6 tablespoons of the court bouillon into a small saucepan and boil until reduced by two-thirds. Stir in the heavy cream and boil gently for 2 minutes. Gradually beat in the butter.

Plunge the watercress, including the stem, into boiling water, Drain immediately, then refresh in cold water. Drain and squeeze as much water as possible from the watercress. Chop the watercress as finely as possible and add it to the sauce. Keep hot.

Strain the remaining court bouillon and return it to the pan. Add the fish steaks and cook gently in the court bouillon for 12–15 minutes or until the flesh flakes easily. Drain.

Stir the lemon juice into the sauce.

Arrange the reserved watercress leaves around the edge of each plate, pour the sauce over and place the fish on the top. Garnish with watercress sprigs and lemon slices.

BAKED SHRIMP AND SPINACH IN PERNOD SAUCE

Spinach, chard or lettuce leaves wrapped around fish or shellfish helps retain the natural juices and flavor of the seafood.

Serves 4

INGREDIENTS

24 large fresh spinach leaves, central stem removed

24 shelled jumbo shrimp

2 tablespoons butter

¼ cup dry white wine

pinch of cayenne pepper

salt and pepper

2 tablespoons chopped shallot

¼ cup Pernod

⅔ cup fish stock (see page 246)

½ cup heavy cream

2 tablespoons freshly grated Parmesan cheese

Preheat the oven to 375°.

Pour boiling water over the spinach leaves. Drain, then immediately drop them into ice water. Dry well. Wrap the shrimp in the leaves and arrange them in a single layer in a shallow baking dish, greased with half the butter. Pour over the white wine and add the cayenne and seasoning. Cover and bake for 20 minutes. Drain the juices and reserve. Transfer the shrimp to a flameproof serving dish and keep hot.

Melt the remaining butter and sauté the shallot until soft. Stir in the Pernod and bring to the boil. Add the fish stock and cooking liquid, and boil rapidly until reduced by half. Add the cream and continue boiling until reduced and slightly thickened.

Adjust the seasoning. Pour the sauce over the shrimp and sprinkle with Parmesan cheese. Cook under a preheated broiler until golden brown.

SHRIMP AND SPINACH ROULADE

SHRIMP AND SPINACH
ROULADE

*This dish can be served warm or chilled as an appetizer or light lunch dish.
Cherry tomatoes make an interesting garnish in contrast to the green spinach.*

Serves 4 – 6

Wash the spinach well and cook in a covered pan with just the water clinging to
the leaves for 5 minutes or until soft. Drain in a colander and press out all excess
water. Finely chop, then place in a bowl with the nutmeg, cheese and seasoning. Mix well.

Grease a 10½-× 5½-× 1-inch jelly roll pan, then line with wax paper. Preheat
the oven to 375°.

Beat the egg whites until stiff. Beat the egg yolks into the spinach mixture,
then gradually fold in the whites. Pour into the jelly roll pan. Shake to level the
mixture. Bake for about 15 minutes or until firm to the touch.

Meanwhile, to make the filling, melt the butter in a saucepan and sauté the
mushrooms until soft. Stir in the flour and cook for 1 minute. Remove from the
heat and gradually stir in the milk. Return to the heat and cook gently, stirring,
until thickened and smooth. Stir in the tomatoes, shrimp, dill and lemon juice,
and cook until heated through. Season well.

Invert the roulade onto a sheet of wax paper and carefully remove the lining
paper. Spread the sauce over the roulade. Starting from one short edge, roll up
using the paper to lift the roulade. Serve warm or cold.

INGREDIENTS

1½ lb fresh spinach
pinch of grated nutmeg
3 tablespoons grated Parmesan
   cheese
salt and pepper
6 eggs, separated
3 tablespoons butter
¾ cup chopped mushrooms
3 tablespoons flour
1½ cups milk
3 tomatoes, peeled, seeded and
   finely chopped
1½ cups shelled shrimp (9 oz)
1½ teaspoons chopped fresh dill
   (optional)
3 tablespoons lemon juice
cherry tomatoes, to garnish
   (optional)

QUENELLES OF HALIBUT WITH SAFFRON SAUCE

*Quenelles are like poached mousseline dumplings and can be made
from fish, shellfish, meat, poultry or game. The saffron sauce adds a
delicate golden hue to this dish.*

Serves 4

INGREDIENTS

*½ lb halibut fillet, skinned and well
    chilled*

1 chilled egg white

⅔ cup heavy cream, well chilled

1 tablespoon lemon juice

salt and pepper

2 cups fish stock (see page 246)

chervil or parsley sprigs, to garnish

Saffron sauce

1 tablespoon butter

4 tablespoons chopped shallots

⅔ cup fish stock (see page 246)

2 generous pinches saffron threads

½ cup dry white wine

½ cup heavy cream

Roughly chop the fish and place in a blender or food processor. Purée until smooth, then slowly add the egg white and cream while the machine is running. When the mixture is firm, stop the machine, add the lemon juice and season, then mix again. Chill until required for cooking.

With two wet spoons, shape the mixture into 12 ovals (quenelles). Poach the quenelles in the fish stock for 5–7 minutes, until just firm to the touch. Drain and keep warm. Reserve the fish stock for another recipe.

Meanwhile to make the sauce, melt the butter and sauté the shallots until soft. Add the fish stock, saffron and white wine, then simmer gently for 5 minutes more. Add the cream and simmer gently for 5 minutes more. Strain.

Pour the sauce onto 4 individual plates, arrange 3 quenelles on each.

CREAMY SEAFOOD PIE

Any firm white fish may be used for this recipe such as haddock, cod, flounder or halibut. The vegetables may be varied or omitted. Shrimp can also be added to the fish and a little cheese stirred into the sauce.

Serves 6

Preheat the oven to 400°

Cook the potatoes in boiling salted water for 20 minutes. Drain well. Add half the butter and mash. Season and beat in the egg. Set aside.

Place the fish fillets, milk, onion, carrot, peas and bay leaf in a saucepan. Season lightly, bring to the boil, cover and simmer for 15 minutes. Remove the pan from the heat and discard the onion and bay leaf. Strain and place the fish and vegetables in a baking dish. Set aside.

Melt half the remaining butter in a saucepan and stir in the flour. Cook for 1 minute, then remove from the heat and gradually stir in the strained milk. Cook, stirring constantly, until the sauce is thick and smooth. Stir in the nutmeg and cream. Adjust the seasoning, then pour the sauce over the fish and vegetables. Mix together in the dish and sprinkle the parsley over.

Spread the potatoes over the filling to completely cover and dot the surface with the remaining butter.

Bake for 10–15 minutes or until the potato topping has browned.

INGREDIENTS
2 lb potatoes, peeled
8 tablespoons butter
salt and pepper
1 egg, beaten
2 lb white fish fillets, skinned and boned
2 cups milk
1 small onion, halved
½ cup diced carrot
¼ lb peas (1 cup)
1 bay leaf
2 tablespoons unbleached flour
pinch of grated nutmeg
2 tablespoons light cream
2 tablespoons chopped parsley

BROILED MACKEREL WITH SAGE SAUCE

This is a delicious way to serve mackerel and it is very quick and easy to prepare. If fresh sage is unavailable, fresh parsley or dill are preferable to using dried sage.

Serves 4

Cut the fins from the mackerel and cut 3 diagonal slits in the skin across both sides of the fish. Season the fish inside and out, then place in a dish large enough to hold them in a single layer.

Mix the oil, lemon juice and wine together and pour over the fish. Cover and leave to marinate in a cool place for 1½ hours, turning the fish occasionally.

Remove the mackerel from the marinade. Cook under a hot broiler for 5–8 minutes each side, depending on the thickness of the fish, or until the flesh flakes easily.

Transfer to a warm dish, cover and keep hot. Carefully remove the oil from the top of the marinade. Pour the cooking juices into a saucepan, add the vermouth and sage leaves and simmer for 2–3 minutes. Season to taste and pour over the mackerel. Serve at once.

INGREDIENTS
4 mackerel, cleaned
salt and pepper
⅔ cup olive oil
2 tablespoons lemon juice
7 tablespoons dry white wine
7 tablespoons dry vermouth
1 teaspoon very finely chopped fresh sage

QUENELLES OF HALIBUT WITH SAFFRON SAUCE

TAGLIATELLE WITH SEAFOOD AND CHAMPAGNE SAUCE

*A scrumptious sauce made with salmon, monkfish and dry
champagne transforms fresh pasta into a special-occasion dish.*

Serves 4

INGREDIENTS

*16 fresh mussels, scrubbed and
  beards removed*

⅔ cup fish stock (see page 246)

1 red mullet, about ¾ lb filleted

½ lb monkfish fillet

½ lb fresh salmon fillet, skinned

4 raw jumbo shrimp, shelled

4 sea scallops

½ lb fresh tagliatelle (see page 251)

6 tablespoons butter

salt and pepper

*2 oz leek, cut into fine julienne strips
  (¼ cup)*

*⅔ cup champagne or dry sparkling
  white wine*

1¼ cups heavy cream

pinch of cayenne pepper

*12 fresh basil leaves, shredded
  (optional)*

*freshly grated Parmesan cheese, to
  serve*

Discard any open mussels which do not close when tapped. Place the mussels and fish stock in a pan, cover and cook over high heat for several minutes or until the mussels open. Discard any closed mussels. Leave to cool in the stock, then remove the mussels from their shells. Strain the stock through fine cheesecloth and reserve.

Cut the fish fillets into 1½-inch strips. Remove the vein from each shrimp and cut in half. Cut the scallops in half horizontally.

Cook the tagliatelle in boiling salted water with a dash of oil for 2–3 minutes or until al dente.

Meanwhile, melt half the butter and sauté the leek and shrimp for 30 seconds. Add the fish fillets, champagne and reserved stock, then simmer for 1 minute. Carefully remove all the fish from the pan and keep warm.

Boil the liquid rapidly until reduced by half. Add the cream and boil rapidly until reduced and thickened. Adjust the seasoning and add the cayenne pepper. Return the fish to the sauce with the mussels, scallops and basil. Warm through gently for about 3 minutes.

Drain the tagliatelle and toss in the remaining butter, then season. Serve with the sauce and Parmesan cheese.

KEDGEREE

*A classic English breakfast dish of smoked fish in creamy rice, seasoned
with cayenne pepper and nutmeg. Serve for brunch with freshly
squeezed orange juice. Other suitable fish are smoked cod or hake.*

Serves 4

INGREDIENTS

1 lb Finnan haddie fillets

½ cup long-grain rice

salt and pepper

*2 eggs, hard-boiled, shelled and
  chopped*

2 tablespoons lemon juice

pinch of cayenne pepper

pinch of grated nutmeg

⅔ cup light cream

4 tablespoons butter, diced

2 tablespoons finely chopped parsley

parsley sprigs, to garnish

Place the Finnan haddie in a large shallow pan with just enough water to cover and poach for about 15 minutes or until tender. Drain, skin, and roughly flake the fish.

Meanwhile, cook the rice in boiling salted water for about 15 minutes or until tender. Drain.

Preheat the oven to 350°.

Carefully mix the fish, rice and eggs together. Stir the lemon juice, cayenne pepper and nutmeg into the cream. Stir it into the rice and fish mixture and adjust the seasoning. Spoon the mixture into a buttered baking dish, dot with the butter and cook for 25 minutes. Stir in the chopped parsley and garnish with parsley sprigs.

TAGLIATELLE WITH SEAFOOD AND CHAMPAGNE SAUCE

SQUID RISOTTO

The risotto may be pressed into a buttered mold, left to stand for a few minutes, then unmolded onto a serving plate, if wished.

Serves 4

INGREDIENTS

1 lb squid
¼ cup olive oil
1 cup chopped red onions
2 garlic cloves, crushed
2 cups arborio rice
1 red pepper, seeded and chopped
⅔ cup dry white wine
2½ cups fish stock (see page 246)
2 teaspoons tomato paste
salt and pepper
1 teaspoon lemon juice
2 tablespoons finely chopped parsley

To prepare the squid, carefully remove the tiny silvery ink sacs inside each body and place in a small bowl. Pour a small amount of boiling water over and press the sacs to squeeze out the ink. Leave to soak.

Wash the squid well and cut the tentacles from the bodies. Peel away the purplish skin from the bodies and pull out the transparent spine and discard the innards. Cut the tentacles from the head and wash well. Discard the heads. Cut the bodies into small rings.

Heat the oil in a large heavy-bottomed saucepan and sauté the onion and garlic until soft. Add the rice and cook, stirring, until transparent. Add the red pepper and squid rings and tentacles. Stir well, then stir in the wine and bring to the boil. Stir in half the fish stock, cover and simmer for 5 minutes. Strain the inky liquid through fine cheesecloth and add to the risotto with the tomato paste. Stir well, then add the remaining stock. Simmer for 10 minutes more or until the liquid has been absorbed and the rice is creamy. Adjust the seasoning and stir in the lemon juice.

Sprinkle with chopped parsley and serve at once.

SOLE WITH MUSSELS IN TARRAGON CREAM SAUCE

Seafood lovers will delight in this special combination of sole and mussels. Serve on a bed of rice with a lightly steamed green vegetable.

Serves 4

INGREDIENTS

1¼ quarts mussels in their shells
½ cup dry white wine
2 tablespoons finely chopped shallot
fresh thyme sprig
3 parsley sprigs
salt and white pepper
4 sole fillets, total weight about 2 lb, skinned
1 teaspoon finely chopped fresh tarragon or ½ teaspoon dried
⅔ cup heavy cream
small tarragon sprigs and lemon slices, to garnish

Scrub the mussels under cold running water and discard any that do not close when sharply tapped. Remove the beards.

Heat 4 tablespoons of the wine with the shallot, thyme and parsley. Add the mussels, cover and cook over a high heat for 4–5 minutes, shaking the pan frequently. Remove the mussels from their shells, discarding any that have not opened. Strain the juice from inside the mussels with the cooking liquid and return to the rinsed-out pan.

Season the sole fillets, lay them in the liquid and poach gently for 4–5 minutes or until the flesh is just opaque.

Transfer the sole to a warmed plate, add the mussels, cover and keep hot. Stir the remaining wine into the cooking liquid with half the tarragon. Boil until reduced to about 2 tablespoons. Stir in the cream and simmer until thickened. Add the remaining tarragon and reheat gently. Season and coat the base of warmed serving plates with the sauce.

Carefully place the sole on the sauce. Place some of the mussels along the length of the sole and arrange the remainder around the side. Garnish with tarragon and lemon.

CHINESE EGG NOODLES
WITH SHRIMP AND GOLDEN THREADS

Egg noodles are tossed in a piquant sauce in this dish, which is quick to cook and requires very little preparation. Serve as a lunch dish or for a light supper with steamed broccoli or snow peas.

Serves 4

Heat the water in a large saucepan and cook the noodles according to the package directions. Drain and set aside. Heat a wok, then add the peanut oil. The oil is hot enough to stir-fry when a small piece of ginger floats to the top.

Stir in the white scallion parts, garlic and ginger, and stir-fry for 30 seconds. Add the mushrooms, green scallion parts, and shrimps. Stir-fry for a further 30 seconds. Pour in the cornstarch mixture and add the sugar. Stir-fry for 1 minute, then add the beansprouts.

Add the drained noodles, stirring and tossing them until they are coated in the sauce. Sprinkle the sesame oil over and stir-fry for 30 seconds. Serve.

INGREDIENTS
2½ quarts water
½ lb Chinese egg noodles
3 tablespoons peanut or sunflower oil
1½-inch piece fresh ginger root, cut into thin strips
3 scallions, white part finely chopped and the green shoots cut into 1-inch pieces
1 large garlic clove, finely chopped
1 cup sliced mushrooms
½ lb shelled shrimp, coarsley chopped (2 cups)
1 tablespoon cornstarch, mixed with 3 tablespoons light soy sauce and 5 tablespoons medium-dry sherry
½ teaspoon sugar
½ lb beansprouts
1 teaspoon sesame oil

CHINESE EGG NOODLES
WITH SHRIMP AND
GOLDEN THREADS

PAUPIETTES OF SOLE WITH SALMON MOUSSELINE

*Fillets of sole, filled with a delicate salmon mousse and poached in vermouth,
is an elegant and delectable dish to serve for a special dinner party.*

Serves 4

INGREDIENTS

*4 sole fillets, 1¾–2 lb, halved
    lengthwise and skinned*

2 tablespoons butter

salt and pepper

6 tablespoons dry white vermouth

¼ cup water

1 cup light cream

1½ teaspoons chopped fresh dill

2 teaspoons lemon juice

fresh dill sprigs, to garnish

Mousseline

*½ lb salmon fillet, skinned, boned,
    shredded and chilled*

1 chilled egg white

6 tablespoons chilled heavy cream

1 teaspoon chopped fresh dill

1½ teaspoons lemon juice

Preheat the oven to 375°.

To make the mousseline, process the salmon in a food processor until smooth, then add the egg white and mix again. Gradually add the heavy cream, mixing after each addition. Add the dill, lemon juice, and salt and pepper.

Divide the mousseline between the 8 sole fillets. Roll up and secure each one with a wooden toothpick.

Grease a baking dish with the 2 tablespoons butter and arrange the sole in a single layer. Season well, then pour in the vermouth and water. Cover with aluminum foil and bake for 20 minutes, until the fish is white and the mousseline firm. Transfer to a serving plate and keep hot.

Strain the juices into a saucepan and boil rapidly until reduced by half. Stir in the cream, chopped dill, lemon juice and seasoning. Simmer gently to reduce slightly. Do *not* boil. Remove the toothpicks from the sole and serve garnished with dill sprigs and the sauce.

LOBSTER THERMIDOR WITH RICE PILAF

*If using cooked lobster tails, remove the meat from the shells and make
2¼ cups fish stock (see page 246) with the lobster shells added,
then strained.*

Serves 4

Place the wine, onion, carrot, celery, parsley, bay leaf, peppercorns, thyme and tarragon in a very large saucepan with the water. Bring to the boil, cover and simmer gently for 15 minutes. Return to the boil and add about one-quarter of the lobster tails. They must be completely immersed in liquid, so do not add too many at one time. Bring back to the boil, then simmer for 2 minutes. Remove the lobster tails from the pan. Repeat this process until all the lobster tails are cooked. Cool, then remove the shells.

Strain the cooking liquid, then boil rapidly until reduced to about 1¼ cups.

Meanwhile, to make the rice pilaf, heat the oil and sauté the onion until soft. Stir in the rice and sauté until transparent. Add the stock, bring to the boil, cover and simmer for 15–20 minutes or until all the stock has been absorbed. Adjust the seasoning, stir in the chopped parsley and keep hot.

Melt 2 tablespoons of the butter and sauté the mushrooms for 3 minutes. Add the lemon juice and set aside. Melt 2 tablespoons of the remaining butter and sauté the lobster meat for 1 minute. Pour the brandy over and boil until reduced to 1 tablespoon.

Melt the remaining butter and stir in the flour and mustard. Cook, stirring for 1 minute. Remove from the heat and gradually stir in the reduced stock. Bring to the boil, stirring, then simmer for 5 minutes. Mix the cream and egg yolks together and gradually stir into the sauce over very low heat. Cook, over low heat, stirring, until thickened slightly.

Stir in the mushrooms and their juices, and the lobster tails with their juices. Stir in the cayenne and adjust the seasoning. Transfer the mixture to a flameproof dish, sprinkle with the cheese and cook under a hot broiler for a minute or two until golden. Serve at once with the rice pilaf.

INGREDIENTS
3 cups dry white wine
¾ cup sliced onion
½ cup sliced carrot
¼ cup sliced celery
6 parsley sprigs
1 bay leaf
6 peppercorns
¼ teaspoon dried thyme
*1 tablespoon chopped fresh
    tarragon or ½ tablespoon dried*
1 quart water
4 lb lobster tails, preferably raw
6 tablespoons butter
1¼ cups sliced mushrooms
4 teaspoons lemon juice
4 tablespoons brandy
1 tablespoon unbleached flour
½ teaspoon dry mustard
⅔ cup heavy cream
2 egg yolks
pinch of cayenne pepper
salt and pepper
*2 tablespoons freshly grated
    Parmesan cheese*

Rice Pilaf
2 tablespoons olive oil
½ cup finely chopped onion
1 cup long-grain rice
2¼ cups fish stock (see page 246)
salt and pepper
1 tablespoon chopped parsley

PAUPIETTES OF SOLE WITH SALMON MOUSSELINE

SUSHI

Sushi is a Japanese snack food of seasoned rice mixed with a variety of ingredients and served in decorative, edible packages. These recipes are to serve with the seasoned rice on a large platter or individual plates with soy sauce for dipping.

Serves 4

INGREDIENTS

Seasoned Sushi Rice (Shari)
⅔ cup short-grain rice, preferably
 Japanese, rinsed and drained
1 cup water
3-inch piece konbu seaweed
4 teaspoons rice vinegar

Put the rice, water and konbu in a saucepan and leave to soak for 15 minutes. Cover the pan, bring to the boil and simmer for 10 minutes or until tender. Leave to cool. Do not remove the lid during this time. Remove the konbu and stir in the rice vinegar. Chill.

Thin Egg Crêpes (Usu Yaki Tamago)
2 eggs
1 tablespoon sake
1½ teaspoons sugar
¼ teaspoon salt
1½ teaspoons water
vegetable oil for frying

Mix the eggs, sake, sugar, salt and water together until evenly blended. Allow the foam to settle. Lightly oil an 8-inch skillet and place over gentle heat. Pour in half of the egg mixture and swirl it to evenly coat the base of the pan. Cook until the edges of the crêpe begin to dry out. Remove from the heat and allow to cool slightly until you can turn it over. Return to the heat and cook the other side for about 30 seconds. Remove from the pan and leave to cool. Repeat for second crêpe.

Using a sharp knife cut each crêpe into a rectangle. Reserve trimmings to use, shredded, in other sushi.

Tied Golden Rolls
¼ quantity seasoned sushi rice (see
 above)
1 teaspoon toasted sesame seeds
½ teaspoon grated fresh ginger root
1 teaspoon rice vinegar
1 teaspoon sugar
2 thin egg crêpes, trimmed to
 rectangles (see above)
¼ lb smoked salmon, cut into long
 strips

Mix the rice, sesame seeds, ginger, vinegar and sugar together. Shape into 2 even rolls, the same length as the egg crêpes, with wet hands or by rolling up in a damp clean dish towel or piece of cheesecloth.

Place each roll on an egg crêpe and roll up carefully. Tie 4 strips of smoked salmon along the length of each roll at regular intervals. Chill until required, then cut each roll in 4 pieces between the smoked salmon. Serve.

Crab and Avocado Rolls
½ ripe medium avocado, about ¼ lb,
 peeled and mashed
½ teaspoon wasabi powder
2 teaspoons mayonnaise
salt
lemon juice
½ lb crabmeat, flaked
¼ quantity seasoned sushi rice
2 sheets nori seaweed

Mix the avocado with the wasabi powder and mayonnaise. Season to taste with salt and lemon juice. Sprinkle the crabmeat with lemon juice.

Roll the rice into 2 even rolls the length of the nori seaweed. Place a sheet of nori on a work surface, preferably on a sudare mat. Arrange a roll of rice at one end, spread half the avocado mixture along the length of the rice and then arrange half the crabmeat along the length of the nori. Roll up carefully, using the sudare mat. Chill until required. Cut each roll into 6 pieces. Serve.
Note
Wasabi, a pungent horseradish spread, is available in specialty stores as a powder.

Lay the pieces of nori seaweed on a work surface. Divide the rice between each, placing it on the top corner of the nori. Top each with a piece of salmon, cucumber, dill and wasabi. Sprinkle with lemon juice. Fold up the opposite bottom corner of the seaweed to half cover the filling.

Roll the seaweed into a cone shape, dampening the edge if necessary to seal. Chill until required.

Shape the sushi rice into 4 ovals. Sprinkle with a little wasabi and top each with a shrimp. Chill until required.

Salmon and Dill Hand Rolls
2 sheets nori seaweed, each cut into
    4 squares
¼ quantity seasoned sushi rice
    (opposite)
2 oz smoked salmon, cut in 8 pieces
8 slices cucumber or snow peas, cut
    in julienne strips
8 sprigs fresh dill
1 teaspoon wasabi powder mixed
    with 1 teaspoon water
lemon juice

Prawn Sushi
¼ quantity of seasoned sushi rice
    (opposite)
½ teaspoon wasabi powder mixed
    with ½ teaspoon water
4 cooked jumbo shrimp, shelled

SHRIMP AND COCONUT CURRY

This curry is very easy to prepare and quick to cook. The coconut milk is made by grating the white flesh, adding boiling water and leaving it to soak for 20 minutes.

Serves 4

Pour boiling water over the grated coconut and leave to soak for 20 minutes. Place a piece of double cheesecloth in a colander over a bowl. Pour the coconut with all of the water into the cloth, pull the ends of the cloth together and squeeze out as much liquid as possible. Set the liquid aside.

Melt the ghee in a saucepan and sauté the onion until soft. Add the garlic, chilies, mustard seeds, turmeric and coriander.

Mix the cornstarch with the coconut milk and stir it into the onion mixture. Add the lemon juice and salt, and simmer gently for 10 minutes, stirring occasionally. Add the shrimp and simmer for 5 minutes more. Serve hot with boiled rice.

INGREDIENTS
½ lb white coconut flesh, all brown
    husk removed, finely grated
1¼ cups boiling water
4 tablespoons ghee or clarified
    butter
1 cup finely chopped onion
1 garlic clove, crushed
2 dried chilies, crumbled
½ teaspoon black mustard seeds,
    ground
½ teaspoon ground tumeric
1 teaspoon ground coriander
1 tablespoon cornstarch
the juice of ½ a lemon
salt
1½ lb shelled shrimp
hot boiled rice, to serve

POULTRY
AND GAME

Every morning, an astounding variety of seasonal game and fresh poultry is bought at Smithfield Market; the remainder is sent overnight by private suppliers. With such a wide choice you can be adventurous with your cooking. Try quintessential Traditional Jugged Hare, or take your inspiration from the East with Stir-Fried Chicken with Ginger and Snow Peas.

CHICKEN EN PAPILLOTE

Cooking en papillote (in paper packages) ensures that the contents retain their moisture. Serve with the sauce, accompanied by thinly sliced sautéed mushrooms and a julienne of cooked celery and potato.

Serves 4

INGREDIENTS

4 boneless chicken breasts, skinned
1 tablespoon butter
2 tablespoons finely chopped shallots
1 cup finely chopped mushrooms
½ cup blanched and finely chopped
   hazelnuts
1 egg white, lightly beaten
1 tablespoon heavy cream
salt and pepper
2 teaspoons medium-dry sherry
Sauce
2 tablespoons butter
2 tablespoons unbleached flour
1¼ cups chicken stock (see page 247)
2 egg yolks
½ cup light cream
1 tablespoon medium-dry sherry

Preheat the oven to 350°.

Cut a slit in each chicken breast to make a pocket to hold the stuffing. Melt the butter in a skillet and sauté the shallot until soft. Add the mushrooms and cook gently for 2–3 minutes. Cool slightly. Add the hazelnuts, egg white and cream to the skillet and mix well. Season.

Place each chicken breast on a buttered circle of aluminum foil large enough to enclose it. Fill the breast with the stuffing mixture. Sprinkle ½ teaspoon sherry over each piece of chicken and seal the packages. Place on a baking tray and bake for 40 minutes.

Meanwhile, to make the sauce, melt the butter in a saucepan and stir in the flour. Cook the flour for 1 minute. Remove the pan from the heat and gradually stir in the stock. Bring to the boil and simmer for 5 minutes, stirring occasionally. Mix the egg yolks with the cream. Remove the pan from the heat and stir a little of the sauce into the egg mixture. Stir the egg mixture into the sauce and heat. Adjust the seasoning and stir in the sherry. Serve the sauce with the chicken breasts.

PERSIAN-STYLE CHICKEN

*The substantial stuffing for this chicken is fragrant and spicy. Serve
garnished with lemon slices, walnut halves and fresh coriander leaves.*

Serves 4–6

Preheat the oven to 375°.

Wipe the chicken inside and out and pour half the lemon juice inside the cavity. Cook the rice in 1 quart lightly salted, boiling water for 7–8 minutes, then drain thoroughly. Melt ¼ cup of the butter and sauté the onion until golden. Stir in the raisins, walnuts, turmeric and cumin. Remove from the heat and add the drained rice. Mix the ingredients well and season to taste.

Stuff the chicken with the rice mixture and truss, then place in a roasting pan. Pour the remaining lemon juice over the chicken and sprinkle with salt. Spread the remaining butter over the breast. Roast for 1½ hours, basting occasionally. Serve at once.

INGREDIENTS
4 lb chicken
juice of 1 lemon
½ cup long-grain rice
7 tablespoons butter
½ cup chopped onion
½ cup raisins
½ cup chopped walnuts
½ teaspoon ground turmeric
½ teaspoon ground cumin seeds
salt and pepper

ROAST TURKEY WITH LEMON AND ALMOND STUFFING

*Turkey can be enjoyed at times other than just Thanksgiving and is an
ideal choice for a large dinner party. Serve with this
delectable stuffing.*

Serves 8–10

Preheat the oven to 425°.

To make the stuffing, melt the butter and sauté the shallots and celery until soft. Add the turkey liver and cook for 2 minutes. Mix all the remaining ingredients together in a large bowl and add the liver mixture.

Stuff the neck end of the turkey with the stuffing. Truss, and place the turkey on a rack in a roasting pan. Roll any remaining stuffing into balls. Mix the melted butter, lemon juice and wine together and pour over. Roast for 30 minutes, then reduce the temperature to 350° and continue roasting for a further 3–3½ hours. Baste occasionally during roasting. One hour before the end of cooking, cook any remaining stuffing in a roasting tin. Transfer to a warm serving plate and rest for 15 minutes before carving.

To make the giblet gravy, place the giblets and water in a saucepan, bring to the boil, then simmer for 1½–2 hours while the turkey is cooking. Strain. When the turkey is cooked, spoon off most of the fat from the roasting pan. Sprinkle the flour over the pan juices. Brown over high heat, stirring, for 1 minute, then gradually stir in the giblet stock. Season to taste and simmer, stirring, for 10 minutes. Strain into a gravy boat and serve with the turkey.

INGREDIENTS
8–10 lb turkey
8 tablespoons butter, melted
juice of ½ lemon
¼ cup white wine
Lemon and almond stuffing
3 tablespoons butter
½ cup shallots or onion, chopped
1¼ cups finely chopped celery
the turkey liver, finely chopped
1 lb pork sausage
finely grated zest of 2 lemons
2 cups fresh bread crumbs
¾ cup finely chopped almonds
2 tablespoons chopped parsley
½ teaspooon dried thyme
salt and pepper
Giblet gravy
the turkey giblets, minus the liver
5 cups water
1 tablespoon unbleached flour

CHICKEN BREASTS WITH PROSCIUTTO AND MOZZARELLA

*This succulent dish is both quick and easy to prepare. Serve with new
potatoes and a green vegetable, or a crisp green salad.*

Serves 4

INGREDIENTS

2 boneless chicken breasts, halved

8 fresh sage leaves, or 1 teaspoon
    dried sage

salt and pepper

2 tablespoons butter

4 thin slices prosciutto (about 2 oz)

½ lb mozzarella cheese, sliced

fresh sage leaves, to garnish

Cut a slit horizontally along each chicken breast to make a pocket. Insert 2 sage leaves or ¼ teaspoon dried sage into each and season lightly.

Melt the butter in a skillet and sauté the chicken for 15–20 minutes or until tender. Place the chicken breasts in a baking dish and pour the pan juices over. Place a slice of prosciutto over each, then cover with the mozzarella. Broil for 5 minutes, or until the cheese begins to melt and turn golden. Garnish each of the chicken breasts with fresh sage leaves and serve.

CHICKEN ENCHILADAS

*To give the enchilada sauce the correct Mexican "heat," be sure to use
small green Serrano chilies.*

Serves 4–6

INGREDIENTS

Tortillas

2 cups unbleached flour

1½ teaspoons salt

¼ cup shortening

⅔ cup warm water

⅔ cup vegetable oil

Enchilada sauce

3 tablespoons vegetable oil

½ cup chopped onion

3 tablespoons tomato paste

1½ lb canned tomatoes

½ teaspoon sugar

1½ teaspoons salt

3 Serrano chilies, seeded and finely
    chopped

Chicken filling

2 tablespoons vegetable oil

½ cup chopped onion

1 green bell pepper, seeded and
    chopped

3 boneless chicken breasts, skinned
    and cut into 1-inch cubes

½ teaspoon salt

3 oz pitted ripe olives, roughly
    chopped (½ cup)

1⅔ cups grated Cheddar cheese

To make the tortillas, sift the flour and salt into a bowl and cut in the shortening until the mixture resembles bread crumbs. Gradually add the water, mixing lightly with a knife. Knead the dough on a lightly floured surface and divide it into 8 even-sized balls. Place them in a bowl and cover with a damp cloth. Roll out each ball into a 9-inch circle. Heat a large, ungreased skillet or a griddle over moderate heat. Cook the tortillas on both sides, until the dough puffs slightly and light brown flecks appear on the surface.

To make the enchilada sauce, heat the vegetable oil and sauté the onion until soft. Add the tomato paste and sauté for 1 minute. Place the tomatoes, with their juice, in a blender or food processor and blend until smooth. Add to the pan with the sugar, salt and chilies. Bring to the boil and simmer for 15 minutes.

To make the chicken filling, heat the oil and sauté the onion until soft. Add the green pepper and chicken, and sauté for 5 minutes, stirring occasionally. Add the salt and 1¼ cups of the enchilada sauce. Bring to a boil, cover the pan, reduce the heat and simmer for 15 minutes. Add the olives and ⅓ cup of the cheese and simmer for 5 minutes.

Preheat the oven to 350°.

To assemble the enchiladas, heat the ⅔ cup vegetable oil in a skillet. Dip each tortilla into the hot oil for about 10 seconds, until it becomes pliable. Drain slightly, then dip it into the warm enchilada sauce for 1–2 seconds. Fill each "dipped" tortilla by spooning some of the chicken filling across the middle, rolling it up and placing it seam side down in a baking dish.

Pour the remaining sauce over the top and sprinkle with the remaining cheese. Bake for 20 minutes.

TRADITIONAL JUGGED HARE

*This is a classic dish made with the hare's blood as the thickening
agent. If you do not have a freshly shot hare, the blood can be omitted.
Two cottontail rabbits may be substituted for the hare.*

Serves 6

Wash the hare and pat dry with paper towels. Place the bacon in a large heavy-bottomed skillet or casserole and cook gently until the fat runs. Add 4 tablespoons of the butter and brown the hare all over.

Add the onion, carrots, celery, seasoning, bouquet garni and lemon zest. Add the stock and bring it gently to the boil. Reduce the heat, cover the pan tightly and simmer gently for 2½–3 hours or until the hare is tender. Blend the remaining butter with the flour to a smooth paste. Beat it into the liquid, a little at a time, and cook for 5 minutes, stirring, until thickened. Season to taste.

Mix the blood and port together.

Just before serving, remove the skillet from the heat and gradually stir in the port and blood mixture. Serve immediately.

INGREDIENTS
4 lb hare, cut up
3 bacon slices, diced
6 tablespoons unsalted butter
½ cup chopped onion
¾ cup chopped carrots
1¼ cups chopped celery
salt and pepper
bouquet garni
finely grated zest of 1 lemon
3¾ cups chicken stock (see page 247)
2 tablespoons unbleached flour
3 tablespoons port

DUCK WITH COGNAC AND
PEACHES – (A VARIATION OF
DUCK WITH COGNAC AND
NECTARINES)

DUCK WITH COGNAC AND NECTARINES

This is a rich dish and is ideal to serve with steamed vegetables and boiled rice.
Peaches, or other dried fruit, may be used in this recipe if nectarines are unavailable.

Serves 2–3

INGREDIENTS

3 oz dried nectarines (½ cup)

boiling water to cover

2 tablespoons Cognac or brandy

2 tablespoons port

2 tablespoons butter

4 lb trussed duck

¼ orange

salt and pepper

1¼ cups cold water

4 fresh nectarines or peaches, pitted
and cut into slices

Place the dried fruit in a bowl and cover with boiling water. Leave until lukewarm, then stir in the Cognac and port. Leave to soak overnight.

Place the nectarines, the soaking liquid and butter in a small saucepan. Cover and simmer very gently for about 20 minutes, adding more water if the mixture seems too dry. Purée the fruit and reserve. Preheat the oven to 350°.

Prick the duck all over with a fork and place the orange inside the cavity. Place on a rack in a roasting pan. Season and pour half the cold water into the pan. Roast for 30 minutes per 1 lb, increasing the temperature to 425° for the last 15 minutes.

Remove the duck from the oven and discard the orange. Carefully tip the duck so the cavity juices run into the pan, then transfer to a plate and keep hot. Pour off the fat and stir in the remaining water and nectarine purée. Simmer over moderate heat for about 10 minutes.

Warm the sliced nectarines in the oven for 2 minutes. Carve the duck into slices and serve with the nectarine slices. Spoon the sauce over.

SQUAB IN HONEY SAUCE
WITH FRESH FIGS

SQUAB IN HONEY SAUCE WITH FRESH FIGS

*This rich and fruity dish is excellent for entertaining. The squab is
cooked in a casserole flavored with honey, brandy and wine, with fresh
figs added to the sauce just before serving.*

Serves 4

Heat the oil in a large flameproof casserole, add the squabs and brown all over.
Remove from the pan. Sauté the onion and garlic in the oil until soft, then stir in
the brandy and wine. Increase the heat and bring to the boil.

Return the squabs to the casserole, then add the stock, honey, dried figs,
lemon juice and bouquet garni. Cover and simmer over low heat for about 1½
hours. The squabs are cooked when the juices run clear after a skewer or fork
has been inserted into the leg. Remove the squabs from the pan and keep hot.

Strain the cooking liquid into a saucepan. Mix the butter and flour together
and beat into the sauce, a little at a time. Simmer gently for 5 minutes, then
adjust the seasoning. Add the fresh figs and simmer for 1–2 minutes.

Using poultry scissors, cut each squab in half and arrange on a warmed
serving plate. Carefully spoon the sauce and figs over and serve at once.

INGREDIENTS
2 tablespoons olive oil
4 squabs, dressed
½ cup chopped onion
2 garlic cloves, crushed
1 tablespoon brandy
⅔ cup dry white wine
1¼ cups chicken stock (see page
   247)
4 tablespoons honey
2 oz dried figs, chopped (⅓ cup)
4 teaspoons lemon juice
bouquet garni
1 tablespoon butter, softened
1 tablespoon unbleached flour
4 fresh figs, quartered
salt and pepper

73

ROAST GOOSE WITH SAGE, ONION AND APPLE STUFFING

*Sage and onion stuffing is traditionally English and is used for
poultry, pork and lamb recipes. The addition of apple makes it an ideal
accompaniment to roast goose.*

Serves 6–8

INGREDIENTS

8–10 lb goose, trussed weight
salt and pepper
Sage, onion and apple stuffing
4 tablespoons butter
½ cup finely chopped onion
the goose liver, finely chopped
4 cups fresh bread crumbs
½ lb sausage
finely grated zest of 1 lemon
1 teaspoon chopped fresh sage or
    ½ teaspoon dried sage
½ lb tart apple, peeled and coarsely
    chopped
2 tablespoons Calvados or applejack

Preheat the oven to 400°.

Wipe the goose inside and out, remove any lumps of fat from the inside and
dry thoroughly. Season well.

Melt the butter and sauté the onion until soft. Add the goose liver and sauté
until it changes color. Cool the mixture slightly before adding it to the remaining
ingredients. Mix well, then stuff the neck end of the goose loosely.

Truss the goose neatly and place it on a rack in a roasting pan. Prick the lower
legs, breast and sides of the bird. Roast, breast side up, for 20 minutes.

Remove the goose from the oven and turn it over onto the breast. Reduce the
temperature to 325° and roast for 1 hour. Turn the goose onto its back and roast
for a further 1–1¼ hours. The bird is cooked when a skewer or fork is inserted
into the leg and the juices run clear. Pour off the fat several times during
cooking.

When the goose is cooked, leave it in a warm place for 15 minutes before
carving. Serve with giblet gravy (see page 69). A little Calvados or applejack
may be added, if wished.

QUAIL CASSEROLE

*These delicate birds are cooked with orange and flavored with thyme and brandy.
Serve for supper with new potatoes and snow peas.*

Serves 4

INGREDIENTS

3 tablespoons butter
¼ lb bacon, chopped
4 quail
2 oranges, peeled and roughly
    chopped
1 garlic clove, crushed
1½ cups finely chopped shallots
1¼ cups hot chicken stock (see page
    247)
fresh thyme sprig
salt and pepper
1 tablespoon brandy
croutons, watercress and strips of
    orange rind, to garnish.

Preheat the oven to 350°.

Melt 2 tablespoons of the butter in a large casserole and sauté the bacon until
lightly colored. Add the quail and cook on all sides until evenly browned. Stir in
the orange flesh, garlic, shallots, stock, thyme and seasoning. Cover and cook
for 35–40 minutes or until the quail are tender. Transfer the quail to a warmed
serving dish and keep hot.

Skim off any excess fat from the cooking liquid, then strain. Stir in the brandy
and then boil rapidly until the liquid has reduced and is slightly thickened.
Remove from the heat and stir in the remaining butter. Pour the sauce over the
quail and serve garnished with croutons, watercress sprigs and strips of orange
rind.

STIR-FRIED CHICKEN WITH GINGER AND SNOW PEAS

The secret of success when stir-frying is organization. Having all the ingredients prepared and close at hand is essential, as the actual cooking time is surprizingly quick. Snow peas add color and a crunchy texture to this delicious Chinese dish.

Serves 4

INGREDIENTS

3 boneless chicken breasts, skinned and cut into 1-inch squares

1¼ cups peanut oil

2 teaspoons finely chopped fresh ginger root

¼ cup finely chopped scallions

1 large clove garlic, finely chopped

1½ cups thinly sliced mushrooms

½ lb snow peas

scallion curls, to garnish

Marinade

1 egg white, beaten

1 tablespoon cornstarch

2 teaspoons light soy sauce

2 teaspoons rice wine or medium-dry sherry

Sauce

2 tablespoons light soy sauce

3 tablespoons rice wine or medium-dry sherry

1 teaspoon sugar

1 teaspoon cornstarch

Mix the marinade ingredients together and pour over the chicken. Marinate for 30 minutes. Mix all the sauce ingredients together and set aside. Preheat a wok over high heat and add the peanut oil. When the oil is smoking hot, stir-fry the chicken for 2 minutes. Place a sieve over a bowl and pour in the chicken and all of the oil.

Return 3 tablespoons of the oil to the wok, and stir-fry the ginger, scallions, and garlic for 30 seconds. Add the mushrooms and stir-fry for 30 seconds. Add the snow peas and sauce and stir. Return the drained chicken to the wok and stir-fry for a further 1 minute. Garnish and serve at once with Chinese noodles.

GUINEA FOWL CASSEROLE

*A guinea fowl has gray feathers speckled with white, and is a native of
Africa. It is in season throughout the year in England and similar in
taste to pheasant. If unavailable, substitute a chicken. This rich
casserole is also delicious made with 2 or 3 squabs.*

Serves 3–4

Place the onions in a saucepan of cold water, bring to the boil, and drain
immediately. Melt the butter in a round flameproof casserole over gentle heat.
Add the onions and the guinea fowl, and slowly brown the bird on all sides,
taking care not to burn the butter.

Pour the cream over and season. Cover and simmer gently for 1 hour, or until
the bird is cooked, basting occasionally.

Remove the bird from the casserole, and keep hot. Add the lemon juice and
jelly to the sauce, stir until well blended, and adjust the seasoning. Divide the
guinea fowl into portions, arrange on a serving plate, and pour over the sauce.

INGREDIENTS
8 pearl onions
3 tablespoons butter
*2½–3 lb guinea fowl or chicken,
    cleaned and trussed*
1¼ cups heavy cream
salt and pepper
1 tablespoon lemon juice
*1 tablespoon cranberry or red
    currant jelly*

ROAST VENISON WITH WINE-FRUIT SAUCE

*This richly marinated venison is roasted with its tangy citrus sauce
and is an ideal dish for any special occasion.*

Serves 8

Wipe the meat with paper towels and trim off any excess fat. Place the onion,
carrot, celery, garlic, bouquet garni, peppercorns, wine and ⅔ cup oil in a large
dish. Add the venison and baste with the marinade. Cover the dish with plastic
wrap and marinate in the refrigerator for 48 hours, turning several times.

Preheat the oven to 325°.

Drain the venison and reserve the marinade. Brush the meat with oil and
wrap in aluminum foil. Roast for 25 minutes per 1 lb. About 30 minutes before
the end of the cooking time, remove the aluminum foil, sprinkle the meat with
flour and baste with the cooking juices.

Meanwhile, place the marinade in a saucepan and cook, uncovered, for
about 20 minutes, until reduced by half. Strain and reserve.

Cut the citrus zest into thin strips and simmer in ⅔ cup water for 5 minutes.
Drain and reserve. Place the citrus juices and red currant jelly in a pan. Stir over
low heat until the jelly dissolves, then add the port and strained marinade.
Simmer for 10 minutes. Blend the cornstarch to a smooth paste with 2 tablespoons water. Add to the pan, stirring, until thickened. Add the citrus zest and
wine vinegar and simmer for a further 5 minutes.

Place the venison on a warmed serving plate and sprinkle with chopped
parsley. Serve with the hot sauce.

INGREDIENTS
5½ lb haunch of venison
¾ cup chopped onion
½ cup chopped carrot
¼ cup chopped celery
2 garlic cloves, crushed
bouquet garni
6 black peppercorns
3 cups dry red wine
olive oil
flour for dredging
*thinly pared zest and juice of
    1 orange*
*thinly pared zest and juice of
    1 lemon*
water
4 tablespoons red currant jelly
¼ cup port
1 tablespoon cornstarch
1 tablespoon red wine vinegar
chopped fresh parsley, to garnish

STIR-FRIED CHICKEN WITH GINGER AND SNOW PEAS

ROAST DUCK AND POMEGRANATES IN NUT SAUCE

This dish, which is of Persian origin, may also be made with pheasant, goose, chicken or small lamb meatballs. Garnish with rosy pomegranate seeds, fresh limes and walnuts. Serve with tagliatelle or pasta.

Serves 4–6

INGREDIENTS

5 lb duck, giblets reserved

2½ cups water

salt and pepper

1 small onion, chopped

fresh pomegranate, lime slices and walnuts, to garnish

Sauce

4 tablespoons butter

½ cup chopped onion

1 cup ground walnuts

1 cup fresh pomegranate juice

1 teaspoon sugar

2–3 tablespoons fresh lime juice

ROAST DUCK AND POMEGRANATES IN NUT SAUCE

Place the duck giblets (except the liver) and neck into a small saucepan, with the water. Bring to the boil, skim any scum from the surface, cover and simmer gently for 45 minutes.

Preheat the oven to 375°.

Wipe the duck inside and out. Season the cavity and place the whole onion inside. Truss, prick the skin, and rub all over with salt. Place upside down on a rack in a roasting pan and pour in 3 tablespoons of water. Roast for 45 minutes, then turn the duck over and roast for a further 50 minutes. It is cooked when the juices run clear after a skewer or fork has been inserted into the thigh.

Meanwhile, to prepare the sauce, melt the butter and sauté the onion until golden. Remove the pan from the heat and stir in the walnuts. Return the pan to the heat and add the pomegranate juice. Strain the giblet stock and add it to the sauce, with the sugar and lime juice. Cover and simmer gently for 30 minutes or until the sauce has thickened.

Remove the duck from the oven. Pour off the fat and add the juices from the duck cavity to the pan juices. Add both to the sauce. Adjust the seasoning. Simmer, stirring, for 3 minutes. Joint, garnish and serve.

Note Do not be tempted to use an electric juicer for the pomegranates, as the bitter pith will be included. A manual juice squeezer is perfectly adequate.

WILD DUCK WITH ANCHOVIES AND CAPERS

The combination of anchovies and capers produces a tart taste that blends well with the richness of the wild ducks. Use mallard, can or black ducks.

Serves 4

Blend the wine, oil, tarragon, marjoram, peppercorns and salt together. Pour over the ducks, cover and leave in a cool place for 12 hours. Turn the birds every 2 hours onto a different side until all sides have been marinated.

Preheat the oven to 400°.

Remove the ducks from the marinade and dry well. Insert a piece of lemon in the cavity of each bird and season, then put a slice of bacon over each breast. Place in a roasting pan and cook for 20–30 minutes. The birds are cooked when the juices run clear after a skewer or fork has been inserted into the leg.

Meanwhile, strain the marinade into a pitcher and skim the fat from the surface. Heat 1 tablespoon of this fat and sauté the onion until soft. Stir in the strained marinade and the anchovies and boil until reduced by half. Purée the sauce in a blender or food processor, then return to the rinsed-out pan. Stir in the capers.

Remove the trussing string from the ducks, place them onto a warmed plate, cover and keep hot. Remove the excess fat from the pan juices, then pour the juices and cream into the anchovy and caper sauce. Reheat and simmer until reduced to a slightly syrupy consistency. Spoon some of the sauce over the ducks and serve the rest separately in a warmed sauceboat.

INGREDIENTS
1¼ cups full-bodied dry white wine
2 tablespoons olive oil
fresh tarragon sprig
fresh marjoram sprig
6 black peppercorns, crushed
salt and pepper
2 dressed wild ducks, about 1¾ lb each, trussed
½ lemon cut in half
2 bacon slices
½ cup finely chopped onion
10 anchovy fillets, soaked in milk, then drained
2 tablespoons chopped capers
2 tablespoons heavy cream

BROILED QUAIL STUFFED WITH MUSHROOMS

This is an elegant and unusual dish. Each bird is stuffed with mushrooms, shallot and parsley, then broiled until tender.

Serves 2–4

Melt the butter and sauté the mushrooms, shallot and parsley until soft. Season and leave to cool.

Cut each quail down the backbone with poultry scissors. Turn over and press down on the breast to break the breastbone. Loosen the skin over the breast of each bird and stuff it with the mushroom mixture.

Make a small slit in the skin on the breast at the leg end of each bird. Gently bend the legs inward to meet at the breastbone and tuck the end of each leg into the slit in the skin.

Place the quail, breast uppermost, on the broiler rack. Brush with olive oil, then sprinkle with the herbs and seasoning. Cook under a preheated moderate broiler for 12–15 minutes, turning once, until tender and golden brown.

INGREDIENTS
2 tablespoons butter
½ cup finely chopped mushrooms
2 tablespoons chopped shallot
1 tablespoon chopped parsley
salt and pepper
4 quail
1 tablespoon olive oil
1 tablespoon chopped fresh thyme or 1 teaspoon dried
1 teaspoon dried oregano

BRAISED VENISON WITH RED WINE

Serve with small potatoes steamed in their skins and braised fennel.

Serves 6

INGREDIENTS

6 venison steaks, about ½ lb each,
    cut from the shoulder
½ lb salt pork, diced
6 tablespoons unsalted butter
2 tablespoons vegetable oil
1 cup chopped onions
2½ cups chopped carrots
2 cups chopped celery
3 cups chopped turnips
salt and pepper
2 tablespoons unbleached flour
2 tablespoons red currant jelly
Marinade
½ cup chopped onion
6 black peppercorns
sprig of thyme, or ¼ teaspoon dried
    thyme
⅓ cup chopped celery
1 garlic clove, crushed
2½ cups dry red wine
¼ cup vegetable oil

To make the marinade, place the onion, peppercorns, thyme, celery, garlic, red wine and oil in a large shallow bowl. Add the steaks and coat with the marinade. Cover, place in the refrigerator and marinate, turning occasionally, for up to 2 days.

When ready to cook, remove the meat from the marinade and dry with paper towels.

Parboil the salt pork for 10 minutes, then drain on paper towels.

Melt half the butter with the oil in a large flameproof casserole. Add the venison and sauté until evenly browned. Remove from the pan and set aside. Add the salt pork to the pan and sauté until lightly colored. Add the onions, carrots, celery and turnips and sauté until soft.

Place the venison steaks on the bed of sautéed vegetables. Strain over the marinade and season. Cover the pan tightly and simmer for 2–2½ hours or until the meat is tender. Alternatively, cook in an oven preheated to 325° for 2½–3 hours.

Place the meat on a serving plate and keep hot. Strain the cooking liquid into a saucepan. Blend the remaining butter with the flour to a paste, then beat it into the liquid, a little at a time. Cook, stirring, until the sauce thickens. Stir in the red currant jelly and simmer until it has melted. Taste and adjust the seasoning.

Pour a little sauce over the meat and serve the remainder separately.

PEKING DUCK

This delicious Chinese dish first appeared in America and Europe toward the end of the last century. Originally, only the skin was eaten in the pancakes, while the meat was served with another dish.

Serves 4–6

INGREDIENTS

4 lb duck
1 tablespoon brandy
12 scallions
Pancakes
4 cups unbleached flour
2 cups boiling water
2 tablespoons sesame oil
Basting sauce
2 tablespoons honey
2 tablespoons dark soy sauce
⅔ cup cold water
Plum sauce
¼ cup hoisin sauce
¼ teaspoon sesame oil
1 teaspoon honey

Wash and dry the duck thoroughly. Rub the brandy all over the skin. Tie a piece of string under each wing and hang the duck overnight in a cool, dry, airy place.

To make scallion curls for the garnish, trim the root ends and all but 2 inches of the leaves from two scallions. Skin the scallions and cut the green leaves two or three times lengthwise. Drop them into ice water and leave for 2 hours, or until the ends open and curl up. Slice the white part only of the remaining scallions lengthwise into thin strips. Wrap until needed.

To make the pancakes, sift the flour into a bowl and stir in the boiling water. Mix to a dough. Knead in the bowl or on a lightly floured surface for 3 minutes. Cover with plastic wrap or a clean dish towel and rest for 30 minutes.

Preheat the oven to 400°.

Meanwhile, mix all the basting sauce ingredients together. Place the duck on a rack in a roasting pan half filled with cold water. Pour some of the basting sauce over the breast. Roast, breast side up for 35 minutes, basting every 10 minutes. Using two wooden spoons, turn the duck over onto its breast and baste with more sauce. The wooden spoons prevent the skin from being

pierced and the juices escaping. Roast for a further 30 minutes, basting frequently. Turn the duck over onto its back, and cook for a further 10 minutes, basting with the sauce.

While the duck is roasting, make the pancakes. Knead the dough briefly. Divide in half and keep one half covered. Roll the first half into a sausage shape about 16 inches long and cut in into 16 equal-sized pieces. Flatten each piece into a 2½-inch circle. Brush half the circles with sesame oil, then press the remaining circles on top of them, making 8 pairs. Make more pancakes with the remaining dough in the same way, to make 16 pairs. Roll out the circles until they measure 6 inches in diameter. Heat a heavy-bottomed skillet and cook the pancakes in the ungreased pan for 2 minutes on each side. When ready, the pancake will look dry on the underside and have brown flecks. The pancake will puff up when turned over. Remove from the pan, and while still hot, peel the two pieces apart. Keep hot wrapped in a dish towel.

Mix all the plum sauce ingredients together. Remove the skin from the duck in one piece and cut into 2-inch squares. Using 2 forks, pull the meat into shreds. Arrange the meat on a serving platter and garnish with the scallion tassels.

To serve, spread a little plum sauce over a pancake. Top with duck skin and meat, sprinkle with scallion strips, and roll up and eat with your fingers.

ROAST GROUSE WITH BREAD SAUCE, GAME CHIPS AND CHESTNUTS

*Bread sauce, game chips and chestnuts are the traditional English
accompaniment to serve with grouse. Ruffled grouse weigh up to
1¾ lb and you should allow one bird per person.*

Serves 4

INGREDIENTS

4 young ruffled grouse

juice of 1 lemon, strained

salt and pepper

16 bacon slices

4 tablespoons butter

1 teaspoon unbleached flour

Bread sauce

2 cups milk

2 cloves

1 small onion, sliced

salt and pepper

pinch of grated nutmeg

1½ cups fresh bread crumbs

2 tablespoons light cream

Game chip baskets

¾ lb potatoes

oil for deep-frying

salt

4 tablespoons butter

*1¼ lb canned whole unsweetened
   chestnuts, drained*

2 tablespoons pine nuts

white grapes to garnish

To make giblet stock for the gravy, remove the giblets from the grouse. Cover the giblets with water, bring to the boil and simmer for 30 minutes. Set aside.

Preheat the oven to 450°.

Wipe the birds inside and out and truss. Sprinkle with lemon juice and season. Bard with the bacon and place the birds in a roasting pan with the butter. Roast for 15 minutes. Remove the bacon and return the grouse to the oven for a further 5 minutes to brown the breasts. Remove from the pan and keep hot. Skim off the excess fat from the pan juices. Stir in the flour, then strain in the giblet stock. Bring to the boil and boil until well reduced. Season and strain. Remove the trussing string from the grouse.

To make the bread sauce, bring the milk, cloves, onion, seasoning and nutmeg to the boil. Reduce the heat and barely simmer for 10 minutes. Cool and strain. Return the infused liquid to the pan and stir in the bread crumbs and cream. Simmer for 10 minutes, stirring often. Adjust the seasoning.

To make the game chip baskets, finely slice the potatoes on a mandolin, or slice very thinly with a sharp knife. Dip a double wire mesh basket into the hot oil, remove, then line the bottom of the basket with overlapping potato slices. Push the top basket into place and plunge into the hot oil. Deep-fry until crisp and golden. Make 3 more baskets in the same way. Drain on paper towels, sprinkle with salt and keep hot. Melt the butter in a saucepan and add the chestnuts and pine nuts. Stir until heated through, then use to fill the baskets. Garnish.

BROILED POUSSIN WITH GARLIC AND LIMES

A poussin is a very young chicken weighing about 1–1¼ lb.

Serves 4

INGREDIENTS

2 poussins

juice of 3 limes

½ cup olive oil

4 garlic cloves, quartered

salt and pepper

¼ teaspoon ground turmeric

Split the poussins in half by cutting down one side of the breastbone. Open the birds out, turn them over and cut through the other side close to the backbone. Cut the backbone out completely.

Place the poussins in a bowl. Mix the remaining ingredients together, using the juice of 2 limes only, and pour over. Marinate for 1½–2 hours.

Charcoal grill or broil. If cooking over charcoal, baste during cooking with the marinade. To broil, place the pieces in a shallow flameproof dish or broiler pan. Pour the remaining lime juice over the poussins, tuck the garlic pieces under the portions and broil for 20–25 minutes, turning and basting with the marinade. Serve with the pan juices poured over the birds.

PHEASANT WITH CALVADOS AND APPLES

The cock pheasant is a beautiful bird with long speckled tail feathers.
The hen, although smaller, is fatter, with succulent flesh. Young
pheasants may be roasted but older birds should be casseroled.
This recipe combines the rich flavors of the pheasant, Calvados or
applejack and cream. Serve with sautéed apple slices.

Serves 2–3

INGREDIENTS

1 pheasant, about 2 lb trussed weight
salt and pepper
3 tablespoons clarified butter
2 shallots, finely chopped (¼ cup)
6 tablespoons Calvados or applejack
1¼ cups chicken stock (see page 247)
bouquet garni
¼ teaspoon arrowroot
1 tablespoon water
⅔ cup heavy cream
2 tablespoons butter
3 McIntosh apples, peeled and cut
*   into ½-inch-thick slices*
watercress, to garnish

Wipe the pheasant and season well. Heat the clarified butter in a casserole and brown the bird on all sides. Add the shallots and sauté until golden. Add the Calvados, stock and bouquet garni, and bring to the boil. Reduce the heat, cover and cook gently for 1 hour.

Remove the pheasant from the pan, divide into portions and keep hot. Strain the cooking juices, skimming off the fat. Return the juices to the pan. Mix the arrowroot with the water to a smooth paste, then add it to the cooking juices. Stir over a gentle heat for 1 minute, then add the cream. Cook gently, stirring, for 5 minutes. Season to taste.

Melt the butter in a skillet and cook the apples for 5 minutes or until golden but still firm. Arrange the apple slices around the edge of a serving dish. Place the pheasant in the center and pour the sauce over. Garnish with watercress.

PHEASANT WITH CALVADOS
AND APPLES

SPICED SALMIS OF CHICKEN WITH CAPERS

Coriander and cumin flavor this dish. In England, it is made with guinea fowl, birds about 2¼ lb with a flavor similar to a mild pheasant. You can also use 4 rock cornish hens, about 1¼ lb each.

Serves 4

Preheat the oven to 425°.

Cover the breast of each bird with 2 bacon slices and secure with fine string or thread. Put 2 lemon quarters inside each bird. Place in a roasting pan and roast for 30 minutes, basting occasionally. Remove from the pan and allow to cool slightly.

Remove the legs from each bird and carefully remove each breast. Remove and discard the skin from each portion. Roughly chop the carcasses.

Add the butter to the juices in the roasting pan and sauté the onion until soft. Stir in the coriander and cumin and cook, stirring, for 2 minutes. Add the stock and bring to the boil. Transfer to a large saucepan. Add the carcasses, cover and simmer for 30 minutes. Strain.

Add the lemon juice to the stock, then boil rapidly until reduced to about 2 cups. Stir in the capers and adjust the seasoning.

Arrange the joints in a single layer in a flameproof dish. Pour the sauce over and simmer gently for 15–20 minutes or until tender. Transfer to a heated serving dish and serve.

INGREDIENTS
2 young chickens, about 2¼ lb each
4 bacon slices
1 lemon, quartered
2 tablespoons butter
½ cup chopped onion
1 tablespoon ground coriander
2 teaspoons ground cumin
2½ cups chicken stock (see page 247)
2 tablespoons lemon juice
1½ teaspoons capers, drained
salt and pepper

RABBIT WITH TARRAGON CIDER SAUCE

The combination of the tarragon and cider in this sauce provides a sharp, piquant contrast to the rich game flavor of the rabbit.

Serves 4

Preheat the oven to 450°.

Grease the bottom of a roasting pan with 1 tablespoon butter and add the onion. Wrap a slice of bacon around each piece of rabbit and secure with a wooden toothpick. Place the rabbit on top of the onion and roast for 15 minutes.

Mix the cider, chopped tarragon, honey and mustard together and pour it over the rabbit. Reduce the temperature to 325° and continue cooking for 1–1½ hours, until tender.

Melt the remaining butter and sauté the apple until golden brown. Remove the rabbit from the roasting pan and keep hot. Remove the toothpicks. Pour the cooking juices over the apples. Dissolve the cornstarch in the water and stir it into the pan. Simmer gently, stirring, until thickened. Stir in the tomato paste and season.

Pour the sauce over the rabbit and garnish with the tarragon sprigs.

INGREDIENTS
3 tablespoons butter
½ cup chopped onion
4 bacon slices
4–5 lb rabbit, cut up
1¼ cups cider
1 tablespoon chopped fresh tarragon or ½ tablespoon dried tarragon
2 tablespoons honey
1 tablespoon Dijon mustard
2 tart apples, peeled, cored and cut into 8 pieces
1 tablespoon cornstarch
2 tablespoons water
1 tablespoon tomato paste
salt and pepper
fresh tarragon sprigs, to garnish

PARTRIDGE WITH APRICOTS
UNDER A PUFF PASTRY CRUST
(SHOWN HERE IN AN
INDIVIDUAL SERVING DISH)

PARTRIDGE WITH APRICOTS
UNDER A PUFF PASTRY CRUST

These individual pies are ideal as a luncheon dish.

Serves 4

INGREDIENTS

4 partridges
¼ cup olive oil
½ cup chopped shallot
½ cup finely diced carrot
¼ cup diced celery
1 bay leaf
9 sprigs fresh thyme
sprig of fresh parsley
⅔ cup dry white wine
1¼ cups chicken stock
4 tablespoons butter
salt and pepper
2 tablespoons pine nuts
2 tablespoons dry sherry
1 tablespoon cornstarch
squeeze of lemon juice
8 apricots, peeled, halved and pitted,
    or 16 canned halves, in
    unsweetened syrup, well drained
¾ quantity puff pastry (see page
    248)
beaten egg, to glaze

Using a sharp knife, carefully remove the legs from each partridge. Cut a line down the length of each leg bone and carefully ease the flesh away from the bone. Discard the skin. Ease the breasts from each carcass and discard the skin. Roughly chop the meat and then all the carcasses and bones. Heat half the oil in a heavy-bottomed casserole and brown the bones. Remove from the pan.

Add half the shallot, carrot and celery to the pan and sauté until golden. Add the bay leaf, 1 thyme sprig and the parsley, and return the bones to the pan. Pour the white wine over and bring to the boil. Add the stock, then cover and simmer for 45 minutes. Strain and reserve. There should be about 1¼ cups.

Melt the butter and sauté the partridge until golden all over. Season the meat and divide it between 4 individual heatproof deep dishes.

Add the remaining oil to the casserole and sauté the remaining shallot and pine nuts until golden. Stir in the sherry and bring to the boil. Add the reserved stock. Mix the cornstarch in 2 tablespoons water and stir into the sauce. Simmer until thickened. Adjust the seasoning and stir in the lemon juice. Cool.

Preheat the oven to 450°.

Finely chop remaining thyme sprigs. Divide the apricots and thyme between the 4 dishes. Pour the cooled sauce on top.

Roll out the pastry on a lightly floured surface and use to cover the pies. Brush with beaten egg. Re-roll the trimmings and cut out leaves. Arrange on the pies and brush with beaten egg. Bake 20–25 minutes or until crisp and golden. Serve hot.

MALLARD DUCK WITH RED WINE AND ORANGE

*In England this dish is made with widgeon, a wild duck. We have
substituted mallard, a tender domestic duck.*

Serves 4

Preheat the oven to 400°.

Wipe the ducks, season and place half a slice of orange in the cavity of each. Cover the breasts with bacon and truss neatly. Smear the surfaces with butter, place in a roasting pan and roast for 45 minutes, basting occasionally.

Meanwhile, to make the demi-glace sauce, heat the oil and gently sauté the onion, celery and carrot for 15 minutes. Stir in the flour and cook, stirring, until browned, scraping the crusty sediment from the bottom of the pan. Add 2 cups of the beef stock, mushrooms, tomato paste and the bouquet garni. Bring to the boil, reduce the heat, partially cover and simmer for 30 minutes.

Add half the remaining stock, return the sauce to the boil and skim constantly as the fat rises to the surface. Repeat with the remaining stock to give the sauce a glossy appearance. Strain the sauce and adjust the seasoning. This makes 1¼ cups demi-glace sauce.

To make the red wine sauce, melt the butter and sauté the shallots until soft. Add the red wine and the bay leaf, and simmer until reduced slightly. Add the demi-glace sauce with the orange zest and juice. Bring to the boil and simmer for about 5–8 minutes.

When cooked, remove the ducks from the oven cut them into serving pieces and keep hot. Add the pan juices to the sauce, then strain and skim any fat from the surface. Return to the pan and stir in the red currant jelly and season to taste. Simmer, stirring, to reheat. Place the ducks on a serving plate, pour the sauce around them and garnish with orange segments and watercress.

INGREDIENTS
2 mallard ducks, about 1 lb trussed
    weight each
salt and pepper
1 thick orange slice, halved
4 bacon slices
2 tablespoons butter
fresh orange segments and
    watercress, to garnish
Demi-glace sauce
2 tablespoons vegetable oil
¼ cup finely chopped onion
2½ tablespoons finely chopped
    celery
½ cup finely chopped carrot
1 tablespoon unbleached flour
2½ cups beef stock (see page 246)
1 mushroom, very finely chopped
1 teaspoon tomato paste
bouquet garni
Red wine sauce
1 tablespoon butter
2 shallots, finely chopped
½ cup dry red wine
bay leaf
pared zest of ½ orange
juice of 1 orange
1 teaspoon red currant jelly

ROAST TEAL WITH ORANGE BUTTER

*Teal is a small wild duck, often considered the most delicious of all wild
fowl. In this recipe the teal is served hot, but it is also delicious cold.
Allow 1 teal per person.*

Serves 4

To make the orange butter, beat the butter with the orange zest and juice, mustard and seasoning until evenly mixed. Form into a roll on a piece of aluminum foil, then wrap and chill until hard.

Preheat the oven to 425°.

Season the teal, then wrap a bacon slice over each breast. Place in a roasting pan and cook for 8–10 minutes. Remove the bacon and cook for 5 minutes more.

Remove the trussing string from the teal, then transfer the birds to warmed serving plates. Arrange the watercress around the birds. Cut the orange butter into 4 slices and place a slice on each bird. Spoon the cooking juices over and serve at once.

INGREDIENTS
salt and pepper
4 young teal, about ¾ lb each,
    dressed and trussed
4 bacon slices
8 watercress sprigs
Orange butter
8 tablespoons butter, softened
finely grated zest of 2 oranges
juice of 1 orange
½ teaspoon Dijon mustard

TURKEY AND CHESTNUT PIE

*A delicious pie made with hot-water pastry dough which is perfect for picnics or buffets. A
good jellied stock is essential—bouillon cubes simply won't do. If you do not have any
good stock at hand, make the required amount by covering 4 chicken wings with cold
water, add a few flavoring vegetables, bring it to the boil and simmer for 2 hours. Boil it
until reduced to the required amount of stock.*

Serves 6–8

Preheat the oven to 450°.

Roll out two-thirds of the dough to ½-inch thickness and use to line a lightly
buttered 8-inch springform pan.

Mix the turkey, bacon, parsley and half the chestnuts together and season.
Spoon half the mixture into the lined pan. Arrange the remaining chestnuts in a
layer over the filling. Spoon the remaining turkey mixture over the top and
sprinkle with brandy.

Roll out the remaining dough to an 8-inch circle. The top should be slightly
thinner than the base. Cover the pie, seal the edges and crimp. Re-roll the
trimmings and cut into leaves or other decorative shapes. Cut a cross in the
center of the pie and turn back the dough. Insert a small funnel of aluminum foil
into the hole. Brush the pie top with the beaten egg. Position the leaves and
brush with beaten egg.

Bake for 20 minutes. Reduce the temperature to 325°, cover the pie with foil
and cook for a further 2 hours. Remove the foil and cook the pie for 20 minutes
more, or until the pastry is a rich golden brown. Heat the stock gently until it is
just liquid. Remove from the heat and sprinkle the gelatin over the surface.
Leave for a few minutes to soften, then return the pan to the heat and stir until
the gelatin dissolves completely. Pour it into the middle of the pie, then cool
completely. Remove the funnel and serve.

INGREDIENTS
*1 quantity hot-water pastry dough
   (see page 249)*
1¼ lb turkey meat, diced
½ lb slab bacon, diced
2 tablespoons chopped parsley
*1 lb canned whole unsweetened
   chestnuts, drained and halved*
salt and pepper
3 tablespoons brandy
1 egg, beaten
*1¼ cups jellied turkey or chicken
   stock (see page 247)*
1 tablespoon unflavored gelatin

PARTRIDGES WRAPPED IN VINE LEAVES

*Partridges belong to the same family as pheasants. The stuffing in this recipe is made with
mushrooms, bread crumbs, ham and cream and is partly precooked because the roasting
time for partridge is so brief. The bird should be served slightly pink.*

Serves 4

Preheat the oven to 450°.

Wipe the partridges, season and set aside. Melt half the butter and sauté the
onion until soft. Add the mushrooms and cook for 3 minutes or until the
moisture has evaporated. Remove from the heat, place in a bowl, then cool
slightly. Stir in the bread crumbs, ham, parsley and cream, and season to taste.
Stuff the partridges and truss. Smear the breasts with the remaining butter.

If canned vine leaves are used, rinse well in cold water and dry. Remove the
stems and cover each breast with a leaf. Place 3 slices of bacon over each bird
and tie loosely in place with string.

Place the birds in a baking dish and roast for 15 minutes. Remove the birds
from the oven, discard the bacon and vine leaves, and return the partridges to
the oven for 5–10 minutes or until the breasts have browned.

Garnish and serve with the cooking juices and game chips (see page 82).

PARTRIDGES WRAPPED IN VINE LEAVES

INGREDIENTS
4 young partridges
salt and pepper
4 tablespoons butter
½ cup chopped onion
¾ cup chopped mushrooms
½ cup fresh bread crumbs
*1 oz ham, finely chopped
   (2 tablespoons)*
1 tablespoon chopped parsley
1 tablespoon heavy cream
4 large vine leaves
12 bacon slices
*extra vine leaves and lamb's
   lettuce, to garnish*

RAISED GAME PIE

*A favorite recipe for lunchtime snacks or picnics. The game is flavored
with wine, juniper berries, herbs and spices to make a tasty pie.*

Serves 8

INGREDIENTS

1 dressed pheasant, about 1¾ lb
1 dressed wild duck, about 2 lb
1 dressed grouse, about 1 lb
1 dressed partridge, about 1 lb
½ lb parboiled salt pork
1 onion
salt and pepper
1 quantity hot-water pastry dough
(see page 249)
1 egg, beaten, to glaze
Marinade
1¼ cups dry red wine
½ cup olive oil
½ cup wine vinegar
8 juniper berries, crushed
½ cup sliced onion
few parsley sprigs
few thyme sprigs
2 bay leaves
1 garlic clove, crushed
pinch of grated nutmeg
1 tablespoon sugar
1 teaspoon salt
¼ teaspoon Tabasco
Stock
½ cup chopped onion
½ cup chopped carrot
¼ cup chopped celery
1 bay leaf
fresh thyme sprig
fresh rosemary sprig
few parsley sprigs
4 juniper berries
⅔ cup white wine
2 cups chicken stock (see page 247)
2 teaspoons unflavored gelatin

To bone the game birds, carefully remove the breasts from each bird with a sharp knife, cutting away the meat from the legs. Remove all the skin, tendons and fat, then cut the meat into ½-inch strips. Roughly chop the carcasses and discard any skin and fat. Place the bones in a roasting pan.

Mix together all the ingredients for the marinade. Add the game meat, cover and leave in the refrigerator to marinate overnight or up to 24 hours.

Preheat the oven to 425°.

To make the stock, roast the bones for 20 minutes. Add the onion, carrot and celery and roast for a further 10 minutes. Transfer to a large saucepan. Add the herbs, juniper berries, white wine and stock, then bring to the boil. Cover and simmer for 1½ hours. Leave to cool, then strain. Boil the stock rapidly until reduced to 2 cups. Strain through fine cheesecloth then chill. Remove the surface fat.

The following day, preheat the oven to 375°. Remove the strips of meat from the marinade and dry well. Discard the marinade. Coarsely grind the salt pork and onion, then combine with the game. Season generously.

Reserve a scant one-third of the dough and wrap in plastic wrap. Roll out the remaining dough on a lightly floured surface and use to line the bottom and sides of a 9-inch round springform cake pan or raised pie mold, allowing the dough to overlap the rim a little. Spoon the filling into the dough case, pressing it down gently. Brush the edges of the dough with water. Roll out the remaining dough and cover the top of the pie. Press the edges well to seal, then trim off the excess. Crimp the edges. Re-roll the trimmings and use to make decorative leaves. Make a 1-inch hole in the top of the pie and insert a small funnel of aluminum foil in the hole. Brush with beaten egg. Arrange the dough leaves on top and brush with beaten egg.

Bake for 45 minutes. Remove the sides of the pan, and brush the sides of the pie with beaten egg, then return to the oven for 15 minutes. Brush the pie all over with beaten egg and return to the oven for 15 minutes more. To check if the filling is cooked, insert a skewer into the center of the pie, and leave for 10 seconds, then remove; it should be hot. If not, brush the pie with more beaten egg and return it to the oven for 15 minutes more. When cooked, leave the pie until cold.

Sprinkle the gelatin over the stock and leave to soften for 2 minutes. Stir over gentle heat until the gelatin dissolves completely. Leave until cool, then pour into the pie. Chill until required. Serve at room temperature.

CHICKEN AND HAM PIE

*A raised pie is ideal for a picnic, as the filling is set in a rich firm jelly
and encased in a thick pastry crust so it is easy to pack and carry.*

Serves 8

Lightly grease an 8-inch springform pan with a removable bottom. Alternatively, line the bottom and sides of a deep 8-inch cake pan with wax paper. Roll out two-thirds of the dough to ¼-inch thick and use to line the cake pan. Mix the chicken, ham, bacon, herbs and seasoning together. Spoon the filling into the lined pan. Pour over the wine and dot with butter. Roll the remaining dough into an 8-inch circle. Re-roll the pastry trimmings and cut into decorative leaves. Brush the edges of the pie with some of the beaten egg and cover with the dough circle. Crimp the edges to seal.

Preheat the oven to 450°.

Glaze the top of the pie with beaten egg, cut a cross in the center and turn the dough back. Insert a small aluminum foil funnel into the hole. Arrange the dough leaves on top and brush with beaten egg. Bake for 20 minutes. Reduce the temperature to 325°, cover with aluminum foil and bake for 2 hours. Remove the aluminum foil and cook the pie for 20 minutes more. Remove from the oven and cool completely.

Meanwhile, heat the stock gently until it is just liquid. Remove from the heat. Sprinkle the gelatin over and leave to soften for 2 minutes. Place over gentle heat until it has dissolved completely, allow to cool until almost set, then pour into the pie. Chill until required. Remove the funnel before serving.

INGREDIENTS

*1 quantity hot-water pastry dough
(see page 249)*

*1½ lb raw chicken breast, skinned
and diced*

1 lb cooked ham, diced

8 bacon slices, finely chopped

4 tablespoons chopped parsley

½ teaspoon fresh chopped thyme

pinch of grated nutmeg

salt and pepper

3 tablespoons dry white wine

2 tablespoons butter

1 egg, beaten, to glaze

*1¼ cups jellied chicken stock (see
page 247)*

1 tablespoon unflavored gelatin

THE PROVISIONS HALL

CHEESE
AND DAIRY

12

CHEESE AND DAIRY

◆

In the Dairy, over 500 different cheeses are on show and customers may taste before buying. All types of cream are on sale, including crème fraîche from France as well as butter from many countries. What could be nicer for summer lunch than Hot Goat's Cheese Salad with Sage Dressing? For an after-theater snack with friends, why not try Creamy Scrambled Eggs with Caviar?

CREAM OF STILTON SOUP

The Stilton is not actually cooked, but melts as it is stirred into the hot soup. This is a very rich soup, so this quantity will easily serve 4 as an appetizer. It is as delicious made with Roquefort or Danish blue.

Serves 4

INGREDIENTS
1¼ cups milk
1 bay leaf
¼ cup sliced onion
2 tablespoons butter
2 tablespoons unbleached flour
2 cups chicken stock (see page 247)
4 oz crumbled Stilton cheese (½ cup)
salt and pepper

Bring the milk, bay leaf and onion to the boil. Remove from the heat, cover and leave to infuse for 10 minutes. Strain.

Melt the butter in a large saucepan, stir in the flour and cook, stirring, for 1 minute. Remove the pan from the heat and gradually pour in the milk, stirring constantly. Return the pan to the heat and cook, stirring, for 1 minute, then add the stock. Bring the soup to the boil, then let it simmer for 5 minutes.

Remove the pan from the heat and immediately add the cheese. Stir until the cheese melts, then season with pepper and salt if necessary. Serve hot with crusty bread.

CAMEMBERT CROQUETTES

This simple cheese dish makes a delicious appetizer served with plum sauce.

Serves 2

INGREDIENTS
1 round Camembert, about ½ lb
flour seasoned with salt and pepper
1 egg, beaten
salt and pepper
1½ cups fresh bread crumbs
oil for deep-frying

Cut the Camembert into 8 wedges and toss in seasoned flour. Place the egg on a plate and season. Dip the cheese in egg, then coat in the bread crumbs. Coat a second time if necessary.

Chill the cheese for 30 minutes.

Heat the oil in a deep-fat fryer to 350°. Fry the Camembert in two batches for 1–2 minutes or until the coating is golden brown. Drain on paper towels and serve piping hot.

HOT BRIE TARTS

*These little tarts are perfect for a cocktail party because the pastry
can be made in advance. Serve straight from the oven, puffed and golden. Other
suitable cheeses to use are plain brie, Danish blue or Roquefort.*

Makes 28

Roll out the dough on a lightly floured board to ⅛-inch thickness.

Use a 3-inch round cookie cutter and cut out 28 circles and use to line muffin tins. Chill 30 minutes.

Preheat the oven to 425°.

Prick the bases with a fork, cover the bottom of each tin with a small circle of aluminum foil and fill with baking beans. Bake blind for 10 minutes. Remove from the oven, leave for 2 minutes, then remove the beans and paper. Reduce the oven temperature to 350°.

To make the filling, chop the cheese into small pieces. Place in the top of a double boiler or in a bowl set over a pan of simmering water. Add the cream and stir for 3–4 minutes or until the cheese melts. Remove from the heat and allow the cheese mixture to cool slightly. Stir in the beaten eggs.

Pour about 2 tablespoons of the mixture into each pastry case. Bake for 15–18 minutes or until puffed and golden. Serve at once.

INGREDIENTS
*1 quantity basic pie crust dough
  (see page 247)*
1 lb herb brie, rind removed
¼ cup light cream
4 eggs, lightly beaten

CAMEMBERT AND BROCCOLI SOUP

*This rich cheese soup combines beautifully the flavors of the Camembert and
broccoli. Serve before a light main course, such as broiled poultry or fish.*

Serves 4

Melt the butter in a large saucepan and sauté the shallots until soft. Peel the broccoli stems to remove the coarse skin, then chop. Add to the pan and sauté gently for 5 minutes. Add the stock and wine. Cover and simmer for 10–15 minutes or until the broccoli is tender.

Combine the cornstarch with the milk and stir into the soup. Bring to the boil, then simmer gently for 2–3 minutes. Add the Camembert and heat gently until melted, stirring frequently.

Purée the soup, return to the rinsed-out saucepan and adjust the seasoning. Warm through, then ladle into individual soup bowls.

For the garnish, sauté the tiny broccoli flowerets in the butter until tender but still crisp. Arrange on top of the soup with the basil leaves and paprika.

INGREDIENTS
2 tablespoons butter
*¼ cup finely chopped shallots or
  scallions*
½ lb broccoli flowerets
*1¼ cups chicken stock (see
  page 247)*
1¼ cups dry white wine
2 teaspoons cornstarch
⅔ cup milk
*½ lb Camembert, rind removed
  and cubed*
salt and pepper
Garnish
8 tiny broccoli flowerets
1 tablespoon butter
fresh basil leaves
paprika

DILL AND WALNUT YOGURT

This yogurt may be served as an appetizer with pita bread or as an accompaniment to spicy rice dishes.

Serves 4–6

Place the cucumber in a colander and sprinkle with salt, then leave to drain for 30 minutes.

Do not rinse the cucumber, but instead pat dry with paper towels.

Place the yogurt in a bowl and beat for a few moments until smooth. Add the remaining ingredients and mix well. Pour into a serving bowl. Garnish with fresh dill and walnut halves. Chill until required.

INGREDIENTS

1 large cucumber, peeled and diced
½ teaspoon salt
2½ cups plain yogurt
4 teaspoons finely chopped fresh dill or 2 teaspoons dillweed
1 small green chili, seeded and finely chopped
½ cup roughly chopped walnuts (2 oz)
2 tablespoons golden raisins
sprigs of fresh dill and walnut halves, to garnish (optional)

ROQUEFORT MILLE-FEUILLE

This savory pastry slice filled with creamy Roquefort cheese may be cut into small squares for a cocktail party, or cut into large portions for a first course or a snack.

Serves 4–6

Preheat the oven to 425–450°.

Roll out the dough on a lightly floured board to a 15-× 10-inch rectangle. Cut in half lengthwise.

Place the cheese in a bowl, add the butter and mix until well blended, soft and creamy. Stir in the egg and the paprika.

Place half the dough on a dampened cookie sheet (the moisture helps the pastry to rise while cooking). Make sure the cookie sheet is a thick one.

Spread the mixture onto the dough, leaving at least 1 inch of dough uncovered around the edges. Moisten the edge of the dough with a little cold water and top with the second piece of dough. Gently press the edges together to seal. Using a sharp knife, trim the edges evenly and pinch together. Brush with the egg glaze; the salt gives a rich golden color.

Bake for 15–20 minutes or until the pastry is a rich golden brown. Serve immediately.

INGREDIENTS

½ quantity puff pastry (see page 248)
scant 1 cup crumbled Roquefort cheese (5 oz)
2 tablespoons butter
1 egg, lightly beaten
¼ teaspoon paprika
1 egg, beaten with a pinch of salt, to glaze

NESTLED EGGS

*Phyllo pastry "nests" make an attractive serving container for these poached eggs.
They are served with a white wine sauce and garnished with caviar.*

Serves 4

INGREDIENTS

8 tablespoons unsalted butter

4 sheets of phyllo pastry

*1 large carrot, cut into julienne
strips (½ cup)*

*white part of 1 leek, cut into julienne
strips (¼ cup)*

6 tablespoons dry white wine

2 tablespoons chopped shallot

1 egg yolk

salt and pepper

4 eggs

*2 teaspoons salmon caviar or red
lumpfish roe, to garnish*

4 parsley sprigs, to garnish

Preheat the oven to 425°.

Melt 2 tablespoons of the butter and brush the inside of 4 individual 4-inch muffin tins.

Cut each sheet of pastry into 4 pieces. Line each tin with 4 pieces of pastry, brushing with melted butter between each layer. The pastry should be roughly pressed in to look like a "nest." Bake for 7–8 minutes, until crisp and golden. Keep warm.

Melt 2 tablespoons of the remaining butter and sauté the carrot and leek for 1–2 minutes or until just tender. Add 2 tablespoons of the white wine. Reserve.

Place the shallot and remaining white wine in a saucepan. Boil over moderate heat until reduced to 1 tablespoon. Strain into a small bowl and add the egg yolk.

Place in the top of a double boiler or in a bowl over a pan of simmering water and beat until the mixture just holds the trail of the beaters. Remove from the heat. Dice the remaining butter and beat it into the egg mixture a little at a time. Season to taste. Keep warm over the water.

Poach the eggs.

Place the pastry shells on serving plates. Warm the julienne vegetables, then spoon around the edges of the pastry shells. Arrange a poached egg in the center of each and spoon a little of the sauce over.

Garnish with a little caviar and parsley sprigs.

QUAILS' EGGS IN A BASKET

*These quails' eggs served in baskets of choux pastry make a delicious
and attractive first course.*

Serves 4

INGREDIENTS

*1 quantity choux pastry dough (see
page 249)*

*1 tablespoon finely grated Parmesan
cheese*

Filling

*3 oz Swiss chard or spinach leaves,
trimmed weight*

2 tablespoons butter

6 tablespoons heavy cream

grated nutmeg

paprika

salt and pepper

8 quails' eggs

Preheat the oven to 425°.

Spoon the choux pastry dough into 4 equal portions on a dampened cookie sheet. Spread out slightly into 2½-inch circles. Sprinkle with Parmesan cheese and bake for 20 minutes. With a small sharp knife, remove the top third of the "baskets" and place on the cookie sheet. Return to the oven for 5 minutes to crisp.

To make the filling, slice the Swiss chard or spinach leaves into very fine strips. Melt the butter in a skillet and sauté until just tender. Stir in the cream and season well with nutmeg, paprika and salt and pepper.

Boil the eggs for 2 minutes, drain and dip in cold water. Drain and remove the shells. Using an egg slice, slice almost through the eggs to make a fan shape. Remove the egg slices carefully.

Warm the chard gently and pile it into the pastry basket. Arrange 2 eggs on top of each one, sprinkle with paprika and top with the lid.

Yogurt Cheese Balls Marinated in Herbs

*These walnut-sized balls of thick yogurt look very pretty in their jar of
golden olive oil. Eat with salads, using the flavored oil as a salad dressing.*

Makes 16 balls

INGREDIENTS

*1 cup thick plain yogurt or Greek
yogurt*

2½ cups olive oil

*3 large sprigs fresh herbs, such as
rosemary, thyme or marjoram*

Stir the yogurt until smooth, then place it in the center of a large piece of
cheesecloth. Tie into a bundle and secure with string. Place the bundle in a deep
saucepan or casserole (it must not touch the bottom), position a wooden spoon
across the top and tie the bundle to it. Leave to drain overnight.

Unwrap the drained yogurt cheese and shape into 16 walnut-sized balls with
your fingers. Pour the olive oil into a glass jar and carefully drop the cheese balls
into the oil, one by one. Tuck the herbs down the sides of the jar, cover and
leave for at least 2 days before eating.

PHYLLO CHEESE PIE

*Phyllo is a wafer-thin pastry dough used to make sweet and entrée pies.
When using this dough, always keep it under a damp cloth, working with one
sheet at a time as it dries very quickly and becomes impossible to use.*

Serves 6–8

Preheat the oven to 375°.

Melt 6 tablespoons of the butter and sauté the onion until golden. Wash the spinach and cook in the water that clings to the leaves for 5 minutes. Drain thoroughly, then add to the onion and cook, stirring for 5 minutes. Remove from the heat, add the parsley, seasoning and nutmeg. Leave to cool. Add the feta cheese and eggs and mix well.

Melt the remaining butter. Place one sheet of pastry in a greased 12-× 9-inch shallow pan. Brush with the melted butter. Neatly tuck in the edges. Continue to make layers with half the pastry, brushing each one with butter.

Spread the spinach and cheese filling over the pastry, then use the remaining sheets, brushed with butter, to cover the filling. When the last sheet of pastry is in place, brush it well with butter and, using a sharp knife, score the top into a diamond pattern.

Bake for 40 minutes or until golden brown. Cool in the pan for 10 minutes, then serve.

INGREDIENTS
½ lb butter
1 cup finely chopped onion
*2 lb fresh spinach, central stem
  removed*
*2 tablespoons finely chopped
  parsley*
salt and pepper
¼ teaspoon grated nutmeg
½ lb feta cheese, crumbled
3 eggs, lightly beaten
10 sheets phyllo pastry

CREAMY SCRAMBLED EGGS WITH CAVIAR

*This will serve four as a first course or two as a light brunch dish.
Serve with melba toast.*

Serves 4

Lightly grease a skillet with the butter and place over gentle heat. Pour in the eggs, add the remaining butter, crème fraîche and seasoning.

Cook, stirring with a wooden spoon, until the eggs begin to set. Remove the skillet from the heat and continue stirring until the eggs are thick and creamy. Taste and adjust the seasoning.

Spoon the eggs onto individual serving plates and sprinkle the caviar over. Arrange melba toast triangles around the dish and serve immediately.

INGREDIENTS
8 tablespoons butter
8 eggs, lightly beaten
3 tablespoons crème fraîche
salt and pepper
*4 tablespoons caviar, or black
  lumpfish roe*
melba toast, to serve (see page 47)

YOGURT CHEESE BALLS MARINATED IN HERBS

CHICKEN AND MUSHROOM CREPES WITH CRAB SAUCE

*The unusual combination of flavors in this recipe blend together very well.
Serve with a crisp salad for lunch or as a light supper.*

Serves 4

INGREDIENTS

2 tablespoons butter

2 tablespoons finely chopped shallot

*3 boneless chicken breasts, about
    1¼ lb each, skinned and cut into
    ½-inch cubes*

¾ cup roughly chopped mushrooms

salt and pepper

⅔ cup light cream

½ lb crabmeat, flaked

2 tablespoons medium-dry sherry

Crêpes

½ cup unbleached flour

salt

1 egg, beaten

6 tablespoons milk

¼ cup water

1 tablespoon melted butter

vegetable oil for greasing

To make the crêpes, sift the flour and salt into a bowl. Make a well in the center and add the egg. Gradually beat in the milk and water until smooth. Stir in the melted butter.

Heat a 5½-inch crêpe pan over moderate heat. Pour in a little vegetable oil and when hot, add 2–3 tablespoons of the batter. Cook the crêpes for 1 minute on each side. Keep the crêpes warm and layered with wax paper, on a plate set over a pan of simmering water. This amount of batter should make 8 crêpes.

To make the filling, melt the butter and sauté the shallot for 2 minutes. Add the chicken and cook, stirring, until the chicken changes color. Stir in the mushrooms, cover the pan and cook for 3 minutes. Remove the lid, season and stir in 2 tablespoons of the cream. Simmer until the liquid in the pan reduces and thickens slightly.

Meanwhile, to make the sauce, blend the crabmeat and sherry together in a blender or food processor, then blend in the remaining cream.

Spoon the filling onto each crêpe, fold over the edges and place two crêpes, seam side down, on individual plates. Spoon the sauce around each crêpe and serve hot.

SPRINGTIME QUICHE

*This quiche combines the fresh flavor of young vegetables with mint. It
is preferable to use a metal tart pan rather than a white ceramic one, as
metal conducts more heat and will produce a better pastry case.*

Serves 6

INGREDIENTS

*½ lb whole wheat pastry dough (see
    page 249)*

2 tablespoons butter

½ cup chopped scallions

4 large lettuce leaves, shredded

⅔ cup shelled peas

salt and pepper

*1½ teaspoons chopped fresh mint or
    ¾ teaspoon dried*

⅔ cup grated Cheddar cheese

1 whole egg

1 egg yolk

⅔ cup cream

⅔ cup milk

Roll out the dough on a lightly floured surface and use to line a 10-inch fluted tart pan with a removable base. Chill for 30 minutes.

Preheat the oven to 375°.

Melt the butter in a saucepan and sauté the scallions, lettuce and peas over gentle heat for 5 minutes. Season, remove from the heat and stir in the mint.

Sprinkle the cheese evenly over the base of the quiche, then spread the vegetables over the cheese. Beat the egg with the egg yolk, cream and milk. Pour carefully over the vegetables. Bake for 40 minutes or until the quiche is set and golden brown. Serve warm or cold.

HOT GOAT'S CHEESE SALAD WITH SAGE DRESSING

This recipe will make a light appetizer for four or a light luncheon dish for two.

Serves 4

Cut the cheese widthwise into 4 equal slices. Pour the olive oil into a bowl, add the sage leaves and carefully immerse the cheese slices. Cover the bowl and leave overnight.

Make the dressing the day before to allow the flavors to blend. Pour all the dressing ingredients into a screw-top jar. Place the top on the jar and shake well to blend.

Preheat the oven to 400°.

Drain the cheese, leaving the leaves in the oil. Place the bread crumbs in a shallow dish and stir in the dried sage. Coat the cheese slices in the bread crumbs and place on a greased cookie sheet. Bake for 10–12 minutes or until the bread crumbs are light golden. Leave the cheese on the cookie sheet for 2 minutes.

Arrange the lettuce leaves and endive spears on individual serving plates. Carefully transfer the cheese slices to each plate. Shake the dressing and spoon a little over the leaves. Serve warm.

INGREDIENTS

1 goat cheese, weighing ½ lb
1 cup olive oil
12 fresh sage leaves
½ cup fine fresh bread crumbs
pinch of dried sage
12 lettuce leaves
12 spears Belgium endive
Sage dressing
1½ tablespoons white wine vinegar
1 garlic clove, quartered
¼ teaspoon Dijon mustard
2 sage leaves
salt
3 tablespoons olive oil

GOLDEN RICE MOLD
WITH DUCK EGGS AND YOGURT

Do not use a casserole with raised handles because the edge of the pan needs to be placed directly on the serving dish when it is turned over to prevent the rice from cracking. A ring mold may be used, or any mold with 2½-quart capacity.

Serves 6

Place the breasts, cold water and seasoning in a saucepan and bring to the boil. Reduce the heat, cover and cook for 30 minutes or until tender. Remove the skin from the breasts and cut the meat into small pieces. Strain the cooking liquid and reserve 6 tablespoons. Stir the egg yolks, yogurt and oil together.

Preheat the oven to 375°.

Mix the saffron with the hot water and leave to infuse for 5 minutes. Stir it into the yogurt mixture with the cooled cooking liquid. Wash the rice in cold water and drain, discarding any husks or discolored grains. Bring a large saucepan of salted water to the boil. Add the rice, stir and return to the boil. Cook for 3–4 minutes, drain immediately and rinse in cold water. Drain again.

Pour the melted butter into the bottom of the mold and rotate it to coat the sides well. Dip the chicken pieces in the yogurt mixture. Mix half of the rice with the remaining yogurt mixture. Reserve half and spread the remainder over the bottom. Sprinkle two-thirds of the currants and the cumin on top. Spread half of the plain rice over the currants and cumin. Top with some of the chicken pieces. Make another layer of white rice, the remaining currants and cumin and top with yellow rice. Press the mixture down and cover with aluminum foil. Bake for 1 hour. Plunge the bottom into cold water for 1 minute. Unmold and serve with extra butter and yogurt.

INGREDIENTS

2 large duck or chicken breasts,
    about ½ lb each
1¼ cups cold water
salt and pepper
2 duck egg yolks
1 cup plain yogurt
1 tablespoon vegetable oil
½ teaspoon saffron powder
1 tablespoon hot water
1¼ lb basmati rice
6 tablespoons butter, melted
⅔ cup currants
½ teaspoon ground cumin
extra butter and yogurt for serving

FRITTATA WITH FRESH HERBS

*This is a baked omelet which can be served hot or cold, with plain
yogurt for breakfast, lunch or a light snack. Vary the herb
combinations to use whatever is available so you do not have to use
dried herbs.*

Serves 4–6

INGREDIENTS
6 eggs
*4 tablespoons finely chopped fresh
    coriander*
*4 tablespoons finely chopped fresh
    parsley*
1 tablespoon finely chopped chives
*green tops of 2 scallions, finely
    chopped*
1 tablespoon finely chopped fresh dill
pinch of saffron powder
salt and pepper
4 tablespoons butter

Preheat the oven to 350°.

Lightly beat the eggs in a large bowl. Add all of the remaining ingredients, except the butter, and beat together lightly.

Place the butter in a shallow round baking dish.

Melt the butter in the oven. Pour the egg mixture into the hot dish, cover with aluminum foil and bake for 30 minutes. Remove the aluminum foil and return to the oven for a further 15 minutes. Turn the frittata out onto a serving dish, cut into 4–6 wedges and serve.

FETTUCCINI WITH GORGONZOLA SAUCE

*This rich creamy sauce combines the delicious Italian flavors of
Gorgonzola and basil. Fresh parsley, sage and oregano would also go
well with this sauce.*

Serves 4

INGREDIENTS
4 tablespoons butter
6 oz Gorgonzola, crumbled (1 cup)
⅔ cup heavy cream
2 tablespoons dry white wine
1 tablespoon chopped fresh basil
salt and pepper
1 lb fettuccini (see page 251)

Melt the butter in a saucepan. Add the Gorgonzola, then stir over gentle heat for 2–3 minutes, until melted. Pour in the cream and wine, beating vigorously. Mix in the basil, salt and pepper and cook, stirring, until the sauce thickens. Remove from the heat.

Cook the fettuccini in a large pan of boiling, salted water for 2–3 minutes or until al dente. Drain thoroughly.

Gently reheat the Gorgonzola sauce, beating vigorously all the time. Taste and adjust the seasoning. Turn the pasta into 1 large or 4 individual serving bowls and pour over the sauce. Serve at once.

FRIED BRIE WITH CRANBERRY SAUCE

FRIED BRIE WITH CRANBERRY
SAUCE

*The brie for this recipe should not be over-ripe. Serve as an appetizer or
light snack with a crisp green salad.*

Serves 6

To make the cranberry sauce, place the cranberries and water in a saucepan and
bring to the boil. Cover and simmer for 10–15 minutes. Remove from the heat
and stir in the sugar. Return the pan to the heat and simmer for 10–15 minutes
more. Pour into a serving bowl and keep hot.

Sift the flour onto a plate and coat the cheese on all sides. Dip into the beaten
egg, then coat with the bread crumbs. Heat the oil in a deep-fat fryer to 350°.
Deep fry the brie for 1½–2 minutes on both sides, or until the bread crumbs are
golden. Drain well on paper towels. Serve hot accompanied by the cranberry
sauce.

INGREDIENTS
¼ cup unbleached flour
1½ lb brie, cut into 6 wedges
1 egg, lightly beaten
1½ cups fresh bread crumbs
1¼ cups vegetable oil
Cranberry sauce
1½ cups cranberries, fresh or
frozen
6 tablespoons water
6 tablespoons sugar

CHARCUTERIE AND VARIETY MEATS

CHARCUTERIE AND VARIETY MEATS

◆◆◆

Over 60 different salamis deck the charcuterie counter, as well as 40 types of sausage, including Harrods own handmade variety. There are 40 different pâtés and Scottish haggis is also a popular purchase. Sizzling Farmhouse Sausages make a delicious and simple meal and the richer Salade de Foie Gras Chaude is the ideal dish for a special occasion.

PRESSED BEEF TONGUE IN ASPIC

Tongue, pressed and set in aspic, is unmolded onto a serving plate and accompanied by Cumberland sauce in this attractive dish.

Serves 6–8

INGREDIENTS
3 lb salted beef tongue
6 black peppercorns
½ cup chopped celery
2 bay leaves
2 small onions, quartered
1 cup chopped carrot
2 cups jellied chicken stock (see
*   page 247) or commercial aspic*
cranberries, to garnish
lemon slices, to garnish
chervil or dill sprigs, to garnish
Cumberland sauce
pared zest and juice of 1 orange
pared zest and juice of 1 lemon
4 tablespoons red currant jelly
¼ cup port
2 teaspoons arrowroot
2 teaspoons water

Soak the tongue in cold water for 4–6 hours. Drain and place in a large saucepan with the peppercorns, celery, bay leaves, onions and carrots. Cover with cold water. Slowly bring to the boil, skimming off any scum with a slotted spoon. Cover and simmer for 2½–3 hours or until the tongue is tender when pierced with a fine skewer or fork.

Remove the tongue from the liquid and remove the skin, any small bones and gristle.

Pour a little aspic into the base of a soufflé dish. Chill until set. Arrange the cranberries, lemon slices and chervil or dill sprigs in a decorative pattern over the aspic. Cover with a thin layer of aspic and leave to set.

Curl the tongue tightly into the dish and pour the remaining stock over the top. Place a plate, which just fits inside the dish, over the tongue with a heavy weight on top. Chill overnight.

For the Cumberland sauce, simmer the pared citrus zest for 5 minutes. Drain. Dissolve the red currant jelly in the citrus juices over gentle heat, then stir in the port. Blend the arrowroot with the water and stir in. Cook until thickened, then stir in the citrus.

To serve, dip the dish quickly into hot water to loosen, then turn out onto a serving plate. Serve with the Cumberland sauce.

SALADE DE FOIE GRAS CHAUDE

*This salad is ideal to serve as a luncheon dish or an appetizer for a dinner party.
The warm dressing blends well with the crisp lettuce and tomatoes.
Radicchio leaves add a splash of color.*

Serves 4

Wash and dry all the salad leaves and tear into bite-sized pieces. Place in a large bowl with the herbs, beans and tomatoes.

Melt the butter with the oil and sauté the onion rings until golden. Add the mushrooms and toss quickly in the fat. Add to the salad ingredients.

Place all the dressing ingredients into the skillet and heat over gentle heat until warmed through. Season generously.

Add to the salad and toss quickly, coating the leaves evenly with the dressing. Serve at once, topped with slices of pâté de foie gras.

INGREDIENTS

¾ lb mixed salad leaves –
    watercress, chicory, radicchio,
    spinach, endive, etc
2 tablespoons chopped fresh herbs –
    parsley, chives, tarragon, basil,
    etc
¼ lb green beans, trimmed and
    blanched for 2 minutes
2 firm tomatoes, peeled, seeded and
    cut into 8
1 tablespoon butter
1 tablespoon olive oil
1 small red onion, cut into rings
1 cup sliced mushrooms
¼ lb pâté de foie gras aux truffes,
    cut into 12 slices

Dressing

3 tablespoons olive or walnut oil
2 tablespoons raspberry vinegar
1 teaspoon green peppercorns
1 teaspoon strong French mustard,
    with or without seeds
1 teaspoon sugar
salt and pepper

SALADE DE FOIE GRAS CHAUDE

CERVELLES BOURGUIGNONNE

*Poached in stock and served in an onion and mushroom sauce,
brains make an appetizing first course.*

Serves 4

INGREDIENTS

2 sets of calves' brains, or 4 sets of
    lambs' brains
3 tablespoons vinegar
3 tablespoons butter
½ cup diced carrot
½ cup diced onion
¼ cup diced leek
¼ cup diced celery
2 garlic cloves, chopped
few parsley sprigs
few thyme sprigs
1 bay leaf
1¼ cups Burgundy, or other red
    wine
1¼ cups chicken stock (see page 247)
24 pearl onions
4 slices smoked bacon
1 cup chopped mushrooms
1 tablespoon unbleached flour
1 tablespoon tomato paste
salt and pepper
chopped fresh parsley, to garnish

Soak the brains in several changes of lightly vinegared water (about 1 table-spoon to every 5 cups water) for 2 hours. Carefully remove the blood vessels and membrane.

Melt 1 tablespoon of the butter and sauté the carrot, onion, leek, celery, garlic, parsley, thyme sprigs and bay leaf for 5 minutes. Add the wine and stock and bring to the boil. Reduce the heat, then add the brains. Cover and simmer for abut 30 minutes (lambs' brains may be ready in 20 minutes).

Place 1 tablespoon of the remaining butter in a large skillet and gently sauté the onions for about 10 minutes or until golden.

Carefully remove the brains from the cooking liquid. Strain the liquid and return it to the rinsed-out pan with the onions. Boil rapidly for about 5 minutes, until the liquid has reduced by one third.

Meanwhile, cut the bacon into strips and sauté in the pan juices until crisp. Remove from the pan, add the mushrooms and sauté for 1–2 minutes.

Combine the remaining butter with the flour and work it to a smooth paste. Beat it into the onion sauce with the tomato paste and gently simmer until thickened. Adjust the seasoning to taste. Cut the brains into even-sized pieces and add to the sauce with the bacon and mushrooms. Simmer very gently until heated through. Serve at once sprinkled with chopped parsley.

RILLETTES DE CANARD

*This classic French country dish is ideal as an appetizer or for picnics.
Serve with hot toast or French bread.*

Serves 4

INGREDIENTS

½ lb duck breast
½ lb parboiled salt pork
½ lb pork fat
1 garlic clove, chopped
1 bay leaf
few sprigs of fresh thyme
salt and pepper
¼ cup water

Preheat the oven to 275°.

Cut the duck and salt pork into 1-× 2-inch strips and dice the pork fat. Place all the ingredients in an ovenproof casserole with a tight-fitting lid. Cover securely with aluminum foil to prevent evaporation, if wished. Cook for 4 hours, shaking the dish from time to time to prevent sticking.

Strain the contents of the dish through a metal sieve, discarding the bay leaf and thyme. Place the meat in a bowl and, using two forks, pull it into shreds. Adjust the seasoning. Press the meat into 4 ramekin dishes and pour the strained fat over. Cool, then chill until set.

Note

Rillettes d'oie may be made by replacing the duck breast with goose.

JAMBON PERSILLE DE BOURGOGNE

*Serve this dish as a light lunch, first course or take on a picnic,
accompanied by crusty French bread.*

Serves 6

Place the ham, veal and ham hocks in a large saucepan and cover with water. Slowly bring to the boil, then simmer for 10 minutes. Drain and discard the water.

Cut the ham into 2-inch cubes and return to the pan with the veal and ham hocks. Add the bouquet garni, peppercorns and onion with the wine and sufficient water to cover the meat. Bring to the boil, cover and simmer gently for 3 hours. Do not allow the liquid to boil again.

Remove the ham pieces from the stock with a slotted spoon. Flake the meat with a fork. Strain the stock through a piece of cheesecloth or dish towel, then stir in the vinegar.

Pack the flaked meat into a glass serving dish. When the stock begins to set, stir in the parsley. Pour the stock over the meat to cover completely and leave to set. Chill for 24 hours before serving.

INGREDIENTS
3 lb mild cured ham
1 veal knuckle, chopped
2 ham hocks
water, to cover
*bouquet garni, made with parsley
    sprigs, 2 bay leaves, tarragon
    and thyme*
12 black peppercorns
1 small onion, quartered
4¼ cups dry white wine
4 teaspoons tarragon vinegar
*2 tablespoons finely chopped
    parsley*

PORK AND WALNUT PATE

*This tasty pâté, made with brandy, juniper berries and orange zest,
can be served as an appetizer or for a picnic lunch.*

Serves 8

Parboil the salt pork for 7–8 minutes, then drain on paper towels.

Preheat the oven to 325°.

Grind the liver, salt pork and bacon together in a food processor. Place in a mixing bowl and stir in the brandy, wine, eggs, juniper berries, nutmeg, orange zest and seasoning.

Line a 9-× 5-× 3-inch loaf pan or terrine with some of the pork fat. Press one-third of the mixture into the dish and sprinkle half the walnuts over the top. Press half the remaining mixture over the walnuts. Arrange the remaining walnuts over the top and spread with the remaining pâté mixture. Smooth over the top and cover with the remaining pork fat.

Cover with aluminum foil and place in a roasting pan. Add enough boiling water to come halfway up the side of the loaf pan. Bake for 1½–2 hours, depending on the depth of the loaf pan or terrine. When cooked, the pâté will have shrunk from the sides of the dish and the juices will run clear.

Put a plate on top of the pâté and place a heavy weight on top. Cool, then chill until required.

INGREDIENTS
1½ lb salt pork
½ lb pig's liver
12 bacon slices
2 tablespoons brandy
6 tablespoons dry white wine
2 eggs, beaten
*1 tablespoon juniper berries,
    crushed*
pinch of grated nutmeg
*1 teaspoon finely grated orange
    zest*
salt and pepper
½ lb pork fat slices
*⅔ cup roughly chopped walnuts
    (3 oz)*

DUCK PATE WITH GREEN PEPPERCORNS

Green peppercorns are a perfect foil for the rich flavor of duck.

Serves 6–8

INGREDIENTS

4½ lb duck, boned
3 tablespoons brandy
2 teaspoons dried thyme
salt and pepper
½ lb lean veal
2 duck livers
4 tablespoons chopped shallots
pinch of ground allspice
2 eggs, lightly beaten
about 16 bacon slices
2 tablespoons green peppercorns
bay leaf

Preheat the oven to 350°.

Remove the skin and trim the excess fat from the duck. Cut the larger pieces into long strips about ¼-inch wide. Place in a bowl with the brandy, half the thyme and seasoning.

Grind the remaining duck with the veal and liver in a meat grinder or food processor. Stir in the shallots, remaining thyme, allspice and eggs. Season and mix well.

Line the sides and bottom of 9-× 5-× 3-inch loaf pan or terrine with two-thirds of the bacon. Remove the duck strips from the marinade and stir the marinade into the ground mixture. Spread one-third of the ground mixture over the bottom of the pan. Cover with half the duck strips and sprinkle with half the green peppersorns. Spread half the remaining ground mixture over the duck, then cover with the remaining duck strips and peppercorns. Spread the remaining ground mixture over the top. Cover with the remaining bacon and the bay leaf.

Cover with aluminum foil and place in a roasting tin. Pour in enough boiling water to come halfway up the sides of the pan. Bake for 1¾–2 hours, until the pâté has shrunk from the sides of the pan. Drain off the excess liquid. Cover with aluminum foil and place heavy weights on top of the pâté. Leave until cold. If using a loaf pan, turn the pâté out onto a serving plate. If using a terrine, serve from the dish.

FOIE GRAS SAUTE

This foie gras should be firm and a creamy white, tinged with pink. A few diced truffles tossed in melted butter may be used to garnish this dish, if wished.

Serves 4

INGREDIENTS

1 lb fresh duck foie gras, trimmed and cut into 12 thin slices
1 egg, lightly beaten
1 cup fresh bread crumbs
salt and pepper
4 tablespoons clarified butter
Madeira sauce
2 tablespoons Madeira
¾ cup jellied veal stock
1 tablespoon orange juice
2 large oranges, segmented, to garnish

Dip the foie gras slices into the egg, then into the bread crumbs. Season. Melt the butter in a skillet and sauté the foie gras for 1 minute on each side. Remove from the pan and keep hot.

To make the Madeira sauce, stir the Madeira into the skillet, then add the veal stock and orange juice. Boil for 3–4 minutes, until reduced. Adjust the seasoning, strain, and pour around the foie gras. Garnish with the orange segments and serve immediately.

Note

Either goose or duck liver can be used in this recipe.

BOUDIN BLANC

CHICKEN LIVER MOUSSELINE
WITH CRANBERRY SAUCE

The rich fruity flavor of cranberries marries well with this light mousseline.
Serve as an appetizer with croûtes of toast.

Serves 4

INGREDIENTS

3 tablespoons butter
2 tablespoons chopped shallot
1 small garlic clove, chopped
4 oz chopped chicken livers (½ cup)
2 oz chopped chicken breast (¼ cup)
½ cup fresh bread crumbs
1 egg
6 tablespoons heavy cream
salt and pepper
parsley or chervil sprigs, to garnish
Cranberry sauce
½ cup cranberries
1 tablespoon sugar
2 tablespoons Madeira
1 cup chicken stock (see page 247)
3 tablespoons chilled butter

Preheat the over to 350°.

Melt the butter in a saucepan and use a little to grease the inside of 4 individual ⅓-cup dariole molds.

Sauté the shallot and garlic until soft. Cool slightly, then place in a food processor with the chicken livers, chicken breast, bread crumbs, egg, cream and seasoning. Blend to a smooth purée.

Spoon the purée into the dariole molds and cover each one with aluminum foil. Place in a small roasting pan and pour in enough boiling water to come three-quarters of the way up the sides of the molds. Cook for about 25 minutes or until firm to the touch. Remove from the water.

Meanwhile, to make the sauce, place the cranberries, sugar and Madeira in a saucepan and boil until the liquid has reduced to 1 tablespoon. Add the stock and boil rapidly for about 10 minutes, until the sauce is light and syrupy. Remove from the heat, adjust the seasoning and beat in the butter.

Unmold the mousses onto individual plates, spoon the sauce around and garnish with parsley. If wished, serve with small croûtes of toast or fried bread.

BOUDIN BLANC

Boudin blanc are sausages made with chicken and veal and are traditionally served with mashed potatoes and apple slices sautéed in butter and sugar. Accompany with the piquant mustard and Calvados sauce.

Makes 8 sausages

Soak the sausage casings in water in the refrigerator for about 4–5 hours.

Scald the cream, then stir in the bread crumbs, seasoning, allspice and nutmeg and set aside until cold. Melt the butter and sauté the onion until soft. Set aside to cool.

Roughly chop the chicken, veal and salt pork and grind in a meat grinder or food processor. Add the bread crumb mixture, the cooked onion and egg whites. Process again in the meat grinder or food processor.

Attach the sausage casings to the end of the faucet or a funnel and pass cold water through them. Put the sausage mixture into a large pastry bag fitted with a large plain tip and pipe the mixture into the soaked sausage casings. Each sausage shuld be about 6-inches long, so either twist the skin at intervals or tie with fine string. Prick the sausages with a sterilized pin to prevent them bursting during cooking.

To make the cooking liquid, pour the water into a roasting pan, and slowly bring to a simmer. Add the herbs and vegetables, then add the sausages. They must be covered with liquid, so add extra if necessary. Gently simmer for 20 minutes. Do not allow the liquid to boil because the sausages may burst. Remove from the heat and cool in the liquid. Drain and dry on paper towels.

To finish cooking, melt the butter in a large skillet and sauté the sausages for 8–10 minutes or until brown. Alternatively, brush with melted butter and brown under a preheated medium broiler.

For the mustard sauce, melt the butter in a saucepan and sauté the shallot until soft. Stir in the flour and cook for 1–2 minutes, stirring continuously. Slowly add the stock and cream, then stir in the mustard and simmer, covered, for 5 minutes. Stir in the Calvados or applejack and lemon juice, then adjust the seasoning.

INGREDIENTS
about 2 yards sausage casings
½ cup heavy cream
2 cups fresh bread crumbs
salt and pepper
¼ teaspoon ground allspice
¼ teaspoon grated nutmeg
2 tablespoons butter
½ cup chopped onion
½ lb chicken breast
½ lb veal for stewing
½ lb parboiled salt pork
2 egg whites
1 tablespoon butter
Cooking liquid
about 2 quarts
few parsley sprigs
2 bay leaves
½ cup diced carrot
¼ cup diced celery
¼ cup diced leek
Mustard sauce
2 tablespoons butter
2 tablespoons chopped shallot
¼ cup unbleached flour
¾ cup chicken stock (see
   page 247)
½ cup light cream
2 tablespoons coarse French
   mustard with seeds
1 tablespoon Calvados or applejack
1 teaspoon lemon juice
salt and pepper

CHICKEN LIVER PATE

This quick pâté involves a minimum of cooking. Serve as an appetizer or snack.

Makes about 1¼ lb

Melt 4 tablespoons butter and sauté the garlic and chicken livers for 5 minutes. Place them in a blender or food processor, but do not belnd. Stir the brandy into the cooking juices, then add it to the liver and garlic. Blend until smooth.

Melt 6 tablespoons of the remaining butter and sauté the mushrooms for 5 minutes. Drain the mushrooms and reserve. Stir the butter into the chicken livers, cool slightly and season to taste with nutmeg and salt and pepper. Stir in the cream and mix well. Pour into a ¾-quart mold or individual ramekins. Arrange the mushrooms on top. Melt the remaining butter, skim off the milky residue and pour over the mushrooms. Cool, then chill until set.

INGREDIENTS
½ lb butter
2 garlic cloves, crushed
½ lb chicken livers
2 tablespoons brandy or Cognac
½ cup sliced mushrooms
¼ teaspoon grated nutmeg
salt and pepper
2 tablespoons heavy cream

FARMHOUSE SAUSAGES

*This is a tasty recipe for making herb and sage sausages. For a traditional
country-style meal, serve sizzling hot with mustard and mashed potatoes.*

Makes 8 sausages

INGREDIENTS

1 lb lean pork

½ lb parboiled salt pork

3 tablespoons chopped parsley

*1½ teaspoons chopped fresh thyme or
¾ teaspoon dried*

*1½ teaspoons chopped fresh
marjoram or ¾ teaspoon dried*

*¾ teaspoon chopped fresh sage or
¼ teaspoon dried*

salt and pepper

½ teaspoon paprika

pinch grated nutmeg

1 tablespoon brandy

about 4 feet sausage casings

Roughly chop the pork and salt pork and pass through a meat grinder or food processor twice. Combine with all other ingredients except the sausage casings, and mix well. Cover and leave in the refrigerator for up to 24 hours for the flavors to develop.

Soak the sausage casings in water in the refrigerator for 4–5 hours. Attach them to the end of the faucet or a funnel and pass cold water through them.

Spoon the sausage mixture into a large pastry bag fitted with a large plain tip or a sausage stuffer and carefully pipe the mixture into the sausage casing. Each sausage should be about 6-inches long, so either twist the skin at intervals or tie with string.

Sauté or broil the sausages with a little extra fat for 10–15 minutes, until well browned.

TRIPE WITH WHITE WINE SAUCE

*Tripe is a variety meat frequently served in England. In this recipe,
strips of tripe are simmered with vegetables, then deep fried and served
in a white wine sauce. Honeycomb tripe is the most suitable variety.*

Serves 4

INGREDIENTS

2 lb dressed tripe

½ cup chopped onion

½ cup chopped carrot

¼ cup chopped celery

½ lemon, sliced

bouquet garni

boiling water

salt and pepper

flour for coating

3–4 eggs, beaten

6–8 garlic cloves, crushed

3 cups fresh bread crumbs

oil for deep-frying

White wine sauce

2 tablespoons chopped shallots

6 tablespoons dry white wine

6 tablespoons white wine vinegar

12 tablespoons butter, diced

2 tablespoons chopped parsley

Place the tripe in a large saucepan with the onion, carrot, celery, lemon and bouquet garni. Add sufficient boiling water to cover and simmer gently for 15 minutes or until tender. Drain well and dry on paper towels. Set aside until cold. Trim off any skin, then cut the tripe into ½-inch strips.

Season the flour, then use to coat the tripe. Mix the eggs, garlic and seasoning together. Dip the tripe into the beaten egg and then in bread crumbs to coat. Set aside while making the sauce.

Place the shallot, wine and wine vinegar in a saucepan and boil until reduced to 2 tablespoons. Remove from the heat and beat in the butter a little at a time, until each amount turns creamy, but not oily, before adding the next amount. Pass the pan over the heat from time to time if necessary, just to warm the mixture. When all the butter has been added, stir in the parsley and adjust the seasoning. Keep the sauce just warm.

Heat the oil in a deep skillet to 375° and deep-fry the tripe in batches until crisp and golden. Drain on paper towels and serve at once, with the hot sauce.

HAM HOCKS WITH CABBAGE AND RED CURRANTS

*This casserole may be boiled rapidly for about 5 minutes before serving
to reduce the liquid with the cabbage.*

Serves 4

Singe the ham hocks over a candle or gas flame. Scrub well, then tie each one tightly in cheesecloth so it keeps its shape during cooking. Place them in a large pan or pressure cooker and add the carrots, onions, leek, celery, bay leaves, bouquet garni, peppercorns, wine, wine vinegar and enough stock to just cover. If using a pressure cooker, add 1¼ cups stock.

Bring to the boil, then reduce the heat, cover and simmer for up to 6 hours or until the ham hocks are tender when tested with a skewer or fork. If using a pressure cooker, follow the manufacturer's directions and allow about 50 minutes. Remove the ham hocks from the pan and leave until cool enough to handle. Strain the stock and boil rapidly until reduced to about 1¼ cups.

Place the cabbage in a large saucepan, cover with boiling water and bring back to the boil. Drain well. Heat the oil in a large flameproof casserole and sauté the onion until soft. Add the apple, juniper berries, red currants and cabbage. Pour the reduced stock over and season generously.

Preheat the oven to 400°.

Remove the ham hocks from the cheesecloth and split through the center lengthwise without completely cutting them in half. Arrange, skin-side up, on top of the cabbage. Bring to the boil, then transfer it to the oven and cook for about 45 minutes.

Sprinkle with parsley and serve at once.

INGREDIENTS
4 ham hocks
1 cup sliced carrots
2 onions, stuck with 4 cloves each
1 cup sliced leeks
½ cup sliced celery
2 bay leaves
bouquet garni
20 black peppercorns
⅔ cup dry white wine
¼ cup white wine vinegar
*chicken stock (see page 247) (see
    method for quantity)*
2 lb red or white cabbage, shredded
2 tablespoons vegetable oil
½ cup chopped onion
2 tart apples, peeled and chopped
12 juniper berries, crushed
½ cup red currants, fresh or frozen
salt and pepper
chopped fresh parsley, to garnish

HAGGIS

*Haggis, a stuffed sheep's stomach is a popular and traditional Scottish dish served
with "tatties" (potatoes) and "neeps" (rutabagas) and a glass of Scotch whisky.*

Serves 10–12

Place the stomach bag in cold water in the refrigerator until required. Do not keep longer than 4 days. Cover the heart, liver and lungs in cold water, and bring to the boil. Cover and simmer for 2 hours.

Meanwhile, preheat the oven to 400°. Spread the oatmeal out on a cookie sheet and toast for 10 minutes.

When the liver, heart and lungs are cooked, strain and reserve the stock. Finely chop the heart, liver, and about one-third of the lungs. Place in a bowl with the oatmeal, suet, seasoning, cayenne, nutmeg and onions. Add 2 cups of the reserved stock. Drain the stomach bag thoroughly and fill just over half full with the stuffing mixture. Sew up the bag with thread and prick in a few places.

Place a trivet in the base of a large saucepan of boiling water. Lower the haggis into the boiling water, reduce the heat, cover and simmer for 3 hours, pricking the skin occasionally, to prevent the haggis from bursting.

To serve, drain the haggis, place it on a serving dish, slit the skin and spoon out the filling from the bag.

INGREDIENTS
1 sheep's stomach bag
1 sheep's liver, heart and lungs
3½ cups quick-cooking oatmeal
1 cup shredded beef suet
salt and pepper
¼ teaspoon cayenne pepper
large pinch of grated nutmeg
1 cup finely chopped onions

SPINACH-WRAPPED SWEETBREADS IN CREAM SAUCE

Buttered rice or mashed potatoes go well with this dish.

Serves 4

INGREDIENTS

1 lb calves' sweetbreads

lemon slice

2 tablespoons chilled butter

½ cup diced carrot

¼ cup diced celery

2 tablespoons diced shallots

½ cup chopped leek

1 bay leaf

few parsley sprigs

rosemary sprig

pared zest of ¼ lemon

2 cups chicken stock (see page 247)

⅔ cup dry white wine

12 large spinach leaves

½ cup heavy cream

*1 teaspoon strong French mustard
   with seeds*

salt and pepper

Wash the sweetbreads well, and place them in a saucepan of cold water, with the lemon slice. Bring to the boil, then simmer for 3 minutes. Drain, cool, then carefully remove any skin. Melt half the butter and sauté the carrot, celery, shallots and leek until soft. Add the bay leaf, parsley sprigs, rosemary and lemon zest. Arrange the sweetbreads on the bed of vegetables, pour the stock over and bring to a simmer. Cover and simmer gently for about 20 minutes, until firm and tender. Carefully remove the sweetbreads from the pan. Strain the cooking liquid and return it to the rinsed-out pan. Add the wine and boil rapidly for 10–15 minutes or until the liquid has reduced by half.

Meanwhile, blanch the spinach leaves in boiling water. Drain and plunge into ice water. Drain and dry on paper towels. Cut away the coarse stems. Cut the sweetbreads into 12 pieces and wrap each one in a spinach leaf.

Add the cream and mustard to the reduced stock and adjust the seasoning. Place the spinach-wrapped sweetbreads in the sauce and simmer gently for about 5 minutes.

To serve, remove the sweetbreads from the pan and arrange on a serving plate or on 4 individual plates. Beat the remaining chilled butter into the sauce, then spoon a little sauce over the sweetbreads. Place the remaining sauce in a sauce boat and serve hot.

CHARLOTTE D'AUBERGINE AUX ROGNONS

*This eggplant charlotte, filled with kidneys in tomato and basil sauce,
is an attractive dish to serve. Accompany with steamed rice.*

Serves 4

To make the sauce, heat the olive oil and sauté the onion until soft. Add the carrot, celery and garlic and sauté, stirring occasionally, for 5 minutes. Add the tomatoes and seasoning, and simmer gently, uncovered, for about 45 minutes, stirring occasionally. Stir in the basil leaves.

Meanwhile, thinly slice the eggplant. Sprinkle with salt and leave for 30 minutes. Wash and dry well. Heat a little of the oil in a skillet and sauté a few eggplant slices at a time. Keep adding a little more oil and continue until all the eggplant slices are cooked.

Melt the butter and brown the kidneys. Using a slotted spoon, remove them from the pan and add to the tomato sauce. Rapidly boil the kidney juices until reduced to 1 tablespoon, then add it to the tomato sauce. Adjust the seasoning.

Preheat the oven to 400°.

Brush the inside of a 1½-quart soufflé dish with oil. Coat the bottom and sides with some of the bread crumbs, then line the bottom and sides with three-quarters of the eggplant slices. Sprinkle over one-third of the remaining bread crumbs. Spoon the kidney and tomato sauce into the dish, and sprinkle with half the remaining bread crumbs. Top with remaining slices and bread crumbs. Press down gently. Bake, uncovered, for 40 minutes. Unmold and serve.

INGREDIENTS
*2 medium eggplants, about 1 lb
  each*
salt and pepper
about ½ cup olive oil
2 tablespoons butter
*8 lambs' kidneys, cored and
  chopped*
1 cup toasted bread crumbs
Tomato sauce
¼ cup olive oil
½ cup chopped onion
½ cup chopped carrot
¼ cup chopped celery
2 garlic cloves, chopped
4 large tomatoes or 14 oz can
salt and pepper
12 fresh basil leaves, shredded

VEAL SWEETBREADS WITH RED AND YELLOW PEPPERS

*The fresh taste of the peppers contrasts well with the smooth texture of
the sweetbreads and the cream sauce, and the rich color of the peppers
makes this a very impressive-looking dish.*

Serves 4

Wash the sweetbreads well, then place them in a saucepan of cold water with the lemon slice. Bring to the boil, then simmer for 3 minutes. Drain and cool, then carefully remove any skin.

Melt 1 tablespoon of the butter in a saucepan and sauté the carrot, celery, leek and garlic until soft. Add the bay leaf, thyme and parsley sprigs, and arrange the sweetbreads on top of the bed of vegetables. Pour the stock over. Bring to a simmer, then cover and cook for about 20 minutes or until firm and tender. Carefully remove the sweetbreads from the pan.

Strain the stock and return it to the rinsed-out pan. Add the brandy and boil rapidly for about 2 minutes, until the sauce is slightly syrupy. Return the sweetbreads to the pan and simmer very gently to warm through.

Stir-fry the peppers in the oil for 2 minutes. Season to taste.

Spoon the peppers onto a serving plate. Cut the sweetbreads into thick slices and arrange on top of the peppers. Beat the remaining butter into the sauce. Stir in the chopped parsley and chives and adjust the seasoning. Pour over the sweetbreads and serve at once.

INGREDIENTS
1 lb calves' sweetbreads
lemon slice
3 tablespoons butter, chilled
½ cup diced carrot
¼ cup diced celery
½ cup diced leek
2 garlic cloves, chopped
1 bay leaf
thyme sprig
few parsley sprigs
⅔ cup chicken stock (see page 247)
1 tablespoon brandy
*1 red pepper, seeded and cut into
  julienne strips*
*1 yellow pepper, seeded and cut
  into julienne strips*
1 teaspoon oil
salt and pepper
1 teaspoon chopped parsley
1 teaspoon chopped fresh chives

VEAL SWEETBREADS WITH RED AND YELLOW PEPPERS

THE FRUIT AND VEGETABLE HALL

VEGETABLES

VEGETABLES

Regardless of the season, Harrods can always boast a profusion of excellent quality vegetables: strings of garlic and onions, snow peas, asparagus and shiny black eggplants. Ideal for warming winter soups, vegetables also make the perfect accompaniment to a main course dish, such as Pommes de Terre à la Lyonnaise and Broccoli Mornay, or as a meal in itself – Wild Mushroom Ravioli.

SPINACH AND TANGERINE SOUP

The combination of spinach mixed with tangerines makes a nourishing and refreshing soup. This is ideal for serving before a rich course or combined with pita bread for a light lunch.

Serves 4–6

INGREDIENTS

2 quarts chicken stock (see page 247)
½ cup yellow split peas, soaked for 4 hours
2 tablespoons butter
¼ lb scallions, the white and green parts chopped separately
1 teaspoon ground turmeric
½ cup chopped fresh coriander
2 cups finely chopped spinach
2 tablespoons finely chopped parsley
finely grated zest and juice of 1 tangerine
finely grated zest and juice of 2 lemons
1 tablespoon cornstarch
⅔ cup cold water
1 cup plain yogurt
coriander sprigs, to garnish

Bring the chicken stock to the boil, add the yellow split peas and simmer for 15 minutes.

Melt the butter in a small saucepan and gently sauté the white scallions for 5 minutes. Stir in the turmeric, then stir the spiced scallions and butter into the stock and peas. Add the green scallion parts, coriander, spinach, parsley and citrus zest and juice. Cover the pan and simmer for 30 mintues.

Mix the cornstarch with the cold water, then stir into the soup. Cover the pan and simmer for 15 minutes more, stirring occasionally.

To serve, swirl some yogurt into each bowl of soup and garnish with coriander.

WILD MUSHROOM RAVIOLI

*This is a generously seasoned Italian dish containing a wild mushroom
filling and served with a creamy sauce.*

Serves 4

For the filling, if using dried mushrooms, cover with boiling water and leave to
soak for at least 1 hour. Drain, squeeze out the excess moisture and reserve the
liquid. Finely chop the mushrooms.

Melt the butter in a saucepan and sauté the shallots and bacon until the
shallots are transparent and the bacon golden. Add the mushrooms and sauté
for 1 minute. Cool slightly, then add the ricotta, parsley, thyme, lemon juice,
nutmeg, cayenne and seasoning. Season generously.

Divide the pasta dough in half. Roll out each piece of dough to a 16- × 12-inch
rectangle on a lightly floured surface.

Either spoon the filling into a pastry bag fitted with a large plain tip or use a
teaspoon. Starting 1 inch in from the edge of the dough, place small mounds of
the wild mushroom filling at 2-inch intervals, to make 48 mounds. Do not use
too much fillng or the ravioli will split during cooking. Brush in between the
mounds of filling with water. Carefully place the second piece of dough on top
and using a long knife or kitchen ruler, mark lines between each mound of
filling to seal the dough.

Using a serrated pastry wheel or sharp knife, cut between each mound to
make 48 ravioli. Leave on a lightly floured board covered with a clean cloth.
Cook the ravioli in boiling salted water for 5 minutes. Drain well.

To make the sauce, scald the cream (if using dried mushrooms, use ¾ cup
cream and ¼ cup of the reserved mushroom liquid). Remove from the heat and
beat in the egg yolks and nutmeg. Season generously.

Spoon the ravioli into a gratin dish. Pour the sauce over and sprinkle with
Parmesan cheese. Cook under a preheated hot broiler until golden.

INGREDIENTS
*6 oz wild mushrooms (2 cups), or
3 oz dried wild mushrooms
(1 cup), or 3 oz cultivated
mushrooms (1 cup)*
2 tablespoons butter
4 tablespoons chopped shallots
4 bacon slices, finely chopped
¼ cup ricotta or cream cheese
3 tablespoons chopped parsley
*½ teaspoon chopped fresh thyme or
pinch dried*
1 teaspoon lemon juice
large pinch of grated nutmeg
pinch of cayenne pepper
salt and pepper
1 lb pasta dough (see page 251)
Cheese sauce
1 cup light cream
2 egg yolks
pinch of grated nutmeg
*¼ cup freshly grated Parmesan
cheese*

CARROT AND ORANGE SOUP

*This refreshing, bright orange soup may be served hot or cold,
accompanied by thin slices of melba toast.*

Serves 4

Bring the chicken stock to the boil in a large saucepan, add the carrots,
seasoning, orange zest and coriander. Reduce the heat, cover the pan and
simmer for 10–15 minutes, or until the carrots are cooked.

Remove the strip of orange zest and purée the soup.

Add the orange juice and return the soup to the boil. Remove from the heat,
stir in the sour cream, adjust the seasoning and pour into bowls. Sprinkle with
chopped mint and serve immediately.

INGREDIENTS
*2½ cups jellied chicken stock (see
page 247)*
1 lb carrots, finely grated
salt and pepper
pared strip of orange zest
½ teaspoon ground coriander
⅔ cup fresh orange juice
⅔ cup sour cream
2 teaspoons chopped fresh mint

FRENCH ONION SOUP WITH COGNAC

*This classic soup is ideal to serve for lunch or light supper.
A good beef stock is essential when making this recipe and bouillon
cubes can not be substituted.*

Serves 6

INGREDIENTS
5 tablespoons butter
1¾ lb onions, thinly sliced
1 teaspoon sugar
1½ quarts beef stock (see page 246)
⅔ cup dry white wine
salt and pepper
3 tablespoons Cognac
1 loaf French bread
1⅓ cups shredded Gruyère cheese

Melt the butter in a saucepan and gently sauté the onions for 20 minutes, until soft. Sprinkle the sugar over and continue to cook, stirring occasionally, until the onions turn golden brown.

Add the stock and white wine and bring to the boil. Reduce the heat, cover and simmer gently for 1 hour. Season to taste and stir in the Cognac.

About 10 minutes before the soup is ready, cut 6 slices of bread 1-inch thick and toast.

Place the slices of toasted bread in individual flameproof bowls or a soup tureen. Pour the soup over the bread and when the bread floats to the surface, place the cheese on top. Broil under a preheated hot broiler until the cheese is bubbling. Serve immediately with the remaining French bread.

FENNEL AND SALAMI WITH BLACK OLIVES

*Fennel has a refreshing licorice flavor and may be eaten raw or cooked.
This recipe makes an ideal appetizer, or a luncheon dish for two, served
with warm crusty bread.*

Serves 4

Place two radicchio leaves on each plate and fill them with the shredded fennel.
Arrange the slices of salami around one side of each plate and place a fan of
olives on top of the salami.

Mix the lemon juice and walnut and olive oils together, then season to taste.
Pour the dressing over the fennel and serve at once.

INGREDIENTS

8 large radicchio leaves
*3 fennel bulbs, trimmed and finely
  shredded*
16 salami slices (about ¼ lb)
*12 pitted ripe olives, quartered
  lengthwise*
juice of ½ lemon
1 teaspoon walnut oil
1 tablespoon olive oil
salt and pepper

ZUCCHINI MOUSSE

*This is a lightly poached zucchini purée which can be served as an
attractive side dish with meat, poultry or fish.*

Serves 4–8

Preheat the oven to 325°.

Steam the zucchini for 3–5 minutes, until tender, then blend to a purée in a
blender or food processor.

Meanwhile, lightly grease 8 individual timbale molds and coat with 2 tablespoons of the bread crumbs.

Melt 2 tablespoons of the butter in a small saucepan and sauté the onion for 5
minutes or until soft. Cool, then transfer to a bowl. Add the nutmeg and cheese
and season. Beat in the eggs. Heat the milk gently with the remaining butter
until it melts, then pour it into the egg mixture in a steady stream, beating
constantly. Fold in the zucchini purée.

Evenly divide the mixture between the prepared molds. Place in a roasting
pan half filled with hot water. Bake for about 25–30 minutes or until the custard
is lightly set. Cool for 5 minutes, then loosen the edge of each mold with the
point of a knife. Carefully turn out onto a warm serving dish and pour a little hot
tomato sauce over or around each. Garnish with chervil or parsley.

INGREDIENTS

1 lb zucchini, sliced
6 tablespoons butter
1½ cups toasted bread crumbs
½ cup finely chopped onion
pinch of nutmeg
⅓ cup finely grated Gruyère cheese
salt and pepper
4 large eggs, lightly beaten
1¼ cups milk
*tomato sauce, heated (see
  page 251)*
*chervil or parsley sprigs, to
  garnish*

FRENCH ONION SOUP WITH COGNAC

CELERY CREAM WITH TOASTED ALMONDS

A delicately flavored dish which is excellent served with veal and poultry.

Serves 4

INGREDIENTS

3 tablespoons butter
3 tablespoons slivered almonds
¼ cup finely chopped shallots
1 lb celery, trimmed and cut into
 julienne strips
salt and pepper
⅔ cup jellied chicken stock (see page
 247)
1 teaspoon chopped parsley
½ cup light cream

Melt the butter in a large skillet and sauté the almonds for 3 minutes or until golden brown. Remove the almonds from the skillet with a slotted spoon and reserve. Add the shallots and celery to the butter in the skillet and sauté until soft. Season and stir in the stock.

Cover the skillet and cook for 15 minutes.

Stir in the parsley and cream, cover and simmer gently for 10 minutes. Serve hot, sprinkled with the toasted almonds.

BAKED FENNEL WITH TOMATO

*Fennel is available during the fall, winter and spring and has an
unmistakable licorice flavor. To prepare, trim the upper stems and
leaves and remove the outer leaves, as these can be stringy.*

Serves 6

INGREDIENTS

6 tablespoons butter
½ cup chopped onion
1 large garlic clove, crushed
3 fennel, about 1½ lb, halved and
 thinly sliced
1 teaspoon tomato paste
¾ lb ripe tomatoes, peeled and finely
 chopped
salt and pepper
1½ cups fresh bread crumbs
¼ cup freshly grated Parmesan
 cheese

Preheat the oven to 400°.

Melt the butter in a saucepan and sauté the onion and garlic until golden. Add the fennel slices and cook over moderate heat for 10 minutes more.

Stir in the tomato paste and tomatoes. Season to taste and cook for 5 minutes or until reduced slightly.

Spoon the mixture into a gratin dish. Mix the bread crumbs with the Parmesan cheese and sprinkle over the surface. Bake for 15 minutes or until the bread crumbs are golden brown. Serve with broiled fish or meat.

PUMPKIN RISOTTO

The rich orange color and distinctive sweet flavor of the pumpkin is highlighted in this creamy risotto.

Serves 4

Melt 2 tablespoons of the butter in a large, heavy-bottomed saucepan, then add the shallots and sauté for 2–3 minutes.

Add the pumpkin and cook, stirring occasionally, for 5 minutes. Add the rice and cook for 2 minutes more, stirring. Stir in ½ cup of the stock, the orange zest and juice, and the ginger. Simmer, stirring, until all the moisture has evaporated. Add another ½ cup of the stock and cook again until it has evaporated. Continue adding the stock and cooking the rice in the same way until all the stock has been used.

When ready, the rice should be tender but firm to the bite and creamy. The pumpkin should also be tender. Season and stir in the remaining butter. Serve hot.

INGREDIENTS

3 tablespoons butter

2 tablespoons finely chopped shallots

1 lb pumpkin flesh, cut into 1-inch cubes

1 cup arborio rice

2½ cups hot chicken stock (see page 247)

finely grated zest and juice of 2 large oranges

1½ tablespoons finely chopped fresh ginger root

salt and pepper

CAULIFLOWER WITH CARAWAY SEEDS

Cauliflower may be cooked whole or broken into flowerets, the latter being the quickest method. Choose a cauliflower with a firm white head, without any brown patches.

Serves 4

Cook the cauliflower until tender, either by steaming or by boiling in salted water. Melt the butter in a skillet and add the caraway seeds. Heat until the butter foams, then add the lemon juice. Remove from the heat.

Drain the cauliflower and place on a serving dish. Season the butter and pour over the cauliflower. Serve hot.

INGREDIENTS

2 lb head cauliflower, trimmed

4 tablespoons butter

½ teaspoon caraway seeds

1 teaspoon lemon juice

salt and pepper

YOUNG PEAS WITH PROSCIUTTO

The addition of prosciutto turns this vegetable dish into an accompaniment suitable for any occasion.

Serves 4

Cut the prosciutto into thin strips.

Melt the butter in a large saucepan and add the ham, peas, scallions, lettuce, sugar, stock and salt and pepper. Bring to the boil, then cover and simmer gently for 15–20 minutes. Serve in a warmed serving dish with the cooking liquid.

INGREDIENTS

2 oz prosciutto, thinly sliced

4 tablespoons butter

2 lb fresh young peas, shelled

12 scallions, trimmed and sliced

1 head Boston lettuce, shredded

1 teaspoon sugar

⅔ cup chicken stock (see page 247)

salt and pepper

LETTUCE AND PEA SOUP

This light and delicate cream soup captures the flavor of summer.

Serves 4

INGREDIENTS

3 tablespoons butter

½ cup chopped onion

1 Boston lettuce, shredded

1 tablespoon unbleached flour

*1⅓ cups shelled fresh peas, or 10 oz
package frozen peas, defrosted*

*⅔ cup chicken stock
(see page 247)*

2 cups milk

salt and pepper

2 egg yolks

½ cup light cream

mint sprigs, to garnish

Melt the butter in a large saucepan and add the onion and lettuce. Stir, cover the pan and cook over gentle heat for 10 minutes.

Stir in the flour, then add the peas. Pour in the stock and milk, season and bring to the boil. Reduce the heat, cover, and simmer for 20 minutes.

Press the soup through a sieve or purée in a blender or food processor, then return to the pan. Mix the egg yolks with the cream and add a little of the warm soup to the mixture. Add the liaison to the soup and heat, but do not boil. Adjust the seasoning, pour into serving bowls and serve garnished with mint.

TOMATO WATER-ICE WITH
A JULIENNE OF SMOKED
SALMON

TOMATO WATER-ICE WITH A JULIENNE
OF SMOKED SALMON

*This is a pretty and refreshing appetizer to serve at any time of the
year. Alternatively, the smoked salmon may be omitted and the water-
ice served in hollowed-out tomato shells garnished with thin lemon
slices and fresh dill sprigs.*

Serves 4

Rub the tomatoes through a sieve into a bowl. Stir in the lemon juice, Worcestershire and Tabasco sauces, salt and sugar.

Pour the mixture into a shallow container and freeze until frozen around the
edges. Turn into a chilled bowl and beat to break up the ice crystals. Return to
the container and freeze until hard.

To serve, place spoonfuls of water-ice onto individual serving plates. Arrange
the smoked salmon around and garnish with a dill sprig and lemon twist.

INGREDIENTS
1½ lb ripe tomatoes, peeled, seeded
  and chopped
juice of 1 lemon
1 teaspoon Worcestshire sauce
few drops Tabasco
salt
½ teaspoon sugar
¼ lb smoked salmon, cut into
  julienne strips
fresh dill sprigs, to garnish
thin lemon slices, twisted, to
  garnish

SUMMER TERRINE

This terrine of layered vegetables wrapped in spinach leaves is very attractive to serve either whole, or sliced and arranged on individual serving plates.

Serves 4

INGREDIENTS
¼ lb green beans, trimmed
1 cup shelled peas
⅓ lb carrots, cut in thin lengthwise strips
¼ lb young spinach leaves
1 lb cream cheese
2 eggs, lightly beaten
finely grated zest of ½ lemon
1 garlic clove, crushed
2 tablespoons lean ground ham
salt and pepper
6 canned artichoke hearts, diced
½ lemon, thinly sliced, to garnish

Preheat the oven to 325°.

Boil the beans, peas and carrots separately until just tender, then drain and refresh under cold running water. Blanch the spinach leaves for 30 seconds.

Line the bottom and sides of a 9-× 5-× 3-inch loaf pan with the spinach leaves, overlapping the edges.

Beat the cheese until softened, then gradually beat in the eggs, lemon zest, garlic, ham and seasoning.

Layer the cheese mixture in the dish, alternating with the beans, carrots, artichokes and peas, in that order. Finish with a layer of cheese mixture. Fold the spinach leaves over the filling to enclose it.

Cover with aluminum foil and place in a roasting pan. Add boiling water to come halfway up the sides of the pan. Bake for 40 minutes. Remove from the oven and allow to cool completely. Chill for at least 4 hours or overnight. Turn out and garnish with the lemon slices.

ROQUEFORT SALAD

The creamy cheese dressing in this salad is also delicious with hamburgers. It may also be served as a dip with crudités and is a suitable dressing for most green salads.

Serves 4–6

INGREDIENTS
2 Belgium endives, trimmed and separated into spears
1 Boston lettuce, shredded
¾ cup sliced celery
1 apple, peeled, cored and diced
Roquefort dressing
¼ lb Roquefort cheese
⅔ cup sour cream
1 teaspoon olive oil
salt and pepper

To make the dressing, mash the cheese with a fork and add the sour cream. Blend thoroughly in a blender or food processor, then add the oil and seasoning.

Arrange the endive around the edge of a large shallow dish. Place the lettuce in the center of the dish and sprinkle the celery and apple over. Serve with the dressing.

WINTER SALAD

INGREDIENTS

8 radicchio leaves

¼ lb mâche, watercress or arugala

1 large Beligan endive

2 tablespoons raspberry vinegar

salt and pepper

2 tablespoons walnut oil

¼ cup olive oil

walnuts halves or roughly chopped
    walnuts, to garnish

*The variety of colors and shapes in this salad makes it a most attractive
dish, with a strong refreshing flavor. This salad is an ideal
accompaniment to roast game and poultry.*

Serves 4

Wash and dry the leaves and arrange them on a platter.

To make the dressing, pour the raspberry vinegar into a small bowl and
season. Pour in the oils and beat until blended.

Dribble the salad dressing over the leaves just before serving, then sprinkle
with the walnuts.

DEVILED ARTICHOKE HEARTS

INGREDIENTS

6 tablespoons walnut oil

1 teaspoon Dijon mustard

1 tablespoon lemon juice

1 tablespoon finely chopped fresh
    chervil

salt and pepper

1 Boston lettuce, separated into
    leaves

½ lb shelled shrimp

15 oz can artichoke hearts, drained
    and halved

2 tomatoes, peeled, seeded amd
    chopped

*A light salad to serve for a summer luncheon or barbecue.
If fresh chervil isn't available, substitute another fresh herb, such as
chives or parsley.*

Serves 4

In a bowl, beat the walnut oil with the mustard, then beat in the lemon juice,
chervil and seasoning.

Arrange the lettuce on four individual plates. Pile the shrimp in the center.
Arrange the artichoke hearts around the shrimp and scatter the tomatoes over
the artichokes.

Spoon the dressing over the artichoke hearts and trickle a little over the
lettuce. Serve at once.

ONIONS A LA GRECQUE

INGREDIENTS

2 lb small white pearl onions

5 tablespoons olive oil

1 teaspoon sugar

⅔ cup dry white wine

2 teaspoons tomato paste

salt and pepper

2 tablespoons chopped fresh
    coriander or parsley

*This adaptable recipe can be prepared as an appetizer or as an
accompaniment to boiled ham or roasted meat or poultry.*

Serves 8

Blanch the onions in boiling water for 1 minute only, then drain and rinse under
cold running water. Carefully remove the onion skins.

Put the onions in a large, heavy-bottomed saucepan with 1¼ cups water and
the remaining ingredients except the chopped coriander. Bring to the boil, then
lower the heat, cover and simmer gently for 30 minutes. Uncover and cook for
15 minutes more or until onions are tender. Taste and adjust the seasoning,
then stir in the chopped coriander. Turn into a warmed serving dish and serve.

STUFFED VINE LEAVES

*This delightful dish may be made with fresh or preserved vine leaves.
When using fresh leaves, soak them for a few minutes in boiling water
until they become limp. If canned leaves are used, pour off the brine,
place the leaves in a bowl and cover with boiling water. Leave
to soak for 20 minutes, drain and rinse under cold water.*

Serves 6

Pour boiling water over the rice and soak for 20 minutes, then drain well. Mix together the beef, pine nuts, currants, onion, parsley, mint, allspice, cinnamon, tomato paste and salt and pepper. Add the drained rice.

Select the large vine leaves for stuffing and use the smaller and torn leaves to line the bottom and sides of a medium-sized pan. Place one vine leaf at a time, vein side up, onto a board and snip off any stem that has been left on. Place 1 tablespoon of filling, or less, depending on the size of the leaf, near the center of the stem. Fold the sides over and roll the leaf into a small rectangular package. If some of the leaves are too small, place one leaf on top of another, half way down, and roll as one. Continue this process until all the stuffing mixture has been used.

Pack the parcels tightly into the prepared pan, pushing the garlic slivers in between. Mix the olive oil, water, lemon juice and sugar together, then pour over the vine leaves. Place a small plate on the top to prevent them unraveling during the cooking process. Bring to the boil, reduce the heat, cover and gently simmer for 2 hours.

Serve either hot or cold, accompanied by plain yogurt.

INGREDIENTS
½ cup long-grain rice
½ lb lean ground beef
2 tablespoons pine nuts
2 tablespoons dried currants
*⅔ cup finely chopped scallion or
  onion*
3 tablespoons chopped parsley
1 tablespoon dried mint
¼ teaspoon ground allspice
¼ teaspoon cinnamon
2 tablespoons tomato paste
salt and pepper
1 lb vine leaves, prepared
3 large garlic cloves, slivered
⅔ cup olive oil
⅔ cup water
juice of 2 lemons
1 teaspoon sugar

STUFFED VINE LEAVES

CABBAGE SAUTEED WITH CUMIN AND BACON

*This dish is a good accompaniment to pork or sausage. Buy whole
cumin seeds and grind in a mortar with a pestle for the best flavor.*

Serves 4

INGREDIENTS

4 tablespoons butter
½ cup chopped onion
3 smoked bacon slices, chopped
1 teaspoon ground cumin seed
*1½ lb white cabbage, core removed
    and shredded*
freshly ground black pepper

Melt the butter and sauté the onion until soft. Add the bacon and cook over
gentle heat for 10 minutes more. Stir in the cumin, then add the cabbage and stir
until it is completely covered in butter. Season with black pepper but do not add
salt.

Cover and cook over gentle heat for 20 minutes, stirring occasionally. Adjust
the seasoning, and serve hot.

FAVA BEANS BAKED
WITH ALMONDS IN SOUR CREAM

A tasty side dish to serve with ham.

Serves 4

INGREDIENTS

2 tablespoons butter
2 tablespoons chopped shallot
2 bacon slices, finely chopped
2 tablespoons slivered almonds
½ lb fava beans, shelled weight
2 tablespoons dry white wine
2 tablespoons water
salt and pepper
*large pinch of chopped fresh dill, or
    ½ teaspoon dillweed*
1 egg yolk
⅔ cup sour cream or crème fraîche

Melt the butter in a flameproof casserole and gently sauté the shallot and bacon
for 5 minutes. Stir in the almonds, fava beans, wine, water, seasoning and dill.
Cover and simmer for 10 minutes.

Mix the egg yolk with the sour cream.

When the beans are tender, remove the pan from the heat and cool for 2
minutes. Mix a tablespoon of the cooking liquid with the egg yolk and sour
cream, then gradually stir the cream mixture into the beans. Cook over gentle
heat for 4–5 minutes, stirring, but do *not* allow the sauce to boil. Serve hot.

BRAISED ENDIVE WITH HAM

*Belgian endive may be cooked or eaten raw. Trim each head
and remove the bitter core by inserting a knife into the base and cutting
around the inner core. Select even-sized endive heads for this dish.*

Serves 4

Melt the butter in a large skillet and add the endive. Tip the pan to one side and spoon the melted butter over the endive. Season, then cover and sweat over moderate heat for 20 minutes or until the endive is tender.

Add the ham and adjust the seasoning. Pour in the lemon juice and cook for 2 minutes more to let the flavors develop. Serve hot.

INGREDIENTS
6 tablespoons butter
*8 Belgian endives, trimmed and
  cored*
salt and pepper
4 oz finely chopped ham (1 cup)
1 tablespoon lemon juice

KOHLRABI WITH CREAM SAUCE

Cooked in cream, kohlrabi is a tasty dish to serve with meat, fish or poultry

Serves 4

Place the kohlrabi in the top part of a steamer or in a colander over a saucepan of simmering water, cover and cook for about 30 minutes or until tender.

Meanwhile, simmer the shallot in the wine in a covered pan for 5 minutes or until tender. Bring to the boil until the wine has reduced to 3 tablespoons. Stir in the cream and simmer until slightly thickened.

Press the sauce through a sieve, return it to the rinsed-out pan and reheat gently. Gradually beat in the butter, one piece at a time. Stir in the lemon juice. Season and keep warm. Do not allow the sauce to boil or it will curdle.

Remove the kohlrabi from the heat, cool slightly, then rub off the skin. Slice finely and arrange the slices in a warmed serving dish. Spoon over the sauce and garnish with the parsley. Serve hot.

INGREDIENTS
*4 small kohlrabi, about 6 oz each,
  trimmed*
*2 tablespoons finely chopped
  shallot*
¾ cup dry white wine
⅔ cup heavy cream
2 tablespoons butter, diced
1 teaspoon lemon juice
salt and pepper
parsley sprigs, to garnish

GLAZED SHALLOTS

The light sugar glaze in this recipe enhances the shallots' mild taste.

Serves 4

Place the shallots in a saucepan and cover with the cold water. Bring to the boil and blanch for 10 minutes. Drain.

Melt the butter in a saucepan, add the sugar, shallots and salt and pepper. Cover and cook for 15 minutes, until the shallots are tender and well glazed. Stir occasionally to prevent the sugar from burning. Turn into a warmed serving dish and sprinkle with parsley.

INGREDIENTS
1 lb shallots, skinned
water to cover
4 tablespoons butter
2 tablespoons sugar
salt and pepper
chopped fresh parsley, to garnish

CHINESE SALAD

*Some of the vegetables used in Chinese stir-fry dishes are equally good
eaten raw in a salad. The dressing consists of some of the flavorings
used in hot Chinese dishes.*

Serves 6

INGREDIENTS

4 celery stalks

*1 lb 2oz head Chinese cabbage,
   shredded*

1½ cups beansprouts

*¼ lb snow peas, sliced diagonally
   into diamond shapes*

*½ small red pepper, seeded and cut
   into thin rings*

1 cup sliced mushrooms

Dressing

2 teaspoons lemon juice

1½ tablespoons light soy sauce

¾ teaspoon sesame oil

¼ cup sunflower oil

1 teaspoon sugar

*¼ teaspoon finely chopped fresh
   ginger root*

Mix all the dressing ingredients together and set aside for the flavors to blend.

Slice the celery into horseshoe shapes by laying each stalk flat and slice at an angle.

Arrange all the vegetables in a large bowl, add the dressing and toss well before serving.

SPINACH AND RICOTTA RAVIOLI WITH SAGE BUTTER

Spinach and ricotta is a popular combination of flavors in Italian cooking. If fresh sage is unavailable, do not substitute dried. Instead use fresh parsley or basil.

Serves 4

To make the filling, melt the butter and sauté the shallot and garlic until soft. Add the spinach and cook over high heat, stirring constantly, until softened and the liquid evaporates. Set aside until cold, then finely chop.

In a bowl, mix the spinach with the cheese, nutmeg, cayenne and seasoning. Divide the pasta dough in half. Roll out each piece of dough on a lightly floured surface to a 16-× 12-inch rectangle. Either spoon the filling into a pastry bag fitted with a large plain tip or use a teaspoon. Starting 1 inch in from the edge of the dough, place small mounds of the spinach filling at 2-inch intervals, to make 48 mounds. Do not overfill or the ravioli will burst during cooking. Brush in between the mounds with water. Carefully place the second piece of dough on top and, using a long knife or kitchen ruler, mark lines between each mound to seal the dough.

Using a serrated pastry wheel or sharp knife, cut between each mound to make 48 ravioli. Reserve on a floured board covered with a clean cloth until required. Cook the ravioli in boiling salted water for 5 minutes drain well.

To make the sage butter, melt the butter and sauté the sage leaves until the butter just starts to turn pale gold. Pour over the ravioli. Add Parmesan cheese and plenty of freshly ground black pepper. Toss well and serve at once.

INGREDIENTS
1 tablespoon butter
4 tablespoons chopped shallot
1 garlic clove, crushed
½ lb fresh spinach, tough center stem removed
4 oz ricotta cheese (½ cup)
2 tablespoons freshly grated Parmesan cheese
pinch of freshly grated nutmeg
pinch of cayenne pepper
salt and pepper
1 lb pasta dough (see page 251)
¼ cup freshly grated Parmesan cheese, to serve
Sage butter
about 8 tablespoons butter
24 large sage leaves, shredded

BROCCOLI MORNAY

The sauce in this dish may also be served with fish and chicken.

Serves 4

Cook the broccoli until tender, either by steaming or by boiling.

To make the sauce, melt the butter in a saucepan over gentle heat. Stir in the flour and cook for 1 minute. Remove the pan from the heat and gradually stir in the milk. Cook, stirring, for 5 minutes, then stir in the grated cheese and seasoning.

Drain the broccoli, place in a serving dish and pour over the sauce. Serve at once.

INGREDIENTS
1 lb broccoli, trimmed
Sauce
2 tablespoons butter
¼ cup unbleached flour
1½ cups milk
½ cup grated Cheddar cheese
salt and pepper

HOT CHICORY AND SMOKED BACON SALAD

*A hot salad dressing turns this into a salad with a difference. Serve as a
unique appetizer.*

Serves 4–6

INGREDIENTS

7 tablespoons sunflower or olive oil

4 smoked bacon slices, diced

*2 slices white bread, crusts removed
and diced*

1 head chicory, outer leaves removed

Hot vinegar dressing

2 tablespoons white wine vinegar

1 teaspoon Dijon mustard

salt and pepper

1 large garlic clove, sliced

Heat 1 tablespoon of the oil in a skillet and cook the bacon until crisp. Remove
with a slotted spoon and keep hot. Add the bread to the skillet and sauté until it
is crisp and golden, using more oil if necessary. Remove the croutons from the
skillet and keep hot.

Arrange the chicory in a salad bowl.

To make the hot vinegar dressing, place the vinegar, mustard, salt and
pepper and garlic in a small saucepan and stir well. Add the remaining oil and
cook until hot but do not boil. Remove the garlic.

Pour the dressing over the chicory, tossing the leaves until they are well
coated. Sprinkle the bacon and croutons over and serve immediately.

HOT CHICORY AND SMOKED BACON SALAD

GREEN BEANS WITH CREAMY HAZELNUT DRESSING

Green beans add a crisp sweetness and vivid green coloring to a salad.
Cook them either by steaming, or by plunging them into boiling water.
Whichever method you use, only cook for a moment so that they
retain their crunch and color.

Serves 4

Preheat the oven to 400°

To make the dressing, beat together the sour cream and mayonnaise until blended, then gradually beat in the lemon juice. Add salt to taste.

Place the hazelnuts on a cookie sheet in the oven for a few minutes or until golden brown. Do not allow them to become too dark. Rub the hazelnuts in a dish towel to remove the skins and chop roughly.

Arrange the beans on individual serving dishes. Spoon the dressing over the beans, sprinkle with hazelnuts and garnish with lemon slices.

INGREDIENTS
½ cup hazelnuts
1 lb green beans, trimmed and
cooked
lemon slices, to garnish
Creamy hazelnut dressing
⅔ cup sour cream
½ cup mayonnaise (see page 250)
juice of ½ lemon
salt

EGGPLANT LASAGNE

This vegetarian version of lasagne makes an interesting change. To remove
the bitter juices, the eggplant should be sliced, sprinkled with salt and placed
in a colander for 20 minutes, then rinsed before cooking.

Serves 6–8

Roll out the pasta and cut into 6- × 4½-inch sheets. Bring a large pan of salted water to the boil with half the olive oil. Cook a few sheets of pasta at a time. Drain immediately and place in a bowl of cold water.

Heat the remaining oil and butter in a pan and sauté the onion until soft. Stir in the tomato paste and the tomatoes. Season, and add the eggplant, wine and oregano. Cover the pan and simmer gently for 10 minutes, or until the eggplant is tender.

Place a layer of drained pasta in the bottom of a greased shallow baking dish. Spread some of the eggplant mixture over the pasta, then a layer of the Bel Paese and the mozzarella mixed together. Continue to make layers in this way, ending with a layer of pasta.

Preheat the oven to 400°.

To make the sauce, melt the butter in a small saucepan, stir in the flour and cook for 1 minute. Remove from the heat and gradually stir in the milk. Add the bay leaf, seasoning and nutmeg and cook, stirring, over gentle heat for 5 minutes. Spread the sauce evenly over the top of the lasagne and sprinkle with the Parmesan cheese. Bake for 20–25 minutes, or until the topping is golden brown.

INGREDIENTS
½ lb pasta dough (see page 251)
2 tablespoons olive oil
salt and pepper
2 tablespoons butter
1 cup finely chopped onion
2 tablespoons tomato paste
1 lb ripe tomatoes, peeled
1 lb eggplant, prepared as above
⅔ cup dry white wine
1 teaspoon dried oregano
½ lb Bel Paese cheese, grated
½ lb mozzarella, grated
¼ cup grated Parmesan cheese
Béchamel sauce
2 tablespoons butter
¼ cup unbleached flour
2 cups milk
1 bay leaf
a pinch of ground nutmeg
2 tablespoons finely grated
*   Parmesan cheese*

HOT CHICORY AND SMOKED BACON SALAD

PUMPKIN PANCAKES WITH SAUTEED APPLES

This recipe combines two flavors of produce which is abundant in the autumn and makes an interesting brunch dish.

Serves 4

To make the pumpkin purée, remove the seeds and stringy membrane from the pumpkin then place on a lightly greased cookie sheet and bake in an oven preheated to 350° for 45 minutes – 1 hour or until tender. Remove the flesh with a large spoon and purée in a blender or food processor.

Sift all the dry ingredients together into a bowl. Make a well in the center and add the orange zest, egg, pumpkin purée and milk. Beat to a stiff batter.

Melt the butter and sauté the apple slices until golden and just softened. Keep hot. Heat a griddle or large skillet over a moderate heat. Brush with melted butter and pour 2–3 tablespoons of the pumpkin batter onto the surface, spreading slightly. Cook 2 or 3 at a time.

Cook for 1–2 minutes or until bubbles appear at the edges. Carefully turn over and cook for a further 1–2 minutes or until golden brown and just firm to the touch. Keep hot while you make the remaining pancakes. Serve at once, with the sautéed apple slices and maple syrup.

INGREDIENTS
½ cup diced pumpkin flesh
½ cup finely ground cornmeal
½ cup unbleached flour
1 teaspoon baking powder
¼ cup light brown sugar
½ teaspoon cinnamon
¼ teaspoon ground ginger
pinch grated nutmeg
salt
1 teaspoon grated orange or lemon zest
1 egg
about ¼ cup milk
4 tablespoons butter
2 large dessert apples, peeled, cored and sliced
maple syrup, to serve

OKRA WITH RICH TOMATO SAUCE

There are a number of different species belonging to the mallow family, but the best known is okra.
Be careful not to cut into the flesh when trimming.

Serves 4

Heat the oil and sauté the onion until soft. Add the garlic and cook for a further 5 minutes.

Stir in the coriander. Add the okra and gently stir until it is coated in oil. Cook the okra for 2 minutes. Stir in the tomato paste. Add the tomatoes and bring to the boil. Season well, then add the water. Return to the boil, cover, reduce the heat and simmer gently for 45–50 minutes, checking that there is sufficient water. Add the lemon juice and cook for 10 minutes more, or until the okra is tender. Serve either hot or chilled.

INGREDIENTS
3 tablespoons olive oil
½ cup sliced onion
1 large garlic clove, crushed
1 teaspoon ground coriander
1 lb okra, trimmed of hard stems
1½ tablespoons tomato paste
1 lb tomatoes, peeled and roughly chopped
salt and pepper
1¼ cups water
juice of ½ lemon

CELERY ROOT AND POTATO GRATIN

*Celery root is a knobbly tuber. Its flavor is similar to celery and
combines well with potato, making this dish an excellent
accompaniment to roast meat and game.*

Serves 4

INGREDIENTS

*1 lb potatoes, peeled and cut into
¼-inch slices*
6 tablespoons butter
*1 lb celery root, peeled and cut into
¼-inch slices*
salt and pepper

Preheat the oven to 375°.

Rinse the potato slices in cold water, then dry thoroughly. Melt the butter in a skillet and lightly sauté half of the potato slices for 1 minute on each side. Arrange in a gratin dish and season.

Sauté the celery root and the remaining potato slices in the same way. Place the celeriac layer on top of the potatoes, season and place the remaining potatoes on top of them. Pour over any melted butter remaining in the pan. Bake for 1 hour.

LATKES

*Latkes are potato cakes made with grated potatoes and served as a
snack. They are traditionally served at Chanukah among Jews.*

Makes 12

INGREDIENTS

1½ lb potatoes, peeled
3 eggs, beaten
2 tablespoons unbleached flour
¼ teaspoon salt
½ cup grated onion
6 tablespoons butter
3 tablespoons peanut oil

Grate the potatoes and squeeze as much water out of them as possible, by hand, or by squeezing them in a piece of cheesecloth. You should have about 2 cups grated potatotes. Place in a bowl with the eggs.

Sift the flour with the salt and add it to the potato mixture. Stir in the onion and mix well.

Melt 2 tablespoons of the butter with 1 tablespoon of the oil in a skillet. Form spoonfuls of the potato mixture into 3-inch wide pancakes.

Fry 4 pancakes at a time for 5 minutes on each side or until cooked and golden brown. Drain on paper towels and keep hot while cooking the remaining latkes in the same way. Serve immediately.

POMMES DE TERRE A LA LYONNAISE

*Pommes de terre à la Lyonnaise is delicious served with a simple main
course, such as broiled meat, poultry or fish.*

Serves 4

INGREDIENTS

*2 lb potatoes, peeled and sliced
¼-inch thick*
6 tablespoons butter
1 cup thinly sliced onions
salt and pepper
1 tablespoon chopped parsley

Rinse the potato slices in cold water and dry them thoroughly. Melt 4 tablespoons of the butter in a large skillet and cook the potatoes over moderately low heat for 20 minutes, turning regularly, until light golden brown.

Meanwhile, melt the remaining butter in another pan and cook the onions until golden. Add the onions to the potatoes, season to taste, and cook together for 2 minutes. Make sure the potatoes are cooked through: if not cook a little longer. Transfer to a serving dish and sprinkle with chopped parsley.

"SEAWEED"

*This crunchy, sweet "seaweed" is often served in Chinese restaurants,
preceding or accompanying the main dishes. Few people realize,
however, they are in fact eating cabbage.*

Serves 4

To prepare the cabbage, roll 2 leaves together into a tight cigar shape and shred
the leaves as finely as possible using a Chinese cleaver or sharp knife. Continue
in this way until all the cabbage has been used.

Half fill the wok with oil, then heat over a high heat. When the oil is hot, add
the cabbage and stir-fry for 2 minutes. Do not allow the cabbage to become too
dark or it will taste bitter. Drain on paper towels. Place in a serving dish and
sprinkle with sugar, salt and almonds. Serve immediately.

INGREDIENTS
*½ lb dark green cabbage leaves (the
outer leaves of the cabbage),
thick stems removed*
peanut oil for frying
1 teaspoon sugar
pinch of salt
2 tablespoons slivered almonds

FENNEL AND RED ONION SALAD
WITH TARRAGON DRESSING

*The rich combination of color and flavor makes this an attractive side
dish or salad to serve.*

Serves 4

Place the onion and fennel in a bowl.

To make the tarragon dressing, mix the vinegar with the salt and pepper and
tarragon. Beat in the olive oil.

Pour the dressing over the onion and fennel, cover with plastic wrap and
leave for 1 hour.

INGREDIENTS
*1 large red onion, thinly sliced into
rings*
4 fennel, trimmed and thinly sliced
Tarragon dressing
2 tablespoons white wine vinegar
salt and pepper
1 teaspoon chopped fresh tarragon
¾ cup olive oil

POMMES DE TERRE SOUFFLE

*These delicate potatoes are light and puffy and guaranteed to impress.
Serve with roast game birds or fillet of beef.*

Serves 4

Peel the potatoes and cut into slices ⅛-inch thick, then soak in a bowl of cold
water for at least 1 hour. Drain the potatoes and pat dry with paper towels.

Heat the oil to 325° and lower half the potato slices into the oil. When the
slices rise to the surface, remove them and allow to drain and cool thoroughly
on paper towels. Repeat with the remaining potato slices.

Just before serving, heat the oil to 395° and plunge in the first batch of
potatoes. They should puff up almost immediately and turn golden brown. Lift
them out of the oil, and again drain on paper towels. Repeat with the second
batch of potatoes. Serve immediately.

INGREDIENTS
1 lb waxy potatoes
vegetable oil for deep frying

PEPPERS WITH PINE NUT STUFFING

*Red, green and yellow peppers are used for this colorful dish.
Serve with a fresh tomato sauce and accompany with rice.*

Serves 4–6

INGREDIENTS

½ cup long-grain rice

8 peppers, stems removed

6 tablespoons butter

½ cup chopped onion

3 scallions, the white and green parts
    chopped separately

¾ lb lean ground beef

¼ cup pine nuts

⅓ cup raisins

3 tablespoons finely chopped parsley

1 tablespoon tomato paste

¼ teaspoon ground allspice

¼ teaspoon cinnamon

salt and pepper

2½ cups beef stock (see page 246)

Preheat the oven to 350°

Cook the rice in lightly salted boiling water, until just tender. Drain. Slice the tops off the peppers and reserve. Scoop out all the seeds and pith, then discard.

Melt all but 1 tablespoon of the butter in a skillet and sauté the onion and the white of the scallions until golden.

Mix all the remaining ingredients together in a bowl, except the beef stock, and add the rice and cooked onions.

Stand the peppers in a baking dish and stuff with the rice mixture. Replace the tops and dot with the remaining butter. Pour the stock around the peppers and bake for 1 hour. Serve hot.

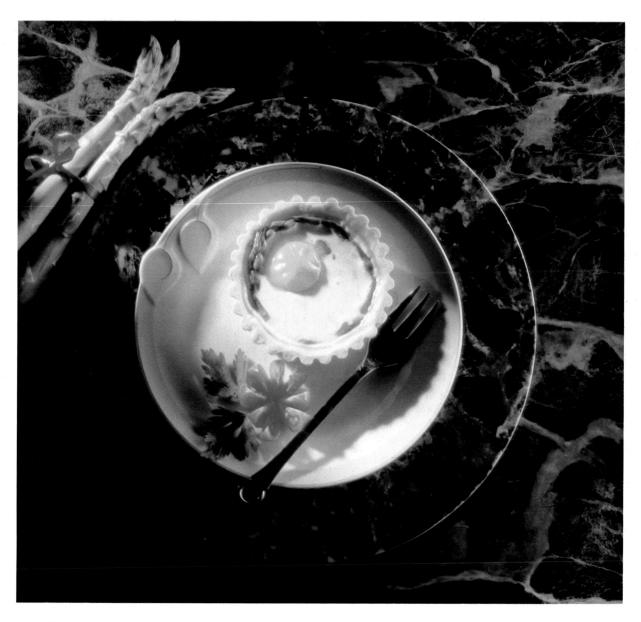

MINIATURE ASPARAGUS TARTS

*Asparagus is one of the most delicious vegetables. This elegant recipe
doesn't mask the fresh asparagus taste and is simple to prepare.*

Serves 4

Butter four 4-inch tart tins. Roll out the pastry and line the tins. Prick the bottom
of each, then cover and chill for 30 minutes.

Preheat the oven to 400°.

Bake blind for 15 minutes, then remove the beans and paper. Reduce
temperature to 350°.

Meanwhile, cook the asparagus in boiling salted water for about 10 minutes
or until just tender. Drain. Bend the asparagus spears around the edge of the
pastry cases, leaving the centers free. Break an egg into the center of each case.
Pour a little cream over each egg and dot with butter. Season and sprinkle with
the cheese. Bake for 6–8 minutes, or until the egg is just set. Serve warm.

INGREDIENTS
*½ quantity basic pie crust dough
(see page 247)*
8 thin asparagus spears
4 eggs
¼ cup light cream
2 tablespoons butter
salt and pepper
*2 teaspoons freshly grated
Parmesan cheese*

RED AND YELLOW PEPPERS WITH SCALLOPS

*This appetizer may be served hot or cold. The peppers are cooked in
their skins, under a hot broiler or directly over a gas flame.*

Serves 4

INGREDIENTS

1 medium red pepper

1 medium yellow pepper

1 lb bay scallops, defrosted if frozen

¼ cup finely chopped shallots

3 tablespoons butter

salt and pepper

2 tablespoons chopped parsley

½ cup dry white wine

Place the whole peppers under a hot broiler, turning often, for 20 minutes. When the peppers are soft, remove from the broiler and cut in half and place in a colander. Remove the skins while the peppers are still hot and discard the stems and seeds. Cut into ¼-inch wide strips and arrange on a plate in alternate colors in a "sun-ray" pattern, leaving a space for the scallops.

Meanwhile, to prepare the scallops, place them in a pan with the shallots, butter and a little salt and pepper. Add half the parsley and the wine and bring to the boil. Reduce the heat, cover the pan, and simmer for 5 minutes. Strain the contents of the pan, and reserve. Bring the liquid to the boil and boil for 5–8 minutes or until reduced. If the dish is to be served hot, return the scallops to the liquid and heat them through.

Pile the scallops into the center of the pepper strips and pour the liquid over. Garnish with the remaining parsley and serve.

GINGERED BEETS

A spicy side dish to serve with roasted chicken or turkey.

Serves 4

INGREDIENTS

1 lb beets

2 tablespoons butter

*2 tablespoons finely chopped candied
    ginger*

2 pineapple slices, chopped

3 tablespoons white wine vinegar

2 tablespoons sugar

salt and pepper

Trim the stems to within 1-inch of the beet and leave whole. Cook in boiling salted water for 30–90 minutes, according to size. The skin will rub off easily when cooked. Drain well, peel and cut into ¼-inch dice.

Melt the butter in a large saucepan, add the beets, ginger, pineapple, vinegar, sugar and seasoning. Heat through, stirring, before serving.

THE FRUIT AND VEGETABLE HALL

FRUIT

Delicious to round off a meal, or to eat alone, fresh fruit can always be bought at Harrods. Fruits can be used to great advantage in main course dishes, such as Chicken Breasts with Mangoes and Almonds, or as an exquisite end to a meal, such as Kumquats Poached in Rose Water. Melon and Strawberries in Champagne is ideal for a special occasion.

RABBIT WITH PRUNES AND RAISINS IN RED WINE SAUCE

For a stronger flavor, marinate the rabbit with the wine and vegetables in the refrigerator in a covered dish for up to 48 hours. When ready to cook, remove the rabbit and dry well. Drain and dry the vegetables and reserve the marinade.

Serves 5–6

INGREDIENTS

4-5 lb dressed rabbit, cut into serving pieces
¼ cup unbleached flour
salt and pepper
2 tablespoons olive oil
1 tablespoon butter
½ cup chopped onion
¼ cup chopped celery
½ cup chopped carrot
1 garlic clove, chopped
⅔ cup red wine
1¼ cups chicken stock (see page 247)
bouquet garni
4 bacon slices, cut into thin strips
12 prunes, pitted
2 tablespoons raisins
chopped fresh parsley, to garnish

Coat the rabbit pieces in the flour, seasoned with salt and pepper. Heat the oil with the butter in a skillet and sauté the rabbit until golden brown. Transfer to a flameproof casserole.

Add the onion, celery, carrot and garlic to the skillet and sauté until soft. Add the red wine and bring to the boil, scraping any sediment from the sides and bottom of the pan. Pour the wine and vegetables over the rabbit pieces. Add the stock and bouquet garni, cover and simmer for 45 minutes.

Fry the bacon strips without any extra fat until crisp. Remove the rabbit pieces from the casserole. Strain the cooking juices, then return them to the rinsed-out pan. Add the rabbit, bacon, prunes and raisins. Cover and simmer for 15 minutes more. Remove the lid and simmer for a further 15 minutes. Adjust the seasoning. Garnish with the chopped parsley.

MELON AND PROSCIUTTO RISOTTO

MELON AND PROSCIUTTO RISOTTO

The combination of melon and prosciutto is universally popular as a chilled appetizer. In this recipe, the combination is equally delicious presented in a creamy risotto and smothered with freshly grated Parmesan cheese. The rice should be al dente, retaining a chewy core, but the risotto will be creamy and should be served immediately.

Serves 6

Measure 1⅔ cups of the melon, purée and reserve.

Melt the butter in a large saucepan over moderate heat and sauté the onion until golden. Add the rice and stir well until all the grains are coated with the melted butter. Add the wine, a little at a time, stirring frequently.

Cook, uncovered, stirring until the wine has almost been absorbed by the rice. Increase the heat and add the chicken stock, about ⅔ cup at a time. Bring to the boil, then reduce the heat and simmer.

From the moment the rice is added, the risotto will take 20–25 minutes to cook. About 5 minutes before the rice is cooked, add the puréed melon and the cream, stirring constantly.

When the risotto is cooked it will have a creamy consistency. Remove the pan from the heat and season. Add the remaining melon and ham to the risotto.

Serve with extra pieces of melon and the Parmesan cheese.

INGREDIENTS

1 large ripe honeydew melon, cut into lengthwise slices, peel removed, seeded and cubed

6 tablespoons butter

½ cup chopped onion

4½ cups arborio rice

⅔ cup dry white wine

about 1 quart hot chicken stock (see page 247)

1 cup light cream

salt and pepper

¼ cup thinly sliced prosciutto, diced

1 cup freshly grated Parmesan cheese

STUFFED PAPAYAS

Papaya may be used in either sweet or savory recipes. As the fruit and leaves contain an enzyme that tenderizes meat, it is an ideal fruit to use in savory dishes. For this dish, choose papayas with mottled green and yellow skins, as they should be slightly under-ripe.

Serves 4

Peel the papayas, cut them in half lengthwise and remove the black seeds with a teaspoon. Parboil the fruit in gently boiling, salted water for 10 minutes, then drain upside-down on paper towels.

Preheat the oven to 350°.

Heat the oil in a large skillet and sauté the onion, garlic and bacon together until the onion is soft. Add the pork and chili and sauté until browned, stirring to break up the meat. Add the tomato paste and cook, stirring, for 2 minutes. Pour over the white wine and stir in the tomatoes. Bring to the boil, reduce the heat and simmer for 5 minutes. Season, remove from the heat and allow the mixture to cool slightly.

Grease a baking dish just large enough to hold the papaya shells and place them, cavity side up, in the dish. Pile the meat mixture into the center of each papaya.

Sprinkle with Parmesan cheese and dot with butter. Bake for 30–40 minutes or until the papaya is tender. Heat the tomato sauce and serve with the sauce poured around each papaya.

INGREDIENTS
2 papayas
2 tablespoons vegetable oil
½ cup chopped onion
1 large garlic clove, crushed
1 slice bacon, finely chopped
1 lb lean ground pork
1 Seranno chili, seeded and finely chopped
1 tablespoon tomato paste
½ cup dry white wine
¾ cup peeled, seeded and chopped tomatoes
salt and pepper
3 tablespoons freshly grated Parmesan cheese
1 tablespoon butter
2 cups tomato sauce (see page 251)
parsley, to garnish

QUINCE-FLAVORED LAMB

Lamb has an affinity with certain fruits and quince is one of them. The combination of fresh ginger, lemon and quince blends well with the sweetness of the lamb. Serve with plain boiled rice.

Serves 6

Trim the fat from the lamb. Heat the oil in a large casserole and sauté the onion until soft. Add the meat and brown on all sides. Stir in the ginger. Season, then add the water and saffron. Bring to the boil, cover and simmer for 2 hours.

Add the sliced quince and lemon juice, and continue to simmer the lamb for 30 minutes or until the quince is tender.

Adjust the seasoning and serve hot.

INGREDIENTS
4 lb shoulder of lamb
2 tablespoons oil
½ cup chopped onion
½ teaspoon finely chopped fresh ginger root
salt and pepper
2 cups water
¼ teaspoon saffron powder
1 lb quince, cored and sliced
juice of ½ lemon

STUFFED PAPAYAS

GRANNY SMITH'S SALAD

*The name of this salad is derived from the Granny Smith, a
particularly crisp and juicy apple. This cheese and apple salad is an
ideal luncheon dish, served with crusty French bread.*

Serves 4

INGREDIENTS
3 Granny Smith apples
lemon juice
1 cup chopped celery
1 cup diced cheese, such as Gruyère
1 small scallion, finely chopped
celery leaves, to garnish
Dressing
⅔ cup plain yogurt
¼ cup mayonnaise (see page 250)
2 teaspoons lemon juice
salt and pepper
1 teaspoon chopped parsley

For the dressing, beat the yogurt until smooth, then beat in the mayonnaise. Add the lemon juice, seasoning and parsley.

Thinly core and slice the apples, but do not peel. Sprinkle with lemon juice to prevent discoloration. Place 2 of the sliced apples in a bowl and add the celery, cheese and scallion. Pour over the dressing and toss well.

Arrange the remaining apple slices on a serving dish and place the salad in the center. Garnish with celery leaves.

Crunchy Apple Salad

Prepare the salad as above, omitting the scallion and substituting ½ cup coarsely chopped walnut or toasted blanched almonds. Sprinkle the nuts over the top of the salad just before serving so they retain their crunchiness.

APRICOT AND MONKFISH KABOBS

APRICOT AND MONKFISH
KABOBS

*Monkfish is ideal for kabobs, as the flesh is firm and doesn't flake easily.
Serve with hot pita bread or boiled rice.*

Serves 4

Place the fish in a bowl. Mix together the lime juice, olive oil, garlic, onion, turmeric and seasoning. Pour the marinade over the fish and marinate for at least 1 hour, turning the fish twice.

Wrap the bacon around the apricots. Thread pieces of fish, peppers, mushrooms and wrapped apricots alternately onto 4 skewers.

Brush the kabobs with the marinade and cook under a preheated broiler for 15–20 minutes, turning and basting frequently. Serve garnished with lime wedges and red pepper strips.

Orange and Sole Kabobs

Slice 4 skinned sole fillets in half lengthwise. Prepare a marinade of the finely grated zest and juice of 1 orange, 1¼ cups olive oil, 1 crushed garlic clove and 2 tablespoons finely chopped parsley.

Place the fish in a bowl, pour the marinade over and marinate for at least 1 hour.

Meanwhile, peel and segment two large oranges and trim 8 mushrooms.

Remove the sole from the marinade with a slotted spoon and roll up tightly, starting at a short end. Thread the fish, orange segments and mushrooms on 4 well-oiled skewers.

Brush with the marinade and cook as above. Serve garnished with orange twists.

INGREDIENTS

1½ lb monkfish, skinned, boned
    and cut into 1½-inch cubes
¼ cup lime juice
⅔ cup olive oil
1 garlic clove, crushed
½ cup chopped onion
¼ teaspoon ground turmeric
salt and pepper
6 bacon slices, halved
12 dried apricots, soaked overnight
    and drained
3 small red, green or yellow
    peppers, seeded and cut into
    squares
8 mushrooms
lime wedges and red pepper strips,
    to garnish

155

VEAL WITH PORT AND FIGS

The natural sweetness of this sauce blends very well with veal. If available, the fresh figs make a stunning garnish. Warm the figs in the oven for a few minutes, cut through the stem into 6 sections, leaving the base whole, then open them out like a flower.

Serves 4

INGREDIENTS

6 dried figs, stems removed and coarsely chopped

6 tablespoons port

½ cup water

6 tablespoons butter

4 veal scallops

1 tablespoon raspberry vinegar

¾ cup bone stock (see page 246)

salt and pepper

4 fresh figs, to garnish (optional)

Place the dried figs in a bowl and pour the port over. Soak for 1 hour, then place in a saucepan with the water and 2 tablespoons of the butter. Bring to the boil, reduce the heat and simmer gently for 15–20 minutes, stirring occasionally. Do not allow the mixture to stick to the bottom of the pan.

Remove from the heat and stir in 2 tablespoons of the remaining butter. Purée the mixture, then rub it through a sieve so no seeds remain.

Melt the remaining butter in a skillet and cook the veal for 2 minutes on each side. Remove and keep hot on a serving dish. Deglaze the pan with the vinegar, then stir in the stock. Bring to the boil and boil rapidly until reduced by a third. Add the fig purée and boil again until reduced slightly. Season to taste, then strain the sauce. Serve the veal with the sauce and garnish with figs, if desired.

PORK WITH PINEAPPLE AND CASHEW NUTS

This stir-fried dish is an impressive but simple recipe to prepare when guests arrive unexpectedly. Serve with boiled rice or noodles.

Serves 4

INGREDIENTS

2 tablespoons cornstarch

1 teaspoon ground ginger

¼ cup dry sherry

2 lb pork loin, cut into ¾-inch cubes

oil for deep-frying

3 tablespoons vegetable oil

½ cup finely chopped onion

1 garlic clove, finely chopped

¼ lb pineapple chunks, fresh or canned, drained

½ red pepper, seeded, sliced and the slices cut in half

4 oz cashew nuts, lightly toasted (⅔ cup)

⅔ cup chicken stock (see page 247)

2 tablespoons soy sauce

Mix the cornstarch, ginger and sherry together to form a smooth paste. Add the pork and stir well to coat the meat. Cover and leave at room temperature for 1 hour.

Heat the oil in a deep-fat fryer to 375°. Fry the pork in batches for 5 minutes, until crisp and golden. Drain on paper towels.

Meanwhile, heat the vegetable oil in a large skillet and sauté the onion and garlic for 2 minutes. Stir in the pineapple and red pepper and cook, stirring, for 1 minute. Stir in the nuts, stock and soy sauce. Add the pork, bring to the boil and simmer for 1–2 minutes. Serve at once.

ARABIAN RICE

This rice pilaf combines meat with dried fruits and pulses. Serve with extra butter and plain yogurt.

Serves 6

Cook the lentils in boiling water for 20–25 minutes or until tender. Drain. Cover the rice with cold water and leave to soak for 15 minutes, then drain. Melt 3 tablespoons butter and sauté half the onion until golden. Set aside.

Mix the beef with the remaining onion, season and form into small meatballs, the size of a cherry. Add the meatballs to the cooked onion and sauté until browned. Stir in the dates and currants. Mix the saffron with the hot water and add to the meat and fruit mixture.

Cook the rice in a large pan of well salted, boiling water for 5 minutes, then drain thoroughly.

Heat the cold water and 4 tablespoons butter in a heavy-bottomed saucepan over moderate heat. Spread a layer of the rice over the bottom of the pan, then a layer of meat and fruit, then lentils. Continue making layers ending with the rice, then push a wooden spoon through the layers to make an air hole. Wrap the lid with a dish towel and steam over moderate heat for 40 minutes. At the end of the cooking time, stand the bottom of the saucepan in cold water, to prevent further cooking. Serve with extra butter.

INGREDIENTS
½ cup brown lentils
1 lb basmati rice
7 tablespoons butter
½ cup finely chopped onion
½ lb lean ground beef
salt and pepper
4 oz pitted, chopped dates (½ cup)
⅔ cup currants
½ teaspoon saffron powder
1 tablespoon hot water
¼ cup cold water

CALF'S LIVER WITH GREEN GRAPES AND MADEIRA

Seasoned with sage and served with a slightly sweet sauce, calf's liver, is a delicious, light main course. Accompany with boiled rice. If fresh sage is unavailable, substitute tarragon or parsley.

Serves 4

Melt half the butter and sauté the onion until golden. Add the stock and Madeira, season and bring to the boil. Boil rapidly for about 4–5 minutes, until reduced and of a slightly syrupy consistency. Add the grape halves and warm through gently. Adjust the seasoning.

Melt the remaining butter in a large skillet. Season the liver, then sauté with the shredded sage leaves for about 3–5 minutes, turning once.

Remove from the skillet and serve at once with the Madeira sauce. Garnish with sprigs of fresh sage.

Calf's Liver with Sautéed Apples
Thinly slice and core two medium-sized tart apples. Proceed as in the recipe above, substituting apple slices for the green grapes and brandy for the Madeira. If fresh sage is unavailable, substitute parsley.

INGREDIENTS
4 tablespoons butter
¼ cup finely chopped onion or shallot
¾ cup chicken stock (see page 247)
½ cup Madeira
salt and pepper
24 large green grapes, peeled, halved and pits removed
1 lb calf's liver, very thinly sliced
4 fresh sage leaves, thinly shredded
4 sprigs sage leaves, for garnish

CHICKEN BREASTS WITH MANGO AND ALMONDS

The flavor of mango is most agreeable with beef and chicken dishes, both hot and cold, for relishes and chutneys, and a wide range of desserts.

Serves 4

INGREDIENTS

3 boneless chicken breasts, skinned and cut into 1-inch squares

1¼ cups peanut oil

1½ teaspoons chopped fresh ginger root

1 large garlic clove, finely chopped

2 large scallions, white part finely chopped and green part cut into pieces

1 large mango, peeled and cut lengthwise into strips

scallion tassels, to garnish

Marinade

1½ teaspoons cornstarch

1 egg white, beaten

2 teaspoons light soy sauce

1 teaspoon rice wine or medium-dry sherry

Sauce

¼ cup water

1 tablespoon light soy sauce

2 tablespoons rice wine or medium-dry sherry

1 teaspoon sugar

1 teaspoon cornstarch

⅓ cup slivered almonds, toasted

Mix together the ingredients for the marinade and pour over the chicken. Cover and marinate in the refrigerator for 30 minutes.

Heat a wok over high heat, then add the peanut oil. When the oil is hot enough for a piece of ginger to float to the surface, add the chicken and marinade, and stir-fry for 30 seconds.

Place a sieve over a bowl, and pour the chicken and all of the oil into it. Leave to drain thoroughly, then return 2 tablespoons of the oil to the wok. Stir-fry the ginger, garlic and white scallion parts for 30 seconds. Return the chicken to the wok and stir-fry for 1 minute. Transfer the chicken to a serving dish.

Pour 1 tablespoon of the oil into the wok, heat and add the mango. Stir-fry for 30 seconds, then add all the sauce ingredients except the almonds. Cook for a further 30 seconds or until the sauce thickens.

Stir in the green scallion parts and the toasted almonds. Pour over the chicken. Garnish with the scallion tassels.

KUMQUATS POACHED IN ROSE WATER

Kumquats resemble tiny, olive-shaped oranges. Their peel is sweet, but the flesh is sharp. This sharpness counteracts the sweetness of the prunes, apricots and honey in this compôte.

Serves 6–8

INGREDIENTS

½ lb prunes

½ lb dried apricots

¼ lb kumquats, sliced with seeds removed

juice of 2 oranges

3 tablespoons honey

1 tablespoon rose water

Place the prunes and apricots in a bowl with sufficient water to cover them by ½ inch. Leave to soak overnight.

Place the prunes and apricots, with their soaking water in a saucepan. Bring to the boil and simmer for 10 minutes, then add the kumquats, orange juice and honey. Simmer for a further 10 minutes. Add the rose water, remove the pan from the heat and pour into a serving bowl. Serve hot or cold.

CHICKEN BREASTS WITH MANGO AND ALMONDS

LYCHEE AND MELON BASKET WITH GINGER CREAM

*This dessert is attractive without appearing too contrived. The flavors
and colors blend beautifully. If you wish to serve more than 4–6
people, double the recipe but make only one "basket," slicing the fruit
and arranging it around the basket.*

Serves 4–6

INGREDIENTS

1 large ripe green-skinned Spanish
    melon
½ lb fresh lychees, peeled and pitted,
    or canned lychees, well drained
    and pitted
Ginger cream
1¼ cups heavy cream
6 tablespoons chopped candied
    ginger
¼ cup advocaat
finely chopped zest of 1 lemon

Lay the melon on its side. Cut a small slice from the bottom so it will sit securely on the dish. Insert a sharp knife just above where the stem was and cut lengthwise, almost to the center. Leave a space of 1 inch of the melon uncut and continue cutting lengthwise to the end of the melon. Repeat on the other side. Make the melon handle by cutting across the melon leaving 1 inch uncut across the center. Remove the two end wedges of melon. Cut away the flesh about ½ inch from the rind, inside the handle. Cut the flesh into cubes or balls and reserve.

Scoop out the flesh of the melon with a melon baller or cut into cubes. Cut the edge of the basket into a scallop pattern.

Pile the melon and lychees into the basket and place on a serving dish. Chill.

To make the ginger cream, lightly whip the cream, then gradually stir in the remaining ingredients until they are well mixed. Spoon into a bowl and serve with the melon basket.

SPARKLING MELON AND LIME SOUP

A light, refreshing dessert to serve on a hot summer evening.

Serves 4

Dissolve the sugar in the water over gentle heat. Add the lime zest, bring to the boil, then simmer for 2–3 minutes. When cold, strain the syrup into a blender container. Add the lime juice and melon and purée until smooth. Chill until required.

Just before serving, stir in the champagne and garnish with the prepared fruit and leaves.

INGREDIENTS
¼ cup sugar
⅔ cup water
pared zest and juice of 1 lime
2 cups diced melon flesh
6 tablespoons chilled champagne or
   sparkling white wine
Garnish
julienne mango strips
fresh raspberries or strawberry
   slices
tiny mint sprigs, scented
   geranium or lemon balm leaves

MANGO AND PAPAYA PARFAIT

*This is an elegant dessert made with fresh mango and papaya, two of
the Caribbean's most mouth-watering fruits.*

Serves 6–8

Purée the mango and papaya flesh in a blender or food processor. Stir in the lemon juice.

Place the egg yolks and sugar in the top of a double boiler. Beat for about 5 minutes or until the mixture is pale, light and thick. Remove the bowl from the heat and continue beating for a further 2 minutes.

Whip the cream until stiff. Fold the fruit purée into the egg yolk mixture, then add the cream. Mix until evenly blended. Pour into a rigid plastic container and freeze for 3 hours or until firm. Alternatively, freeze the parfait in a decorative mold. Dip the mold in very hot water for about 30 seconds before turning out.

INGREDIENTS
1 small ripe mango, peeled, pitted
   and roughly chopped
1 ripe papaya, peeled, seeded and
   roughly chopped
1 tablespoon lemon juice
4 egg yolks
1 cup confectioners' sugar
1 cup heavy cream

MELON AND STRAWBERRIES WITH CHAMPAGNE

*This is a perfect summer dessert. The melon halves form individual
serving dishes. For a picnic, prepare the fruit, wrap in plastic wrap
and add the champagne when ready to serve.
Use strawberries, raspberries, seedless grapes and cherries to fill the
center of the melon.*

Serves 4

Cut the melons in half and scoop out the seeds.

Hull the strawberries and place in each melon half. Sprinkle the sugar over the fruit if wished, and pour about ¼ cup champagne over each serving. Eat at once, served with the remaining champagne.

LYCHEE AND MELON BASKET WITH GINGER CREAM

INGREDIENTS
2 cantaloupe, crenshaw or other
   small melon
1½ lb strawberries, or other soft
   fruit
4 teaspoons superfine sugar
   (optional)
1 bottle chilled champagne or
   sparkling dry white wine

PORT WINE JELLY WITH FROSTED GRAPES

*This clear shimmering jelly, served with sparkling frosted grapes, is
both light and refreshing. To ensure a cloudless jelly, allow the liquid
to drip through the cheesecloth in its own time – one squeeze and a
murky mixture will be the result.*

Serves 6–8

INGREDIENTS
pared zest of 4 lemons
1¼ cups lemon juice
3¾ cups water
1¼ cups superfine sugar
⅔ cup port
*⅓ cup plus 1 teaspoon unflavored
    gelatin, dissolved in ¾ cup hot
    water*
4 egg whites
4 egg shells, crushed
¾ lb dark and green grapes

Place the lemon zest, juice, water, 1 cup sugar and port in a saucepan and stir
well. Place the pan over a gentle heat and stir until the sugar dissolves. Stir in
the gelatin.

Beat three egg whites until frothy, then add the egg shells to the egg whites
and gently beat them into the jelly mixture. Continue beating until the mixture
comes to the boil.

Stop beating as the foam begins to rise and remove the pan from the heat.
Return the pan to the heat and repeat this procedure twice, allowing the foam to
rise and fall without any further beating. Cool for 10 minutes.

Place a sieve lined with a double thickness of cheesecloth over a large bowl.
Slowly pour the jelly into the sieve, allowing the foam to fall in last. Set the sieve
over another bowl and slowly pour the strained jelly onto the egg shells and
whites. Leave the mixture to seep through. Gently remove the sieve and pour
the jelly into a dampened 1¼-quart mold. Leave overnight in a cool place to set.

To frost the grapes, wash and dry them, then cut into clusters. Beat the
remaining egg white lightly with a fork, but do not allow it to foam. Put the
remaining sugar into a shallow bowl, or onto a sheet of wax paper. Using a
small brush, paint the grapes with egg white, then roll them in the sugar. Allow
to dry.

To serve, dip the mold up to the rim in hot water for 5 seconds, then place a
plate upside down over the mold. Invert the two, giving a good shake halfway
over. Lift off the mold and decorate with the frosted grapes.

GINGER WATER-ICE

*The flavor of this water-ice is reminiscent of the ginger beer sold in
stone bottles years ago. For those who dislike ginger, follow the recipe,
omitting the ginger, and you will have a refreshing lemon water-ice.*

Makes 1¼ pints

INGREDIENTS
1 cup sugar
2 cups water
¾ cup lemon juice
*1½ tablespoons very finely chopped
    candied ginger*

Dissolve the sugar in the water over gentle heat, stirring frequently. Increase
the heat and boil for 5 minutes. Remove the syrup from the heat and allow to
cool.

Set the freezer to its coldest setting. Stir in the lemon juice and stem ginger.
Pour the syrup into a shallow container and freeze until it starts to freeze around
the edges. Turn into a chilled bowl and beat to remove the ice crystals. Return to
the freezer and freeze until solid.

Remove from the freezer 15 minutes before serving to soften.

GRAPE TARTS

*These elegant tarts are decorated with black and green grapes and
glazed with marmalade and brandy.*

Makes 12

INGREDIENTS

1½ quantity tart pastry dough (see
    page 248)
1 egg, beaten
3 tablespoons superfine sugar
6 tablespoons heavy cream
½ cup ground almonds
finely grated zest and juice of
    ½ large lemon
few drops of almond extract
3 tablespoons lemon marmalade,
    sieved
1 tablespoon brandy
1 tablespoon water
½ lb seedless green grapes

Roll the dough out ⅛-inch thick on a lightly floured surface with a lightly
floured rolling pin. Cut out 2½-inch circles with a round cutter and use to line 12
tart pans or muffin tins. Prick the base of each tart lightly, then cover and chill
for at least 30 minutes.

Preheat the oven to 400°

Bake blind for 8–10 minutes or until the dough has set and is lightly colored.
Reduce the oven temperature to 350°.

Meanwhile, lightly beat together the egg, sugar, cream, ground almonds,
lemon zest and juice and almond extract. Divide equally between the pastry
cases. Bake for about 10 minutes or until the filling is lightly set and colored.
Cool slightly, then carefully transfer the tarts to a wire rack to cool completely.

Gently heat the marmalade with the brandy and water, if necessary, until the
marmalade melts. Leave to cool. Arrange the grapes in the tart cases, then
carefully spoon the marmalade glaze over. Serve cold.

PEARS POACHED WITH QUINCES AND CASSIS

Serve with lightly whipped cream and almond tuiles.

Serves 4

INGREDIENTS

2¼ cups dry white wine
½ cup crème de cassis
2½-inch cinnamon stick
3 tablespoons superfine sugar, or to
    taste
2 quinces, peeled, cored and sliced
4 firm but ripe pears, peeled

Mix the wine, crème de cassis, cinnamon stick and sugar together in a saucepan
which is large enough to hold the pears standing upright. Heat to simmering
point. Add the quinces, then the pears, standing them upright. Cover and
poach for about 20 minutes or until the pears are just tender. Leave the pears to
cool in the liquid. Transfer to a dish with a slotted spoon, cover and chill.

Remove the cinnamon stick from the pan, then purée the liquid in a blender
or food processor. Cover and chill for at least 2 hours.

Just before serving, adjust the sweetness with more sugar, if necessary.
Arrange the pears on individual serving plates with some of the purée spooned
on the side. Leave at room temperature for about 15 minutes before serving.

SOUTH PACIFIC SHERBET

SOUTH PACIFIC SHERBET

*A delectable trio of tropical fruit sherbets which can be served on individual
plates or arranged into a pyramid shape with alternating colors.*

Serves 12–14

Place the mango purée, kiwi fruit purée and the pineapple juice in 3 bowls.

To make the sugar syrups, place the water in 3 heavy-bottomed saucepans, add the respective amounts of sugar, stir until dissolved, then boil for 5 minutes. Cool the syrup, then add to their respective purées and juices.

Add the lemon juice and zest to the kiwi sherbet and the orange flower water to the pineapple sherbet.

Pour the mixtures into separate shallow containers and freeze for 2½ hours. Remove from the freezer, turn into chilled bowls and beat to break up the ice crystals. Return to the freezer and leave until frozen.

To serve, remove from the freezer and allow to soften for 30 minutes in the refrigerator. Place scoops of sherbet onto freezer trays and place in the freezer for 30 minutes to harden. Arrange on individual dishes or in a pyramid and decorate with mint or fruit, if wished.

Note

Due to the varying acidity of each fruit, a different concentration of sugar syrup is required for each one to ensure a smooth texture and a complementary balance of flavors.

INGREDIENTS

Mango sherbet
*2 ripe mangoes, peeled, pitted and
    puréed*
1¼ cups water
⅔ cup sugar
Kiwi fruit
4 kiwi fruits, peeled and puréed
2 cups water
1 cup sugar
*juice and finely grated zest of
    1 lemon*
Pineapple sherbet
2 cups pineapple juice
1 teaspoon orange flower water
⅔ cup water
½ cup sugar

GOOSEBERRY ICE CREAM IN BRANDY SNAP CASES

The rich smoothness of the ice cream is complemented by the crunchy texture of the brandy snap cases.

Serves 8

Place the gooseberries, sugar, orange zest and water in a saucepan, cover and poach over low heat until they are soft. Remove the orange zest, then rub the gooseberry mixture through a sieve. Cool, cover and place in the refrigerator for about 1 hour. Add a few drops of green coloring, if necessary.

Lightly whip the cream, then fold into the mixture. Pour into a shallow container, cover and freeze for 45 minutes. Tip the gooseberry mixture into a chilled bowl and beat to break down the ice crystals. Return to the container, cover and repeat once more. Return to the container and leave until frozen.

Meanwhile, to make the brandy snap cases, gently heat the syrup, butter and sugar together, stirring occasionally until the sugar dissolves. Remove from the heat and stir in the remaining ingredients, except the orange zest.

Preheat the oven to 350°. Drop about 3 tablespoons of the mixture onto a lightly buttered cookie sheet, leaving plenty of room for the mixture to spread. Bake for 7–10 minutes, until golden brown. Quickly but carefully remove the cooked mixture with a spatula and, while still hot, mold it around the base of an oiled orange, large apple or small bowl or dish. Leave to set. Remove the mold and leave the baskets to cool on a wire rack. Bake and shape the remaining mixture in the same way.

About 30 minutes before serving, transfer the ice cream to the refrigerator. Scoop the ice cream into the baskets and decorate with shreds of orange zest.

INGREDIENTS
2 lb gooseberries, topped and tailed
¾ cup superfine sugar, or to taste
2 long strips orange zest, plus extra for decoration
3 tablespoons water
few drops green food coloring (optional)
2 cups chilled heavy cream
Brandy snap cases
3 tablespoons corn syrup
3 tablespoons butter
7 tablespoons superfine sugar
3 tablespoons unbleached flour
¾ teaspoon ground ginger
¼ teaspoon orange juice
½ teaspoon finely grated orange zest

ORANGE CURACAO ICE CREAM

A perfect dessert for a dinner party. This ice cream is made beforehand and served either in glass dishes or orange shells. Garnish with spirals of orange zest and serve with brandy snaps.

Makes about 1¼ pints

Set the freezer to the lowest setting. Beat the egg yolks with the sugar until pale. Gradually beat in the orange zest and juice and the curaçao, then mix in the cream.

Place the mixture in a shallow container and freeze until the ice cream begins to set around the edges. Turn it into a chilled bowl and beat to break up the ice crystals until smooth. Return it to the shallow container and freeze until firm.

If a smoother ice cream is preferred, repeat the beating and freezing process once or twice more.

Remove from the freezer about 15 minutes before serving to soften slightly.

INGREDIENTS
5 egg yolks
¾ cup sugar
finely grated zest and juice of 2 oranges
2–3 tablespoons curaçao or Grand Marnier
1¼ cups heavy cream, lightly whipped

GOOSEBERRY ICE CREAM IN BRANDY SNAP CASES

THE BAKERY

DESSERTS, CAKES AND BREADS

DESSERTS

With their tempting arrays of tarts, cheesecakes, flans and mousses, Harrods never fails to provide a delicious dessert for an impromptu dinner party. Far more enjoyable to make yourself, puddings are always popular, and who could resist Hazelnut and Passion Fruit Roulade, Crème Brulée with Cherries, or Grand Marnier Mousse with Chocolate Crust?

FRESH DATE AND BANANA PUDDING

INGREDIENTS

1½ lb fresh dates, weighed before
    pitting
3 large bananas, peeled and sliced
1¼ cups heavy cream
finely grated zest of 1 orange
3 tablespoons orange juice
2 tablespoons orange flower water

There is no added sweetener in this dessert as the natural fruit sugar in the dates and bananas is sufficient. If fresh dates are unavailable, substitute dried.

Serves 8

Skin, pit and halve the dates, then arrange half of them in a serving dish. Place the sliced bananas on top, then cover with the remaining dates.

Pour the cream into a bowl and gradually stir in the orange zest, juice and flower water, stirring constantly to prevent the cream from separating. Pour the flavored cream evenly over the layers of fruit and leave in a cool place for at least 30 minutes for the flavors to develop.

CHOCOLATE-SHERRY CHEESECAKE

INGREDIENTS

10 tablespoons butter
3 tablespoons corn syrup
½ lb graham crackers, crushed to
    make 2⅔ cups
2 oz semi-sweet chocolate
few drops of vanilla extract
1 lb cream cheese
3 eggs, separated
1 cup superfine sugar
2 tablespoons sherry
2 tablespoons unflavored gelatin
1¼ cups heavy cream

The extra flavor of sherry makes this an out-of-the-ordinary cheesecake. Because this is served chilled, it can be made a day in advance.

Serves 8–10

Place 8 tablespoons of the butter and 2 tablespoons syrup in a pan and heat until the butter has melted. Stir in the crackers and mix well. Press the mixture into a greased 10-inch springform pan. Chill.

Melt the chocolate with the remaining butter, remaining syrup and vanilla extract in the top of a double boiler, stirring occasionally until melted and glossy.

Beat the cream cheese until smooth, then beat in the egg yolks, sugar and sherry. Sprinkle the gelatin over 1¼ cups cold water and leave to soften for 2 minutes. Stand in a pan of hot water and stir until dissolved. Cool slightly.

Beat the egg whites until stiff. Whip the cream until it just holds its shape. Stir the cooled gelatin into the cream cheese mixture in a steady stream. Using a large metal spoon, fold in the cream, then the egg whites.

Pour the mixture into the lined pan. Quickly drizzle the chocolate sauce over the top and swirl with a skewer. Chill until set.

CREME BRULEE WITH CHERRIES

*This is a crème brûlée with a fruity variation. Once the caramel
topping has been cracked, it opens to reveal the velvety cream. A layer
of dark cherries in kirsch is found underneath.*

Serves 6

Place the cherries, water and superfine sugar in a saucepan over moderate heat.
Stir to dissolve the sugar, then bring to the boil, reduce the heat and simmer for
3 minutes. Mix the arrowroot with the cold water and stir into the cherries.
Simmer for 2 minutes, stirring occasionally. Pour the cherries into a shallow
ovenproof serving dish, or ramekins, and leave to cool. Stir in the kirsch.

Meanwhile, scald the cream. Mix the egg yolks with the vanilla extract, then
gradually beat in the hot cream. Strain the mixture into a saucepan. Cook over
very gentle heat, stirring constantly, for 10 minutes or until the mixture
thickens. Do not allow the mixture to boil or it will curdle. Cover the cream with
a circle of wax paper and leave until cool and thickened. When cool, remove the
paper and spoon over the cherries, making sure that they are covered completely. Cover with plastic wrap and chill for at least 3 hours.

Sprinkle the superfine sugar evenly over the surface. Place under a hot broiler
and cook for about 7 minutes or until the sugar melts, bubbles and darkens
slightly. Leave to cool, then chill before serving.

INGREDIENTS
¾ lb Bing cherries, pitted weight
⅔ cup water
¼ cup superfine sugar
2 teaspoons arrowroot
2 teaspoons ice water
2 tablespoons kirsch
2¼ cups heavy cream
5 egg yolks
few drops vanilla extract
¼ cup superfine sugar

RAINBOW SOUFFLE

Raspberries and pistachio nuts add color as well as an interesting taste to this creamy soufflé. This is an ideal dessert to serve for any festive occasion.

Serves 6–8

INGREDIENTS

6 eggs, separated

1 cup superfine sugar

2 tablespoons unflavoured gelatin

¼ cup cold water

2 cups heavy cream

2 teaspoons vanilla extract

⅔ cup raspberry purée

½ cup pistachio nuts, pounded in a mortar

few drops of green food coloring

Decoration

4 oz semi-sweet chocolate

rose leaves (optional)

1¼ cups heavy cream, stiffly whipped

additional chopped pistachio nuts

Beat the egg yolks and sugar in the top of a double boiler over hot water for 10 minutes or until pale and thick and the mixture just holds the trail of the beaters. Remove from the heat and beat for a further 2 minutes.

Sprinkle the gelatin over the water in a bowl and leave to soften for 2 minutes. Stand in a pan of hot water and stir until dissolved. Cool slightly, then gradually stir into the egg mixture.

Whip the cream until it just holds its shape, then fold into the egg mixture. Divide the mixture evenly between three bowls.

Stir vanilla extract into one bowl of mixture, raspberry purée into another, and pistachios and a little green food coloring into the third. Beat the egg whites until stiff. Divide between the bowls and fold in carefully.

Pour the raspberry mixture into a 1¾-quart glass soufflé dish with a wide strip of wax paper tied around the top and secured with string. Place in the refrigerator for about 10 minutes or until lightly set. Pour the vanilla soufflé mixture over the top and chill again. Finally, pour over the pistachio mixture and chill for about 4 hours, until firm.

Meanwhile, to make the decoration, melt the chocolate and paint the underside of the rose leaves with the chocolate. Leave to set, then carefully remove the leaves. Fill a pastry bag fitted with a star tip with the cream. Carefully peel off the paper from the soufflé. Decorate around the top edge with the chocolate rose leaves, whirls of cream and pistachio nuts.

CHOCOLATE SNOWBALL

This luscious dessert should be left for at least 24 hours before eating. The outer layer forms a crust while the center remains a soft fudge.

Serves 4–6

INGREDIENTS

4 oz semi-sweet chocolate

1 teaspoon instant coffee

3 tablespoons boiling water

½ cup superfine sugar

8 tablespoons unsalted butter, diced

2 eggs

1 tablespoon dark rum

1 cup heavy cream

candied rose petals and violet petals, to decorate (optional)

Preheat the oven to 350°. Line a 3-cup heatproof bowl with foil.

Break up the chocolate and place it in a saucepan. Dissolve the coffee in the water, then add it to the pan with the sugar. Heat gently until the chocolate melts. Transfer the chocolate mixture to a bowl and beat well with an electric hand-held mixer or a balloon whisk. Slowly beat in the butter until evenly combined, then beat in the eggs one at a time. Stir in the rum.

Pour the mixture into the bowl. Bake for about 40 minutes or until risen and firm, but still slightly wobbly like a soufflé with a thick, cracked crust.

Cool at room temperature, then press down with your fingertips to level the surface. Cover and chill for at least 24 hours. Unmold onto a serving plate.

Whip the cream until it holds its shape. Fill a pastry bag fitted with a star tip with the cream and pipe rosettes on the pudding until it is completely covered. Decorate with a sprinkling of crystalized petals, if wished.

CLEMENTINE CHARLOTTE MALAKOFF

CLEMENTINE CHARLOTTE MALAKOFF

*A tempting dessert flavored with clementines and orange liqueur.
The final result looks as spectacular as it tastes. If clementines are out
of season, use tangerines.*

Serves 6

Mix 2 tablespoons of the Grand Marnier with the water. Quickly dip the ladyfingers in the liquid, then line the bottom and sides of a 1-quart charlotte mold, trimming to fit.

Roughly chop 3 clementines and reserve the fourth for decoration.

Beat the butter and sugar together until pale, light and fluffy. Beat in the remaining liqueur and the ground almonds.

Whip ¾ cup of the cream until it just holds its shape, then fold it into the creamed mixture with the chopped clementines. Pour this mixture into the mold and smooth the top. Chill for about 3 hours or until firm.

Whip the remaining cream until stiff and fill a pastry bag fitted with a star tip. Quickly dip the bottom of the mold into hot water, then turn the dessert out onto a serving plate. Pipe whirls of cream around the top edge and decorate.

INGREDIENTS

6 tablespoons Grand Marnier

2 tablespoons water

20–24 ladyfingers

*4 clementines, peeled and
    segmented*

½ lb unsalted butter, softened

½ cup confectioners' sugar

1 cup ground almonds

1 cup heavy cream

MERINGUE BASKET (WITH SUMMER FRUITS)

*Melt in-the-mouth meringue and luscious seasonal fruits make the
perfect light dessert for summer entertaining.*

Serves 6–8

INGREDIENTS
*4 egg whites
2 cups confectioners' sugar
1¼ cups heavy cream
2 tablespoons kirsch or orange
　flavored liqueur
½ lb fruit, such as pitted grapes,
　pitted cherries, hulled
　strawberries and raspberries or
　sliced peaches*

Preheat the oven to 200°.

Line three cookie sheets with aluminum foil (turn rimmed cookie sheets upside down and use the bottoms), and draw a 7½-inch circle on each. Turn the paper over so that the circle is visible but does not come into contact with the meringues and mark them.

Put 3 egg whites in the top of a double boiler over simmering water. Sift in 1½ cups of the confectioners' sugar.

Beat the egg whites and sugar vigorously over the simmering water until the mixture stands in very stiff peaks. Do not allow to get too hot or the meringue will crust around the edges.

Fit a pastry bag with a large star tip. Spoon in one-third of the meringue mixture.

Pipe rings of meringue about ½-inch thick inside two of the circles on the paper. Fill the bag with the remaining meringue and, starting from the center, pipe a continuous coil of meringue on the third sheet of paper. Bake for 2½–3 hours to dry out.

Beat the remaining egg white until stiff, then sift and fold in the remaining confectioners' sugar. Put into the pastry bag. Remove the cooked meringue rings from the paper and put one on top of the other on top of the bottom layer, piping a ring of fresh meringue between each. Return to the oven for 1½–2 hours more. Slide onto a wire rack and peel off the bottom paper when cool. Just before serving, stand the meringue basket on a flat serving plate. Beat the cream and liqueur until stiff then fold in the prepared fruit, reserving some pieces for decoration. Fill the basket with the cream and fruit mixture and decorate with the remaining pieces of fruit.

RUM SOUFFLE OMELET

*This fluffy soufflé omelet is delicious as a special treat for one or to
round off a light supper for two.*

Serves 1

INGREDIENTS
*2 eggs, separated
1 teaspoon superfine sugar
1 tablespoon dark rum
1 tablespoon butter
1 tablespoon apricot jam, warmed
2 tablespoons confectioners' sugar*

Put the egg yolks in a bowl with the superfine sugar and rum. Mix well together. Beat the egg whites until they are stiff and standing in peaks.

Melt the butter in a heavy-bottomed omelet pan until foaming. Quickly fold the egg whites into the egg yolk mixture, then pour into the foaming butter.

Cook over moderate heat for 2–3 minutes, until the underside of the omelet is golden brown, then place the pan under a preheated hot broiler and cook for a few minutes more until the top is golden brown.

Slide the omelet onto a sheet of aluminum foil placed on a warmed serving plate. Spread with the warmed jam, then tip the foil to fold the omelet over.

Sift the confectioners' sugar thickly over the top of the omelet then mark in a criss-cross pattern with hot metal skewers, if liked. Remove the foil and serve.

GRAND MARNIER MOUSSE WITH CHOCOLATE CRUST

*A rich orange mousse enclosed in a thin crust of chocolate. Great care is
needed when turning out of the pan in order not to damage the
chocolate band.*

Serves 4–6

Melt the chocolate in the top of a double boiler over simmering water. Pour it
into a buttered 1½-quart charlotte mold and swirl evenly over the bottom and
sides, spreading with a knife if necessary. Leave to set.

Place the orange zest and juice, egg yolks, superfine sugar and Grand
Marnier in a bowl over hot water. Beat for about 10 minutes until pale and thick.
Remove from the heat and beat for a further 2 minutes.

Sprinkle the gelatin over the water and leave to soften for 2 minutes. Stand in
a saucepan of hot water and stir until dissolved. Cool slightly, then fold it into
the egg mixture.

Beat the egg whites until stiff. Whip the cream until it just holds its shape.
Using a large spatula, fold the cream, then the egg whites into the egg mixture.

Pour into the lined mold and chill for about 3 hours or until set.

Just before serving, very carefully loosen the edge of the chocolate case with a
sharp pointed knife and turn onto a serving plate.

INGREDIENTS
6 oz semi-sweet chocolate
*finely grated zest and juice of
   1 orange*
2 eggs, separated
6 tablespoons superfine sugar
2 tablespoons Grand Marnier
2 teaspoons unflavored gelatin
1 tablespoon water
⅔ cup heavy cream

APRICOT BAVARIAN CREAM

*Bavarian creams are among the lightest and creamiest fruit desserts.
The apricot purée adds a delicate flavor.*

Serves 6–8

Place the apricots in a small saucepan and cook in their soaking water to cover
for 25–30 minutes or until tender. Place the apricots in a blender or food
processor and blend with sufficient cooking liquid to make a thick purée. Set
aside to cool.

Beat the egg yolks and ¾ cup of the sugar together in a bowl until thick. Beat
in the cornstarch. Gradually beat in the warm milk. Place in the top of a double
boiler over simmering water and cook, stirring, until the custard coats the back
of a wooden spoon. Remove from the heat.

Pour the lemon juice into a bowl, sprinkle the gelatin over and leave to soften
for 2 minutes. Stand the bowl in a saucepan of hot water and stir until dissolved.
Stir into the hot custard with the apricot purée.

Beat the egg whites until stiff, then beat in the remaining sugar. Fold into the
custard using a large metal spoon. Chill until just beginning to set, stirring
occasionally.

Whip the cream until it just holds its shape and fold into the custard. Pour the
mixture into a rinsed-out 1¾-quart metal mold and chill for at least 3 hours or
until set.

To unmold, quickly dip the base of the mold into hot water. Run the tip of a
sharp knife around the edge and turn out onto a serving plate.

INGREDIENTS
*½ lb dried apricots, soaked
   overnight*
5 eggs, separated
1 cup superfine sugar
2 teaspoons cornstarch
2 cups milk, scalded
3 tablespoons lemon juice
1 tablespoon unflavored gelatin
⅔ cup heavy cream

COEURS A LA CREME

*This delicate dessert, ideally served with tiny wild strawberries,
derives its name from the heart-shaped dish in which it is made. The
holes in the base of the dish allow the whey to drain away.*

Serves 6

INGREDIENTS
¼ lb ricotta, sieved
½ lb cream cheese
1 cup crème fraîche
a few drops vanilla extract
2 tablespoons superfine sugar
⅔ cup heavy cream, lightly whipped
¼ lb small wild strawberries
strawberry leaves, to garnish
heavy cream, to serve

Mash the ricotta and cream cheese together. Stir in the crème fraîche, vanilla extract and superfine sugar and fold in cream.

Rinse 12 pieces of cheesecloth in water and wring out well. Line 6 heart-shaped coeur à la crème molds with a double layer of cheesecloth, pressing it well into the corners.

Spoon the cheese mixture into the lined molds and place on a large plate to catch the liquid. Cover with plastic wrap to avoid the dessert absorbing any odors or flavors from the refrigerator. Drain overnight. Discard the liquid.

Invert onto individual serving plates and gently remove the cheesecloths.

Arrange the strawberries around the hearts and serve with extra cream.

HAZELNUT AND PASSION FRUIT ROULADE

*If passion fruit is unavailable, use 2 peeled and chopped kiwi fruit or
½ lb hulled strawberries or raspberries.*

Serves 6

Preheat the oven to 350°. Butter a 10½-× 15½-inch jelly roll pan, then line with wax paper.

Beat the egg yolks and sugar in the top of a double boiler over simmering water for 10 minutes or until pale and thick. Remove from the heat and beat for a further 2 minutes.

Beat the egg whites until stiff, then gradually beat in the corn syrup. Fold the egg whites into the egg yolk and sugar mixture, then fold in the hazelnuts. Pour the mixture evenly into the pan. Bake for 12–15 minutes, until firm to the touch. Cover with aluminum foil and cool in the pan.

Whip the cream until stiff, then fold in the passion fruit seeds.

Dust a sheet of wax paper with confectioners' sugar. Turn the cake out onto the paper and carefully remove the lining paper. Spread with the cream and roll up from one short edge, using the wax paper to lift the cake. Carefully transfer to a serving plate and dust with more confectioners' sugar.

INGREDIENTS
5 eggs, separated
¾ cup superfine sugar
2 tablespoons corn syrup
3 oz ground hazelnuts (½ cup)
3 passion fruit, seeds reserved
1¼ cups heavy cream
*confectioners' sugar, sifted, to
    decorate*

(Left) COEURS A LA CREME.
(Below) HAZELNUT AND
PASSION FRUIT ROULADE

SPICED FIG AND ORANGE PUDDING

*This spicy pudding is a possible alternative to a traditional English
Christmas plum pudding. Served with rum butter and decorated with
holly, it looks and tastes seasonal.*

Serves 8

INGREDIENTS
⅔ cup unbleached flour
½ teaspoon baking powder
1 cup shredded beef suet
2½ cups fine fresh bread crumbs
1 cup finely chopped dried figs
1 cup finely chopped dried dates
½ cup seedless raisins
⅓ cup candied mixed peel
⅓ cup finely chopped ginger
pinch each of ground cinnamon,
    cloves and ginger
large pinch of grated nutmeg
finely grated zest and juice of
    1 orange
2 eggs, lightly beaten
3 tablespoons dark rum
Rum butter
8 tablespoons unsalted butter,
    softened
½ cup light brown sugar, packed
finely grated zest of ½ an orange
3–4 tablespoons dark rum

Sift the flour and baking powder into a large bowl. Stir in the suet, bread crumbs, dried fruits, ginger and spices. Add the orange zest and juice, the eggs and rum, and mix well. Spoon the mixture into a 1¼-quart pudding bowl or mold. Cover with pleated wax paper and aluminum foil, then tie string around the rim of the bowl to secure.

Place a trivet in a heavy-bottomed saucepan, lower the pudding into the pan and pour in enough boiling water to come two-thirds of the way up the sides of the bowl. Cover and steam over gentle heat for 4 hours, topping up with more boiling water if necessary.

To make the rum butter, cream the butter and sugar until pale, light and fluffy. Beat in the orange zest. Gradually beat in the rum. Chill if required.

Turn the pudding out onto a serving dish and serve hot with the rum butter.

RHUBARB AND ORANGE CRUMBLE

*A traditional English pudding, this is delicious served warm or cold
with custard or vanilla ice cream.*

Serves 6

INGREDIENTS
2 lb rhubarb, trimmed and chopped
juice of ½ orange
finely grated zest of 1 orange
½ cup light brown sugar
2 tablespoons finely chopped candied
    ginger, (optional)
Topping
¾ cup unbleached flour
¾ cup whole wheat flour
½ teaspoon baking powder
⅔ cup light brown sugar
¾ cup chopped blanched almonds
8 tablespoons butter

Preheat the oven to 350°.

Bring the rhubarb, orange juice and zest and sugar to the boil in a saucepan. Cover and simmer for 15 minutes. Cool slightly, then stir in the ginger. Pour the mixture into a 1¾-quart baking dish.

To make the topping, sift the flours and baking powder together. Tip any bran from the sieve back into the bowl. Add the sugar and almonds and mix well.

Cut the butter into the flour until the mixture resembles bread crumbs, then spread it over the fruit. Bake for 35–40 minutes or until the crumble is golden and crisp. Serve hot or chilled.

SUMMER FRUITS IN A BLUEBERRY RING

*In this dessert, whole strawberries, raspberries and cherries are set in
blueberry jelly in a ring mold, with fresh fruit piled into the center.*

Serves 8–10

Place the blueberries in a saucepan with the sugar and cook gently for 10–15
minutes, until the fruit is soft. Remove from the heat and rub the fruit through a
fine nylon sieve. Pour the purée into a measuring cup and add sufficient cold
water to make the purée up to 2½ cups.

Pour the hot water into a small bowl and sprinkle the gelatin over. Leave to
soften for 2 minutes, then place the bowl in a pan of hot water and stir the
gelatin until dissolved. Stir it into the blueberry purée and stir well. Stir in the
strawberries, raspberries and cherries.

Pour the jelly into a 1¼-quart rinsed-out ring mold. Leave to set 3–4 hours.
Unmold onto a serving dish and pile the fruit for decoration into the center.

If available, arrange blueberry leaves under the jelly and a few bunches of
blueberries outside the ring.

INGREDIENTS
1 lb blueberries
⅔ cup sugar
½ cup hot water
7 teaspoons unflavored gelatin
½ lb strawberries, hulled
½ lb raspberries
½ lb pitted Bing cherries
Decoration
½ lb strawberries with their leaves
½ lb pitted Bing cherries
½ lb raspberries
*small bunches fresh blueberries
(optional)*
blueberry leaves (optional)

179

BISCUITS AND CAKES

— ◆ —

No-one takes their tea more seriously than the British, which is probably why Harrods stocks such a varied selection of cakes and cookies. Traditional Madeira and Dundee Cakes are four o'clock favorites, while Florentines and Orange and Hazelnut Vacherin are irresistible alternatives.

SIMNEL CAKE

Simnel cake is traditionally served on Easter Sunday, the 11 balls of marzipan representing the 11 faithful disciples.

Makes one 8-inch cake

INGREDIENTS

2 cups unbleached flour

½ teaspoon baking powder

pinch each ground cinnamon, cloves
    and nutmeg

1⅓ cups currants

1 cup golden raisins

⅓ cup raisins

½ cup mixed candied peel

⅓ cup candied cherries, quartered

½ lb butter, softened

1 cup light brown sugar

4 eggs, plus 1 egg, beaten to glaze

finely grated zest of 1 lemon

1–2 tablespoons brandy

3 tablespoons apricot jam, warmed
    and sieved

1 egg white, beaten

Marzipan

3 cups ground almonds

1¼ cups confectioners' sugar, sifted

¾ cup superfine sugar

1 tablespoon lemon juice

1 tablespoon orange flower water

2–3 drops vanilla extract

1 egg

1 egg yolk

Glacé Icing

1 cup confectioners' sugar, sifted

1 tablespoon warm water

1 teaspoon orange flower water

To make the marzipan, mix the ground almonds, confectioners' and superfine sugar together. Add the remaining ingredients and mix to a smooth paste. Knead the marzipan lightly but do not over-work or the almonds will become oily. Divide in half and shape into rounds. Wrap in a double layer of plastic wrap and set aside.

Preheat the oven to 350°. Double line an 8-inch springform cake pan with wax paper. Sift together the flour, baking powder and spices. In a separate bowl, mix the dried fruits, peel, candied cherries and 3 tablespoons of the sifted flour together.

Cream the butter and sugar together until pale, light and fluffy.

Roll out half the marzipan into a circle, just under 8-inches wide. Wrap the remaining marzipan in plastic wrap and refrigerate until needed.

Add the eggs to the creamed butter, beating well after each addition. Add a little flour if the mixture starts to separate. Add the lemon zest and fold in the flour. Fold in the fruit mixture and stir in the brandy. Spoon half the mixture into the pan. Place the marzipan layer over the cake mixture, then spoon the remaining cake mixture on top, making a slight hollow in the center.

Wrap the outside of the cake pan with a double layer of brown paper and secure with string. Bake for 3 hours. Do not test the cake in the normal way with a skewer, as the marzipan layer tends to stick to it and gives the appearance of underdone cake mixture. Simply press the top of the cake with your fingers—it should feel firm. Cover the top of the cake with wax paper if it becomes too brown. Leave to cool in the pan for 30 minutes, then turn out onto a wire rack to cool. Wrap in foil and leave for 24 hours before decorating.

Divide the remaining marzipan in half. Roll out one half into an 8-inch circle to fit the top of the cake. Turn the cake over, trimming the bottom, if necessary. Glaze the top with apricot jam and place the marzipan circle on top. Divide the remaining marzipan in half. Divide one half into 11 small balls and set aside. Divide the second half in half again and roll each half into strips, long enough to go around the top of the cake. Twist these strips together and press around the

outer edge of the cake. Place a circle of wax paper over the circle of marzipan. Brush the ring and marzipan balls with beaten egg. Place the cake under a hot broiler, for 1–2 minutes, to brown the marzipan. Remove the paper carefully, then grill the marzipan balls until brown.

Make the glacé icing by sifting the confectioners' sugar into a bowl and adding the water and orange flower water. Mix until smooth, then pour immediately into the center of the cake. leave to set for 2–3 hours before placing the marzipan balls around the edge and adding any decorations. Tie a ribbon around the outside of the cake, if wished.

SIMNEL CAKE

181

DUNDEE CAKE

*Dundee cake originated in the Scottish city of Dundee, also famous for
its marmalade. Candied orange peel and orange zest are used in the
making of this popular fruit cake, which is easily recognized by the
circles of blanched almonds on the surface. In England, Dundee cake is
traditionally made in a round, deep cake pan. This recipe, however,
has been adapted for a loaf pan.*

Makes one loaf cake

INGREDIENTS
½ lb butter
grated zest of 1 lemon
grated zest of 1 orange
1 cup superfine sugar
1 cup raisins
1 cup currants
1 cup golden raisins
⅔ cup candied mixed peel
2½ cups unbleached flour
1½ teaspoon baking powder
pinch of salt
½ cup ground almonds, slightly
    packed
4 eggs
2 tablespoons brandy or dark rum
46 blanched almond halves
2 tablespoons milk

Preheat the oven to 325°. Lightly grease a 9-× 5-× 3-inch loaf pan and line with
wax paper.

Cream the butter and gradually work in the citrus zest. Add the sugar and
cream together until pale, light and fluffy. Place the raisins, currants, golden
raisins and mixed peel in a bowl. Sift the flour with the baking powder and salt
twice, then add ½ cup to the dried fruits. Mix well to ensure they are completely
covered in flour.

Add the ground almonds to the butter and sugar and mix well, then gradually add the eggs, one at a time, beating well after each addition. Gradually
fold in half the remaining flour, then add the fruit little by little. Fold in the
remaining flour, then add the brandy. Spoon the mixture into the loaf pan and
smooth the surface. Dip the blanched almonds into the milk, then arrange them
on the top of the cake.

Bake on the center shelf for 2–2¼ hours. The cake is cooked when a small
skewer inserted into the center comes out clean. Cool in the pan for 10 minutes,
then turn out onto a wire rack and leave until cold.

CARAWAY SEED CAKE

*Most Victorian English cookery books include a recipe for seed cake.
This plain buttery cake, with a hint of caraway, is best eaten a day after baking.*

Makes one loaf cake

INGREDIENTS
½ lb butter
1 cup superfine sugar
2 cups unbleached flour
½ teaspoon baking powder
1 egg
3 eggs, separated
1 teaspoon vanilla extract
1 tablespoon brandy
1 tablespoon caraway seeds

Preheat the oven to 350°. Lightly grease a 9-× 5-× 3-inch loaf pan.

Beat the butter with half the sugar until pale, light and fluffy. Sift together the
flour and baking powder. Gradually add 1 whole egg and 3 egg yolks to the
creamed butter and sugar, beating well between each addition. If the mixture
starts to separate, add a little flour. Stir in the vanilla extract and the brandy,
then gradually fold in the sifted flour. Add the caraway seeds and mix lightly.

Beat the egg whites until they form stiff peaks. Gradually add the remaining
sugar and beat for another 30 seconds or until glossy. Gently fold the beaten egg
whites into the cake mixture.

Pour the mixture into the prepared loaf pan and bake on the center shelf for 1
hour. The cake is cooked when a small skewer inserted into the center comes
out clean. Cool in the pan for 10 minutes, then turn out onto a wire rack and
leave until cold.

CROQUEMBOUCHE

CROQUEMBOUCHE

*This tower of tiny choux pastry buns is the traditional wedding cake in France.
The buns are built up around a metal cone which is removed when they are set.*

Serves 18–20

Preheat the oven to 375°.

Roll out the dough to line a 7-inch fluted French flan case. Prick the dough and bake for 20 minutes, until golden brown. Cool on a wire rack. Increase the oven temperature to 425°. Fill a pastry bag fitted with a small plain tube with the choux pastry mixture. Pipe small buns onto greased cookie sheets, leaving space for spreading. You should have about 60–70 buns. Bake for 15 minutes, then reduce the temperature to 375° for 10–12 minutes more, until the buns are puffy and golden brown. Make a small hole in the bottom of each bun and cool on a wire rack. Whip half the cream and use to fill the buns.

Place the sugar and water in a heavy-bottomed saucepan. Stir over a low heat until the sugar dissolves. Add the cream of tartar and boil steadily, without stirring, until it registers 300° or brittle strands will hang from a fork. Place the pan in hot water to stop further browning.

Butter the cone and place it on wax paper. Spear each bun onto a fine skewer and dip in the caramel. Build the buns up around the cone until it is completely covered. Pour over remaining caramel and leave to set, whip half the remaining cream and pile in the center of the pastry bottom with fresh fruit of your choice. Carefully remove the cone from the buns and place on top of the pastry bottom.

Spoon the remaining cream into a pastry bag fitted with a star tip. Pipe rosettes at random between the buns and decorate.

INGREDIENTS

*1 quantity rich pie crust dough
    pastry (see page 248)*

*2 quantities choux pastry (see page
    249)*

1 lb sugar cubes

14 tablespoons water

½ teaspoon cream of tartar

2½ cups heavy cream

1 lb fresh fruit

*small fruits or edible flowers tossed
    in egg white and superfine
    sugar, or commercial sugared
    flowers, to decorate*

VIENNESE FINGERS

These chocolate-coated biscuits are a teatime treat.

Makes about 18

INGREDIENTS

10 tablespoons butter

2 tablespoons confectioners' sugar

1 cup unbleached flour

⅛ teaspoon or pinch baking powder

few drops of vanilla extract

2 oz semi-sweet chocolate

Preheat the oven to 375°.

Butter two cookie sheets. Put the butter into a bowl and beat until pale and soft, then beat in the confectioners' sugar. Sift in the flour and baking powder. Beat well, adding a few drops of vanilla extract.

Spoon into a pastry bag fitted with a medium star and pipe finger shapes about 3-inches long onto the cookie sheets, allowing room between each for the mixture to spread. Bake for 15–20 minutes, until crisp and pale gold. Cool on a wire rack for 30 minutes.

When the fingers are cold, place the chocolate in the top of a double boiler over simmering water and stir until the chocolate melts. Remove from the heat and dip both ends of the fingers into the melted chocolate. Leave on a wire rack for 30 minutes to set.

CHOCOLATE, ORANGE AND HAZELNUT VACHERIN

This is the perfect dessert for a special occasion, because it looks and tastes wonderful, and can be prepared in advance. The meringues may be made and stored in an airtight container for 2 weeks.

Serves 8–10

INGREDIENTS

6 egg whites

scant 1⅔ cups superfine sugar

3 oz semi-sweet chocolate

3 tablespoons water

¼ teaspoon instant coffee

3¾ cups heavy cream

finely grated zest of 1 orange

1 tablespoon Grand Marnier

1 tablespoon freshly squeezed orange juice

Hazelnut praline

3 oz hazelnuts (½ cup)

3 tablespoons superfine sugar

1 tablespoon water

Decoration

1 teaspoon confectioners' sugar, sifted

8 hazelnuts

thinly pared orange zest or chocolate curls (optional)

Preheat the oven to 275°. Line 4 cookie sheets with brown paper or parchment.

To make the meringues, beat the egg whites until they are stiff but not dry. Beat in the sugar, one tablespoon at a time, beating well between each addition. Spoon the meringue into a large pastry bag fitted with a ½-inch plain tip. Pipe the meringue in a spiral pattern onto a prepared cookie sheet to form a 8½-inch circle. Pipe the remaining meringue onto the other cookie sheets to make 4 circles. Bake for 1½ hours.

Remove from the oven and allow to cool. Peel off the paper very carefully. Increase the oven temperature to 375°. Butter a cookie sheet.

Meanwhile, to make the praline, place the hazelnuts on a cookie sheet and roast for 10 minutes or until they begin to color slightly. Rub them in a dish towel to remove the skins.

Dissolve the sugar in the water over gentle heat, stirring frequently. Bring to the boil and boil gently for 5 minutes or until the syrup is a light golden color. Stir in the hazelnuts. Immediately pour onto the prepared cookie sheet and leave to cool. When the praline is cold, crush in a blender or food processor or with a rolling pin. Set aside.

Melt the chocolate with the water and instant coffee over gentle heat. Set aside to cool.

Whip a quarter of the cream until it just holds its shape. Fill a pastry bag fitted with a large star tip with the cream and chill.

Beat the cream remaining until stiff, then stir one third into the praline, half the remaining cream into the cooled chocolate mixture and the remaining cream into the orange zest, Grand Marnier and orange juice.

Place one layer of meringue on a serving dish and cover with the praline cream. Place the second layer on top and cover with the chocolate cream, then put the third layer on top, cover with the orange cream and finally top with the remaining layer.

Sift the confectioners' sugar over the top and pipe 8 rosettes of the cream around the edge. Lightly press a hazelnut into each rosette. Sprinkle with orange zest or chocolate curls, if desired.

CHOCOLATE CAKE

This luscious cake consists of layers of light "biscuit de savoie" spread with chocolate ganache and "wrapped" in a chocolate frill.

Makes one 9-inch cake

INGREDIENTS
1 tablespoon cocoa
1 cup unbleached flour
1¾ cups confectioners' sugar, sifted, plus ½ teaspoon
6 eggs separated
11 oz semi-sweet chocolate
¼ cup brandy
¼ teaspoon salt
1 teaspoon superfine sugar mixed with 1 teaspoon unbleached flour
Chocolate ganache
8 oz semi-sweet chocolate
1½ cups heavy cream
¼ teaspoon vanilla extract

Preheat the oven to 350°. Lightly butter three 9-inch cake pans and line with wax paper. Dust with the superfine sugar mixed with the confectioners'.

Sift the cocoa and flour together three times. Beat 1½ cups of the confectioners' sugar with the egg yolks until pale and thick enough to make a ribbon trail. Grate 3 oz of the chocolate, then gradually fold it in with 2 tablespoons of the brandy and sifted flour.

Beat the egg whites and salt until stiff, then beat in the remaining confectioners' sugar. Carefully fold the egg whites into the chocolate egg yolk mixture a little at a time.

Spoon the batter into the pans and bake for 10–15 minutes. The cake is cooked when a small skewer inserted into the center comes out clean. Cool in the pans for 5 minutes, then turn out onto a wire rack and cool, upside down.

When the cakes are cold, brush with the remaining brandy.

To make the ganache, melt the chocolate, remove from the heat and stir in the cream and vanilla extract. Beat until the mixture cools and thickens. Sandwich the layers together with the ganache, then spread over the top and sides.

Cut out a strip of non-stick wax paper long enough to wrap around the cake, and 1½ inches higher than the depth. Melt the remaining chocolate and spread three-quarters of it over the paper strip with a spatula, to the edge of one long side, making a straight edge for the base. Spread roughly to the corresponding edge. Spread remaining melted chocolate onto the wax paper ⅛-inch thick.

When the chocolate strip begins to cool, but before it has hardened, carefully wrap it around the cake with the uneven edge at the top. Press gently into place. Carefully pinch the chocolate above the cake into slight "pleats" using the paper. Leave chocolate to harden, then peel away the paper. Scrape remaining chocolate into curls. Arrange on top and sprinkle with confectioners' sugar.

MADEIRA CAKE

This classic cake is recognized by the large slice of candied citron peel on the top. It is best eaten a day after baking, although it keeps well in an airtight container.

Makes one loaf cake

INGREDIENTS
1 cup potato flour
1 cup unbleached flour
½ teaspoon baking powder
pinch of salt
12 tablespoons butter
¾ cup superfine sugar
3 large eggs
finely grated zest and juice of ½ lemon
1 slice candied citron peel

Preheat the oven to 325°. Lightly grease and flour an 8½-× 4½-× 2½-inch loaf pan.

Sift the flours, baking powder and salt together 2 or 3 times. Beat the butter until soft, then cream it with the sugar until pale, light and fluffy. Beat in the eggs, one at a time, beating well after each addition. If the mixture separates, add a spoonful of the sifted flour. Gradually fold in the remaining flour alternately with the lemon zest and juice.

Spoon into the loaf pan. Smooth the top, make a slight dip in the center and place the citron peel in the indentation. Bake on the center shelf for 1–1¼ hours. The cake is cooked when a small skewer inserted into the center comes out clean. Cool in the pan for 10 minutes, then turn out onto a wire rack to cool.

CLEMENTINE CAKE

This rich but light cake makes a sumptuous dessert. Use tangerines if clementines are out of season.

Makes one 9-inch cake

Preheat the oven to 225°. Lightly grease three 9-inch cake pans. Dust with the extra teaspoon of flour and superfine sugar.

Sift all but 2 tablespoons of the confectioners' sugar into a bowl and add the egg yolks. Beat until pale and thick enough to make a ribbon trail. Add the orange zest and gradually stir in 1 tablespoon of Grand Marnier and the orange juice. Fold in the flour.

Beat the egg whites with the salt until stiff, but not dry, then beat in the reserved confectioners' sugar. Carefully fold the egg whites into the egg yolk mixture. Pour into the prepared pans and bake for 15 minutes. The cake is cooked when a small skewer inserted into the center comes out clean. Cool in the pans for 5 minutes, then turn out onto a wire rack and cool, upside down.

Meanwhile, to make the sugar syrup, place the sugar and water in a saucepan and stir over low heat until the sugar dissolves. Boil for 4–5 minutes or until the temperature reaches 225° on a candy thermometer. Cool the syrup, then stir in the remaining Grand Marnier. Pour over the clementines.

When the cakes are cold, brush the layers with syrup. Arrange the clementines on two layers only, reserving ⅔ cup for decoration. Whip the cream, orange flower water and remaining superfine sugar together. Spread some of the cream over the fruit and assemble the cake with the plain layer on the top. Spread some of the cream around the sides and press on the almonds. Place the remaining cream in a pastry bag fitted with a rose tip. Arrange the clementines on cake and pipe cream rosettes.

INGREDIENTS
1 cup unbleached flour, sifted, plus
* 1 teaspoon*
2 tablespoons superfine sugar
1¾ cups confectioners' sugar
6 eggs, separated
finely grated zest of ½ orange
1 tablespoon Grand Marnier
1 tablespoon orange juice
¼ teaspoon salt
¾ cup sugar
⅓ cup water
3 tablespoons Grand Marnier
2 lb clementines, peeled and
* segmented*
3 cups heavy cream
1 teaspoon orange flower water
6 oz slivered almonds, toasted
* (1 cup)*

CELEBRATION CAKE

For that special celebration, this cake makes a really spectacular centerpiece. The use of fresh flowers adds a delightful touch.

Makes one 10-inch cake

INGREDIENTS
Sponge
¾ lb unsalted butter
1⅔ cups superfine sugar
6 eggs
2½ cups unbleached flour
Filling
½ cup sugar
3 tablespoons water
5–6 tablespoons Grand Marnier
½ lb unsalted butter
4 cups confectioners' sugar, sifted
Almond paste
3 cups ground almonds
¾ cup superfine sugar
1½ cups confectioners' sugar, sifted
almond extract
6 egg yolks
sieved apricot jam
Icing and decoration
8 egg whites
4 lb confectioners' sugar, sifted
1½ tablespoons corn syrup
few drops lemon juice
yellow food coloring
fresh freesias for decoration

Preheat the oven to 350°. Lightly grease a 10-inch springform cake pan.

For the sponge, cream the butter and sugar together until pale, light and fluffy, then beat in the eggs, one at a time, beating well after each addition. Carefully fold in the flour. Spoon the mixture into the pan and smooth the top. Bake for about 1½ hours or until well risen, firm to the touch, and slightly shrunk away from the sides of the pan. Cool in the pan for 10 minutes, then turn out onto a wire rack to cool. Slice into 3 horizontal layers.

To make the filling, put the sugar and water into a small saucepan and heat gently until the sugar dissolves. Bring to the boil and boil for 2 minutes. Remove from the heat and stir in 2–3 tablespoons of the Grand Marnier. Allow the syrup to cool.

Beat the butter until very soft, then gradually beat in the confectioners' sugar, beating well after each addition. Beat in the remaining Grand Marnier, to taste.

Place the bottom layer on a 12-inch round cake board. Brush with some of the syrup, then spread with the filling. Place the center layer of cake on top, brush with more syrup and spread with filling. Brush the cut side of the remaining layer with syrup, then place on top. Press the layers firmly but gently together, making sure that the cake is level.

To make the almond paste, mix the almonds and sugars together in a large mixing bowl. Add a few drops of almond extract and mix together with the egg yolks to make a stiff paste. Knead lightly until smooth. Cut off one-third of the almond paste and set it aside.

Roll out the remaining almond paste to a long strip, long enough and wide enough to fit around the cake. Brush the sides of the cake with apricot jam, then fit the strip of almond paste neatly around the sides, pressing it firmly onto the cake. Roll out the remaining piece of almond paste to a circle large enough to fit the top of the cake. Brush the top of the cake with apricot jam and cover with the almond paste circle, rolling it gently into place with a rolling pin. Leave for 24 hours before icing.

For the icing, lightly beat 6 of the egg whites. Gradually beat in 3 lb of the confectioners' sugar to make a smooth royal icing. Beat in the corn syrup.

Spread a good layer of the icing over the top of the cake with a spatula, working it backward and forward to remove as many air bubbles as possible. Pull a ruler, preferably a metal one, across the top of the cake to smooth the icing. Remove the excess icing from the top edge of the cake. Place the cake on a turntable, or an up-turned cake tin, and spread the sides with icing, spreading it as evenly as possible. Pull a cake scraper around the side to smooth the icing. Leave overnight, in a cool place, to dry. Put the remaining icing into a clean mixing bowl and cover the surface tightly with plastic wrap. Cover the bowl with plastic wrap and refrigerate until the next day. Beat the icing well before using again. Store the icing in this way after each application.

Next day, scrape away the rough icing from the top edge of the cake and from the board with a small sharp knife. Brush loose icing off the cake with a clean, dry, pastry brush. Give the cake three more coats of icing, allowing each coat to dry overnight before applying the next.

For the flowers, beat the remaining egg whites and confectioners' sugar together to make a smooth royal icing, then beat in a few drops of lemon juice.

Put about 1 tablespoon of the icing into a small bowl and color with a few drops of yellow coloring. Place in a paper pastry bag. Put a little of the white icing into another paper pastry bag, flatten the point between your finger and thumb, then cut into a "V" shape. Cut a small hole in the yellow icing bag.

Secure a small square of non-stick baking paper onto an icing nail with a little icing. Pipe five, slightly overlapping, white petals onto the paper to form a flower, then make a center with the yellow icing. Remove the paper from the flower nail and place it on a flat tray. Make about 80 flowers in the same way. Leave the flowers in a cool, dry place for at least 24 hours to harden. Make the flowers when you apply the first coat of icing to the cake.

To decorate, mark a double row of evenly-spaced scallops around the side of the cake, marking the second row about 1½-inches below the first. Pipe a small "blob" of icing on each flower, and press them gently onto the side of the cake, following the first row of scallops.

Place a little icing in a paper pastry bag fitted with a small 8 point star tip, then pipe a row of stars around the side of the cake, following the second row of scallops. Pipe two more rows of stars under the first row, continuing them onto the board. Pipe three rows of stars around the top edge of the cake. Place 8 flowers on top of the cake.

Finally, just before presenting the cake, place a small arrangement of fresh freesias on top of the cake.

SHORTBREAD

Shortbread molds transform this simple recipe into a decorative treat. Press the dough into the mold and chill for 1 hour. Turn out onto the cookie sheet and bake.

Makes 8

INGREDIENTS
1 cup unbleached flour
pinch of salt
2 tablespoons semolina
8 tablespoons butter
¼ cup superfine sugar, plus extra for sprinkling

Sift together the flour, salt and semolina. Cream the butter with the sugar until pale, light and fluffy. Gradually add the flour mixture and mix lightly until the ingredients form into a smooth dough.

Roll out the dough on a lightly floured board to a 7-inch circle, then place on a cookie sheet. Pinch the edge into a pattern and prick the surface with a fork to prevent the dough from rising during cooking. Chill for 1 hour.

Preheat the oven to 325°. Bake for about 45 minutes. While the shortbread is still hot, cut it into 8 even-sized wedges, then sprinkle with superfine sugar and cool on the cookie sheet.

CHOCOLATE AND WALNUT COOKIES

These cookies usually disappear the moment they are placed on the cooling rack, probably because they taste wonderful when slightly warm.

Makes about 24

INGREDIENTS
1½ cups unbleached flour
¼ teaspoon baking powder
pinch of salt
8 tablespoons butter
1 cup light brown sugar
1 egg
few drops of vanilla extract
4 oz semi-sweet chocolate, coarsely chopped
½ cup coarsely chopped walnuts

Preheat the oven at 350°. Lightly butter 2 cookie sheets.

Sift together the flour, baking powder and salt. Cream the butter and sugar together until pale. Beat the egg and vanilla extract together, then gradually beat into the butter and sugar. Fold in the flour, a little at a time, then add the chocolate and the walnuts.

Place heaped tablespoons of the mixture onto the prepared cookie sheets, well spaced to allow room for the cookies to spread during cooking. Press very gently to flatten slightly. Bake for 15–20 minutes or until golden brown around the outside and firm to the touch. Leave to cool for 2 minutes, then transfer to a wire rack.

TREACLE TART

This is a favorite English nursery dessert, which, in spite of the name, is made with corn syrup and not treacle.

Serves 6–8

INGREDIENTS
1 quantity rich pie crust dough (see page 248)
5 tablespoons corn syrup
3 cups white or whole wheat bread crumbs
finely grated zest and juice of ½ lemon

Roll out the pastry and use it to line an 8-inch pie plate. Reroll the trimmings and cut into four ½-inch wide strips, a little longer than the width of the plate. Chill. Heat the syrup over gentle heat and stir in the bread crumbs, then stir in the lemon zest and juice. Remove the pan from the heat and cool for 10 minutes.

Preheat the oven to 375°.

Spread the filling over the dough bottom. Twist the dough strips, one by one, and place across the top, making 8 sections. Press the ends of the dough strips into the edges. Bake on the center shelf for 30 minutes. Serve warm or cold.

IRISH APPLE CAKE

*This apple cake is more like a pudding than a cake. It can be served
warm with a good dollop of whipped cream, or served cold.*

Makes one 9-inch cake

Preheat the oven to 375°. Lightly grease and flour a 9-inch springform pan.

Cream the butter with the sugar and vanilla extract until pale, light and fluffy.
Add the eggs, one at a time, beating well after each addition. Stir in the lemon
zest.

Sift the unbleached flour, potato flour and baking powder together twice.
Gradually fold into the cake mixture, then stir in the milk.

Spoon the mixture into the cake pan. Arrange the apple quarters, rounded
sides up, on top.

Bake the cake on the middle shelf of the oven for 1 hour. The cake is cooked
when a small skewer inserted into the center comes out clean. Cool in the pan
for 10 minutes, then remove the ring.

Heat the apricot jam with the water, then rub it through a sieve. Brush the top
of the cake with the glaze while it is still hot.

If it is to be served cold, leave the cake until it has cooled completely, then
sprinkle the top with confectioners' sugar.

INGREDIENTS
8 tablespoons butter
½ cup sugar
1 tablespoon vanilla extract
3 eggs, lightly beaten
finely grated zest of 1 lemon
1 cup unbleached flour
⅔ cup potato flour
1 teaspoon baking powder
2 tablespoons milk
*3 large apples, peeled, cored and
    quartered*
2 tablespoons apricot jam
1 teaspoon water
*1 teaspoon confectioners' sugar,
    sifted*

LIQUEUR-FLAVOURED CREAM HORNS

*Cointreau, Grand Marnier, Kahlua and Tia Maria are among the
endless variety of liqueurs suitable for this filling. Serve these delicate
pastries with coffee or as part of an English tea party.*

Makes 8

Preheat the oven to 425°.

Roll out the dough on a lightly floured working surface to a strip measuring
26 × 4 inches. Cut the dough lengthwise with a sharp knife into eight ½-inch
ribbons.

Butter 8 cream horn molds. Moisten one edge of each dough strip and wind
each round a horn mold starting at the tip, overlapping ⅛-inch and finishing
neatly on the underside. The pastry should not overlap the metal rim. Brush
with beaten egg.

Dampen a cookie sheet and arrange the cream horns on it, seam-side down.
Bake for 10 minutes, until golden brown.

Cool for a few minutes, then carefully twist each mold, holding the dough
lightly in the other hand, to ease it out of the mold. Leave the horns for about 30
minutes to cool completely.

When cold, fill the tip of each horn with a little jam. Whip the cream with the
liqueur until stiff and fill the horns down to the jam. Sift the confectioners' sugar
on each horn to decorate.

INGREDIENTS
*¼ quantity puff pastry dough (see
    page 248) or 8 oz package frozen
    puff pastry*
beaten egg, to glaze
strawberry jam
1¼ cups heavy cream
*1 tablespoon fruit-flavoured
    liqueur*
confectioners' sugar, to decorate

FLORENTINES

Florentines are a luscious mixture of nuts and dried fruits, coated on one side with semi-sweet chocolate.

Makes 16

INGREDIENTS

4 tablespoons butter

6 tablespoons superfine sugar

½ cup blanched and coarsely chopped almonds

¼ cup blanched and coarsely chopped hazelnuts

1½ tablespoons unbleached flour

⅓ cup mixed candied peel

6 candied cherries, coarsely chopped

3 tablespoons light cream

6 oz semi-sweet chocolate

Preheat the oven to 350°. Lightly grease 2 cookie sheets.

Melt the butter over a gentle heat and add all the remaining ingredients except the chocolate. Stir over a gentle heat for 2 minutes or until the sugar has dissolved and the mixture is well blended.

Place 1 tablespoon of the mixture at a time on the cookie sheets, leaving room between each one because the mixture spreads during cooking. With damp fingers flatten the mixture slightly. Bake 10 minutes, or until golden brown. The mixture will spread during baking, so push the edges into a tidy circle with a spatula. Cool on the cookie sheets for 2 minutes, then on a wire rack.

Melt the chocolate in the top of a double boiler over simmering water. When the florentines are cool, turn them over and coat the undersides with melted chocolate. As the chocolate begins to set, make a wavy pattern across the bottom of each one with a fork. Store in a cool, dry place.

CHOCOLATE ECLAIRS

*Chocolate éclairs are always a welcome treat. Serve these as a dessert
after a dinner party or for a special afternoon tea.*

Makes 12

Preheat the oven to 425°. Line a cookie sheet with aluminum foil.

Spoon the choux pastry into a large pastry bag fitted with a large plain tip. Pipe into twelve 5-inch strips on the cookie sheet. Leave space for the mixture to puff up.

Bake for 35–40 minutes. Reduce the temperature to 375° and bake for a further 20–25 minutes. Remove from the oven and pierce each éclair to allow the steam to escape. Return to the oven for 5 minutes to dry, then cool on a rack.

Whip the cream with the sugar and vanilla until stiff. Spoon into a pastry bag fitted with a small plain tip and fill the éclairs.

Melt the chocolate with the water in the top of a double boiler over simmering water. Stir in the butter. Dip the tops of the éclairs in chocolate and leave on a wire rack until set.

INGREDIENTS

1 quantity choux pastry (see page 249)

2 cups heavy cream

1 tablespoon superfine sugar

few drops of vanilla extract

4 oz semi-sweet chocolate

3 tablespoons water

2 tablespoons butter

BLACK FOREST CAKE

This chocolate and cherry cake is a popular dessert. It is too tempting to resist, with generously piped cream and cherries and chocolate curls.

Serves 8–10

INGREDIENTS

3 large eggs
¾ cup superfine sugar
1¼ cups unbleached flour
¼ cup cocoa
1 teaspoon baking powder
5 tablespoons hot water
2½ cups heavy cream
4–5 tablespoons kirsch
4 oz semi-sweet chocolate curls
¾ lb canned black cherries, pitted
    and well drained

Preheat the oven to 375°. Lightly butter and flour three 8-inch cake pans.

Place the eggs and sugar in the top of a double boiler over simmering water. Beat until the mixture is pale and thick and just holds the trail of the beaters. Remove from the heat and beat for 2 minutes more. Sift the flour, cocoa and baking powder onto a plate. Carefully fold it into the egg mixture, cutting through with a metal spoon until evenly mixed. Gently stir in the hot water.

Spoon the mixture into the cake pans. Bake for 10–12 minutes or until firm to the touch. Turn out, remove paper and cool on a wire rack.

Whip the cream until stiff and place one-third into a bag fitted with a star tip. Place the bottom layer of the cake on a cake plate and sprinkle it with a little kirsch and pipe a band of cream around the edge. Reserve 8–10 cherries for decoration and place the remainder inside the cream.

Place another cake on top of the cherries and sprinkle with kirsch. Spread the cake with cream. Sprinkle the underside of the top cake with the remaining kirsch and invert onto the cream layer.

Cover the top and sides of the cake with cream. Sprinkle with the chocolate curls. Pipe cream around the top edge of the cake and decorate. Chill.

MERINGUES

Light as air, meringues are popular English teatime treats. They can be filled with a variety of creams or used as a base for topping. Stored in an airtight container, they will keep for several weeks.

Makes 10

INGREDIENTS

4 egg whites
1 cup superfine sugar
few drops vanilla extract
Chocolate cream filling
3 oz semi-sweet chocolate
3 tablespoons water
¼ teaspoon instant coffee
1¼ cups heavy cream, lightly
    whipped
Liqueur filling
1¼ cups heavy cream, lightly
    whipped
1 tablespoon superfine sugar
1–1½ tablespoons liqueur (such as
    Grand Marnier, curaçao or
    kirsch)
Fruit filling
1¼ cups heavy cream, lightly
    whipped
1 tablespoon superfine sugar
2 oz strawberries or raspberries,
    puréed (¼ cup)

Preheat the oven to 275°. Line two cookie sheets with brown paper or parchment.

Beat the egg whites until stiff but not dry. Beat in half the sugar, then fold in the remainder with the vanilla extract. Place 20 tablespoonsful of the meringue onto the lined cookie sheets. This amount of mixture will make 2¾-inch wide meringues. Bake for 1½ hours.

Leave the meringues to cool in the oven.

For the chocolate cream filling, melt the chocolate, water and coffee together. Leave until cool, then stir into the cream. Beat the ingredients for the liqueur filling together. Repeat for the fruit filling.

When the meringues are cold, sandwich two halves together with one of the cream fillings.

ECCLES CAKES

*A popular teatime treat in England, Eccles cake are best served while
still warm.*

Makes about 20

Preheat the oven to 425°.

Roll out the dough on a lightly floured board to a rectangle ⅛-inch thick.
Using a 3½-inch round cutter, cut into 20 circles.

Mix the melted butter, brown sugar, currants, mixed peel, spices and lemon
zest together.

Place 1 teaspoon of the mixture in the center of each dough circle. Brush the
edges with egg white. Bring the edge up over the filling and pinch together to
seal. Turn the dough over and roll lightly with a rolling pin, to flatten slightly.
Cut 3 slits in the top, brush with egg white and sprinkle with superfine sugar.

Place the Eccles cakes on dampened cookie sheets and bake for 15 minutes or
until puffed up and golden brown. Cool on a wire rack. Serve warm.

INGREDIENTS

*¾ quantity puff pastry dough (see
    page 248)*
3 tablespoons butter, melted
3 tablespoons brown sugar
⅓ cup currants
3 tablespoons mixed candied peel
*pinch each ground cinnamon,
    cloves and nutmeg*
finely grated zest of 1 lemon
1 egg white, beaten
1 tablespoon superfine sugar

ICED GINGERBREAD

*This is a dark, spicy old-fashioned cake, which may be served with or
without icing.*

Makes 36 squares

Preheat the oven to 325°. Lightly grease a 13-×-9-× 2-inch cake pan.

Sift the flour, ginger, cinnamon and cloves together, then stir in the lemon
zest. Melt the butter and stir in the sugar, molasses and syrup. Remove from the
heat and and leave to cool.

Make a well in the center of the flour, then stir in the eggs, milk and syrup
mixture. Mix until well blended and lump-free. Stir the baking soda into the hot
water and add it to the mixture, with the ginger and almonds.

Pour the mixture into the prepared pan. Bake on the center shelf for 1–1¼
hours. Cool the gingerbread in the pan and leave for a day before cutting or
icing.

To make the icing, sift the confectioners' sugar into a bowl and beat in the egg
white and lemon juice until smooth.

Place the gingerbread on a wire rack with a sheet of wax paper underneath.
Spread the icing evenly over the top of the cake and arrange the slivers of ginger
in rows so when the cake is cut, a piece of ginger will be in the center of each
square. Leave to dry and cut into 36 squares.

INGREDIENTS

3 cups unbleached flour
1 teaspoon ground ginger
1 teaspoon ground cinnamon
½ teaspoon ground cloves
finely grated zest of 1 lemon
12 tablespoons butter
½ cup dark brown sugar, packed
1 cup molasses
½ cup corn syrup
2 eggs, lightly beaten
⅔ cup milk
1 teaspoon baking soda
1 tablespoon hot water
*⅓ cup finely chopped ginger,
    packed*
*⅓ cup blanched and finely chopped
    almonds*
*36 slivers of candied ginger, to
    decorate*
Icing
3 cups confectioners' sugar
1 egg white, lightly beaten
*2 tablespoons freshly squeezed
    lemon juice, strained*

BREADS AND YEAST DOUGHS

In the bustling bakery, customers can choose from over 170 different types of bread, including the ever-popular French baguette and brioche, German black bread, as well as Harrods own English varieties. It's fun to try your hand at such treats as Muffins and Chelsea Buns, and the Easter specialty Hot Cross Buns.

SCONES

Scones may be made with or without golden raisins and should be served slightly warm, preferably with whipped cream and strawberry jam.

Makes 10

INGREDIENTS

2 cups unbleached flour
1½ teaspoons baking powder
pinch of salt
3 tablespoons butter at room temperature
2 tablespoons superfine sugar
½ cup golden raisins
1 egg, lightly beaten
½ cup milk, plus a little extra for glazing

Preheat the oven to 425°. Lightly butter a cookie sheet.

Sift the flour, baking powder and salt together.

Cut in the butter until the mixture resembles bread crumbs, then stir in the sugar and golden raisins. Add the egg and 4 tablespoons of the milk. Lightly mix to a soft dough. Roll out on a lightly floured surface to ¾-inch thick. Using a 2¼-inch plain or fluted biscuit cutter, cut out 10 circles.

Place the scones on the cookie sheet and brush the tops with milk. Bake for 10–12 minutes or until golden. Cool on a wire rack.

Whole wheat cheese scones

Use half unbleached and half whole wheat flour, sifted with a pinch each of cayenne pepper and dry mustard. Stir 1¼ cups of grated Cheddar cheese instead of the golden raisins. Sprinkle with a little cheese, before baking as above.

SCOTTISH OATCAKES

In Scotland, oatcakes are served with cheese and a glass of port to end a meal, with marmalade for breakfast or jam for afternoon tea.

Makes about 36

INGREDIENTS

4 cups rolled oats
¾ cup unbleached flour
1½ teaspoons baking powder
pinch of salt
8 tablespoons butter
2–3 tablespoons milk

Process the rolled oats in a food processor until fine. Mix together the rolled oats, flour, baking powder and salt, then cut in the butter until the mixture resembles bread crumbs. Add sufficient milk to make a stiff dough. Cover the bowl with plastic wrap and rest for 30 minutes. Preheat the oven to 350°.

Roll out the dough on a floured surface ⅛-inch thick. Cut into circles or squares. Place the oatcakes on a cookie sheet and bake in the center of the oven for 20 minutes or until golden brown. Cool on a wire rack.

COTTAGE LOAF

*A cottage loaf is easily recognizable by its shape – a squat round bottom with a
smaller ball on top. The cornstarch glaze gives the loaf a lovely golden crust.*

Makes two 1¼ lb loaves

Dissolve the sugar in the water, then stir in the yeast. Leave to stand in a warm
place for 10–15 minutes, until frothy. Lightly butter and flour two cookie sheets.

Sift the flour with the salt and cut in the butter. Make a well in the center and
pour in the yeast mixture and milk. Mix to a smooth dough. Turn out onto a
lightly floured surface and knead for 10 minutes. Return to the bowl, cover it
with plastic wrap and leave in a warm place for 45–60 minutes or until doubled.

Knead the dough for 5 minutes, then divide it into 2 equal-sized pieces. Take
one third from each piece and roll the larger pieces into round balls. Roll the two
smaller pieces into balls and place one small ball on top of each large ball. Flour
the handle of a wooden spoon and push it through the two balls to secure them
together. Place the loaves on the cookie sheets, cover with plastic wrap and
leave to rise in a warm place for 15 minutes.

Preheat the oven to 450°.

To make the glaze, mix the cornstarch with the cold water, then add the boiling
water. Stir until slightly cooled. Brush the loaves with the glaze and bake for 10
minutes. Reduce the temperature to 400° and bake for a further 20–25 minutes.
The loaf should sound hollow when tapped on the bottom. Cool on a rack.

INGREDIENTS

1 teaspoon sugar
1 cup lukewarm water
two ¼ oz packages active dry yeast
4½ cups unbleached flour
1½ teaspoons salt
1 cup lukewarm milk
2 tablespoons butter
Glaze
¾ teaspoon cornstarch
¾ teaspoon cold water
⅓ cup boiling water

197

HEDGEHOG ROLLS

*Hedgehog rolls are very popular with children. A pair of small scissors is all that is
necessary to make the hedgehog "spines," with currants forming the eyes and nose.*

Makes 16

INGREDIENTS

1 teaspoon sugar

1 cup lukewarm water

1 cup lukewarm milk

two ¼ oz packages active dry yeast

5 cups unbleached flour

1½ teaspoons salt

2 tablespoons butter

48 currants

1 egg, lightly beaten, to glaze

HEDGEHOG ROLLS

Dissolve the sugar in the water and milk, then stir in the yeast. Leave to stand in
a warm place for 10–15 minutes, until frothy.

Sift the flour with the salt and cut in the butter. Make a well in the center,
pour in the yeast mixture and mix to a smooth dough. Turn the dough out onto
a lightly floured surface and knead for 10 minutes. Return the dough to the
bowl, cover with plastic wrap and leave to rise in a warm place for 45–60
minutes, or until doubled in size. Knead the dough for 5 minutes.

Lightly butter and flour two cookie sheets.

Divide the dough into 16 even-sized pieces. Shape each one into an oval.
Press one end slightly flat, then press in the sides to make the hedgehog's face.
Place the piece of dough on a sheet, with the face away from you. Cut into the
dough with a small pair of scissors, starting behind the head, and snip small
points to make hedgehog "spines" all over the body. Place two currants on the
face for eyes, and one for the nose. Glaze with the beaten egg. Cover and leave
in a warm place for 15 minutes. Preheat the oven to 450°.

Bake for 15–18 minutes or until shiny golden brown and the bottom sounds
hollow when tapped. Cool on a wire rack.

CHEESE AND HERB BREAD

*A savory cheese bread flavored with chives and parsley
for unusual picnic fare.*

Makes 1 loaf

Dissolve the sugar in the water, then stir in the yeast. Leave to stand in a warm place for 10–15 minutes, until frothy.

Butter an 8½- × 4½- × 2¾-inch loaf pan. Sift the flour, salt, mustard and pepper into a bowl. Stir in the chives, parsley and three-quarters of the cheese. Add the yeast liquid to the dry ingredients and mix to a soft dough. Turn out onto a floured surface and knead for 10 minutes. Place in a bowl, cover with a plastic wrap and leave to rise in a warm place for about 1 hour, until doubled in size.

Turn the dough onto a floured surface and knead for 5 minutes. Divide the dough into two and shape to fit the pan. Cover with plastic wrap and leave to rise in a warm place for 40–50 minutes, until the dough reaches the top of the pans.

Preheat the oven to 375°.

Sprinkle the top of the loaf with the remaining cheese. Bake for 40–45 minutes, until well risen and golden brown. Turn out and cool on a wire rack.

INGREDIENTS

1 teaspoon sugar
1¼ cups lukewarm water
¼ oz package active dry yeast
3 cups unbleached flour
2 teaspoons salt
1 teaspoon dry mustard
pepper
2 teaspoons snipped fresh chives
2 tablespoons chopped fresh parsley
2 cups finely grated cheddar cheese

BLACK RYE BREAD

*This bread is traditionally made using the sour dough method, which
is time consuming. The quicker version below includes plain yogurt to
give the loaf a pleasantly acidic tang.*

Makes 1 large loaf

Dissolve the sugar in the water and stir in the yeast, then leave in a warm place for 10 minutes, until frothy. Sift the flours, salt and caraway seeds together in a large bowl. Tip the bran remaining in the sieve back into the bowl. Stir in the oil, yeast liquid and yogurt. Mix to a soft dough.

Knead the dough for 10 minutes, then return it to the rinsed-out bowl. Cover with plastic wrap and leave in a warm place for 1–1½ hours or until doubled in size.

Lightly butter a 9¼- × 5¼- × 2¾-inch loaf pan.

Knead the dough for 5 minutes, then shape it to fit the loaf pan. Prick the surface of the loaf with a fork. Cover with plastic wrap and leave in a warm place for about 30 minutes or until the dough reaches the top of the pan.

Preheat the oven to 400°. Bake for 45 minutes. Remove the loaf from the pan and return it to the oven for 5 minutes more. Place on a wire rack and cover with a dish towel until cool.

INGREDIENTS

1 teaspoon sugar
1¼ cups lukewarm water
¼ oz package active dry yeast
1½ cups whole wheat flour
2 cups rye flour
1 teaspoon salt
1 teaspoon caraway seeds
2 teaspoons vegetable oil
⅔ cup plain yogurt

WHOLE WHEAT ROLLS

These soft rolls may be made with all whole wheat flour, or half whole wheat and half unbleached flour. The later combination gives a lighter texture.

Makes 12

INGREDIENTS

1 teaspoon superfine sugar
⅔ cup lukewarm milk
⅔ cup lukewarm water
two ¼ oz packages active dry yeast
1½ cups whole wheat flour, plus 2 teaspoons
1½ cups unbleached flour
1½ teaspoons salt
2 tablespoons butter

Dissolve the sugar in the milk and water, then stir in the yeast. Leave to stand in a warm place for 10–15 minutes until frothy.

Meanwhile, sift the flours together with the salt. Tip the bran from the sieve back into the bowl. Cut in the butter and make a well in the center. Pour in the yeast mixture and mix to a smooth dough. Turn out onto a lightly floured surface and knead for 10 minutes. Return the dough to the bowl, cover with plastic wrap and leave to rise in a warm place for 1 hour or until doubled in size.

Lightly butter and flour two cookie sheets.

Knead the dough for 5 minutes. Divide into 12 even-sized pieces and roll each one into a ball. Flatten the balls of dough with your hand into 3-inch circles. Place the rolls on the cookie sheets, leaving enough space between to allow for expansion during cooking. Cover with plastic wrap and leave to rise in a warm place for 20 minutes.

Preheat the oven to 425°.

Dust the rolls with the remaining whole wheat flour and bake for 15 minutes. Cool on a wire rack.

IRISH SODA BREAD

Brown soda bread and jam is an essential part of the Irish high tea. If you prefer a white loaf, use unbleached white flour only.

Makes 1 large or 2 small loaves

INGREDIENTS

3 cups whole wheat flour
2 cups unbleached flour
1 teaspoon baking soda
1 teaspoon salt
3 cups buttermilk, or plain yogurt

Preheat the oven to 400°. Lightly flour a cookie sheet.

Sift the flours, baking soda and salt together into a large mixing bowl. Tip the bran in the sieve back into the bowl and stir to mix. Pour the buttermilk into the bowl, all at once, and mix quickly and lightly to form a soft dough.

Knead briefly on a lightly floured surface, then shape the dough into 1 large or 2 small balls, flattening each slightly. Cut a deep cross in the dough with a sharp knife. Dust with the flour and place on the cookie sheet. Bake for 35–40 minutes for small loaves, or 45–50 minutes for a large one. When cooked, the loaf will be well browned and sound hollow when tapped on the bottom. Cool on a wire rack and eat the same day, if possible, as it becomes stale quickly.

MUFFINS

*Muffins are traditionally cooked on a griddle, however, a heavy-
bottomed skillet can be used instead. Alternatively, cook on a buttered
cookie sheet in the oven.*

Makes 12

Dissolve the sugar in the milk and water, then stir in the yeast. Leave to stand for 10–15 minutes in a warm place until frothy.

Sift the flour with the salt and make a well in the center. Pour in the yeast mixture and mix to a smooth dough. Turn out onto a lightly floured surface and knead for 10 minutes. Return to the bowl, cover with plastic wrap and leave to rise in a warm place for 1 hour or until doubled in size.

Lightly flour a baking tray.

Turn the dough out onto a lightly floured surface. Roll out to ½-inch thick. Using a 3-inch round cutter, cut out 12 circles. Re-roll the trimmings as necessary. Place the muffins on the baking tray, dust the tops with the 1 teaspoon flour mixed with the semolina. Cover the tray with plastic wrap and leave to rise in a warm place for 40 minutes.

Lightly butter a griddle or heavy-bottomed skillet and warm over moderate heat. Place the muffins on the griddle and cook over low heat for about 7 minutes on each side. Alternatively, bake for 10 minutes in an oven preheated to 425°. Turn the muffins over and bake for a further 4–5 minutes. Cool on a wire rack.

Serve the muffins split in two and buttered. If serving cold, split in half, toast lightly and spread with butter.

INGREDIENTS
1 teaspoon superfine sugar
⅔ cup lukewarm milk
⅔ cup lukewarm water
¼ oz package active dry yeast
3 cups unbleached flour, plus
* 1 teaspoon*
1 teaspoon salt
1 teaspoon fine unbleached
* semolina*
extra flour for dusting the tray

SESAME BREAD STICKS

Serve with soups, appetizers and snacks.

Makes about 20

Stir 1 teaspoon of the sugar into the milk and water, then stir in the yeast. Leave in a warm place for 10 minutes, until frothy.

Sift the flour and salt together and cut in the butter. Stir in the sugar and make a well in the center. Stir in the yeast liquid and mix to a soft dough.

Turn the dough out onto a lightly floured surface and knead for 10 minutes. Return to the rinsed-out bowl, cover with plastic wrap and leave to rise for 1½ hours, or until doubled in size.

Knead for 5 minutes. Break off pieces of the dough, about the size of an egg, and roll out to 12-inch pieces. Place on greased cookie sheets, brush with the egg white and sprinkle liberally with sesame seeds. Cover with plastic wrap and leave in a warm place for 15 minutes. Preheat the oven to 425°, and bake for 12–15 minutes or until very crisp and golden brown. Cool on a wire rack.

INGREDIENTS
2 teaspoons sugar
1 cup lukewarm milk
1 cup lukewarm water
¼ oz package active dry yeast
5 cups unbleached flour
2 teaspoons salt
6 tablespoons butter
beaten egg whites for glazing
seasame seeds for sprinkling

HOT CROSS BUNS

These Easter buns should be served hot, dripping with butter. Halve and toast any that do not get eaten immediately.

Makes 12

INGREDIENTS

⅓ cup superfine sugar

½ cup lukewarm milk

½ cup lukewarm water

two ¼-oz packages dry active yeast

3 cups unbleached flour

1 teaspoon salt

pinch each ground cinnamon, cloves
    and nutmeg

4 tablespoons butter, melted and
    cooled

1 large egg, lightly beaten

⅓ cup currants

⅓ cup mixed candied peel

2 tablespoons honey, to glaze

For the cross

2 tablespoons unbleached flour

2–2½ tablespoons water

Dissolve 1 teaspoon of the sugar in the milk and water, then stir in the yeast and leave to stand in a warm place for about 10 minutes, until frothy.

Sift the flour, salt, spices and the remaining sugar into a bowl and make a well in the center. Pour in the yeast liquid, melted butter and egg. Mix to form a soft dough, then turn onto a lightly floured surface and knead for 5–10 minutes, until the dough is smooth and elastic.

Place the dough in a clean bowl, cover with plastic wrap and leave in a warm place for about 1 hour, until doubled in size.

Lightly grease 2 cookie sheets.

Knead the currants and peel into the risen dough, kneading for 2–3 minutes.

Divide into 12 equal-size pieces and shape each one into a neat roll. Place well apart on two greased cookie sheets. Cover with plastic wrap and leave in a warm place for 30–40 minutes or until doubled in size.

Preheat the oven to 425°.

To make the cross, mix the flour and water together to form a smooth paste. Spoon into a small paper pastry bag and cut a small hole in the bottom of the bag.

Pipe a cross on each bun, then bake 25–30 minutes or until the buns sound hollow when tapped on the bottom. Remove from the oven, immediately brush with the honey and return to the turned-off oven for 3 minutes. Cool on the cookie sheet for 2 minutes, then transfer to a wire rack to cool completely.

MAPLE-FRUIT LOAF

Popular throughout the British Isles, this sticky, fruited bread, spread with butter, makes a nutritious snack.

Makes a 1 lb loaf

INGREDIENTS

1 teaspoon sugar

½ cup lukewarm milk

½ cup lukewarm water

¼ oz package active dry yeast

2 cups unbleached flour

½ teaspoon salt

¼ cup maple syrup

1 tablespoon molasses

1 tablespoon butter

1 cup golden raisins

2 tablespoons mixed candied peel

⅓ cup chopped pecans

1 teaspoon honey

Stir 1 teaspoon of sugar into the milk and water, then stir in the yeast. Leave in a warm place for 10 minutes, until frothy.

Meanwhile, sift the flour with the salt into a large bowl. Heat the maple syrup, mollases and butter together over gentle heat, stirring frequently. Leave until lukewarm. Stir the yeast mixture and the syrup mixture into the flour and mix to a dough. Knead for 10 minutes. Knead in the golden raisins, peel and pecans. Place in the rinsed-out bowl, cover with plastic wrap and leave in a warm place for 45 minutes. The dough will not rise very much at this stage.

Knead the dough for 5 minutes more, then place in a greased 9- × 5- × 3-inch loaf pan. Cover with plastic wrap and leave in a warm place for 45 minutes or until it reaches the top of the pan.

Preheat the oven to 400°. Bake for 45 minutes.

While the bread is hot, glaze the top of the loaf with the honey, and return to the oven for 3 minutes. Cool the loaf in the pan for 10 minutes, then turn it out onto a wire rack. Serve warm or cold, spread with butter.

CHELSEA BUNS

*Chelsea buns are delicious as an accompaniment to morning coffee,
or served as part of a traditional tea.*

Makes 12

INGREDIENTS

1½ cups unbleached flour
½ teaspoon superfine sugar
¼ cup lukewarm milk
¼ cup lukewarm water
¼ oz package active dry yeast
½ teaspoon salt
1 tablespoon shortening
1 egg, lightly beaten
½ cup currants
⅓ cup mixed candied peel
¼ cup light brown sugar
2 tablespoons butter, melted
1 tablespoon honey

Sift ½ cup of the flour into a warmed bowl. Dissolve the sugar in the milk and water, then stir in the yeast. Leave in a warm place for 10–15 minutes or until frothy.

Sift the remaining flour with the salt and cut in the shortening. Make a well in the center and pour in the yeast mixture and the egg. Mix to a dough and knead for 10 minutes. Place the dough in a bowl, cover with plastic wrap and leave in a warm place for 1½ hours or until doubled in size.

Turn the dough out on to a lightly floured surface and knead lightly. Roll the dough out into a 12- × 9-inch rectangle. Lightly butter a baking tray with sides.

Mix the currants, mixed peel and brown sugar together. Brush the dough with melted butter and sprinkle with the fruit mixture to within 1 inch of the edge. Roll the dough tightly, starting from one long edge. Press the edges to seal. Slice the roll into 12 pieces and pack into the baking tray.

Cover with plastic wrap and leave in a warm place for 30 minutes or until risen slightly. Preheat the oven to 350°, then bake for 30 minutes.

Remove from the oven and brush with honey. Leave to cool on the tray.

RUM AND WALNUT GUGELHOPF

*The name Gugelhopf, or Kugelhopf, is derived from the shape of the
fluted ring mold used, kugel meaning ball. This recipe has been
adapted to be made in a bundt pan.*

Serves 8–10

Dissolve the 1 teaspoon sugar in the milk and stir in the yeast. Set aside in a
warm place for about 10 minutes, until frothy.

Pour boiling water over the raisins and currants, stir for 1 minute, then drain
thoroughly and dry on a dish towel. Place in a bowl and sprinkle with the 1
tablespoon of flour. Add the candied mixed peel and walnuts. Mix the vanilla
extract with the ½ cup superfine sugar, and add to the fruit.

Sift the remaining flour with the salt into a bowl and make a well in the center.
Pour in the yeast mixture with the rum, eggs, butter and lemon zest. Mix to a
dough and knead for 10 minutes. Knead in the fruits and nuts.

Place the dough into a large warmed bowl, cover with plastic wrap and leave
to rise in a warm place for 1½–2 hours or until doubled in size.

Lightly butter a bundt pan. Knead the dough for 5 minutes, then place in the
pan. Cover and leave to rise in a warm place for 20–30 minutes or until risen to
the top of the pan.

Preheat the oven to 350°. Bake for 45–50 minutes.

Cool in the pan for 10 minutes, then turn out onto a wire rack to cool.

To make the icing, sift the confectioners' sugar into the top of a double boiler
over simmering water, and stir in the water and the rum. Stir over simmering
water until the icing is just lukewarm. Dribble over the top of the cake and leave
to set.

INGREDIENTS

1 teaspoon superfine sugar

⅔ cup lukewarm milk

two ¼ oz packages active dry yeast

⅔ cup raisins

⅓ cup currants

¾ cup unbleached flour, plus
   1 tablespoon

½ cup candied mixed peel

½ cup coarsely chopped walnuts

few drops vanilla extract

½ cup superfine sugar

pinch of salt

2 tablespoons rum

3 eggs, lightly beaten

10 tablespoons unsalted butter,
   softened

finely grated zest of 1 lemon

Icing

1 cup confectioners' sugar

1 tablespoon hot water

1½ tablespoons rum

RUM AND RAISIN FUDGE

Enriched with cream, milk and butter, this fudge has a fine smooth texture obtained by cooling it, then beating the mixture until thick.

Makes about 2 lb

INGREDIENTS
⅔ cup light cream
⅔ cup milk
4 cups sugar
8 tablespoons butter
1 tablespoon dark rum
½ cup seedless raisins

Pour the cream and milk into a saucepan and heat gently. Add the sugar, butter and rum, then stir until the sugar dissolves. Using a pastry brush dipped in cold water, wash down any sugar crystals that form around the sides of the pan. Do not allow the syrup to boil until the sugar has dissolved. Boil the mixture, without stirring, to the soft ball stage or until a temperature of 240° is reached on a candy thermometer.

Remove the pan from the heat and immediately plunge the bottom into cold water. Leave the fudge to cool for 5 minutes, then beat until thick and creamy. Stir in the raisins. Pour the mixture into a greased 9-inch square pan and leave to cool completely. Mark the fudge into 1-inch squares, cut into pieces and serve.

BUTTERSCOTCH

Butterscotch is traditionally made with butter, light brown sugar and water, but is even more delicious made with added heavy cream. This recipe includes instructions for brittle butterscotch and delicious butterscotch caramels.

Makes about 1¼ lb

INGREDIENTS
2 cups light brown sugar, packed
⅔ cup water
⅔ cup heavy cream
8 tablespoons butter
½ teaspoon vanilla extract

Place the sugar, water, cream and butter in a large, heavy-bottomed saucepan and heat gently for 10 minutes, stirring until the sugar dissolves.

Place a warmed candy thermometer into the pan and heat the syrup, stirring occasionally, to 280° for butterscotch caramels, or to 310° for a harder, brittle butterscotch. Stir in the vanilla extract, remove from the heat and plunge the bottom of the pan into cold water.

Pour the mixture into a greased 8-inch square pan. When cooled, mark into squares with an oiled knife. When completely cold, snap the butterscotch into squares, wrap in wax paper and store in an airtight container.

GAELIC TRUFFLES

208

GAELIC TRUFFLES

These truffles may be made with Scotch or Irish whiskey. Roll them in chopped walnuts, confectioners' sugar, cocoa powder, grated chocolate or chocolate sprinkles. Homemade truffles make an ideal gift when presented in a pretty box.

Makes about 30

Rinse out a saucepan with cold water. Pour in the cream and bring to the boiling point over moderate heat. Remove from the heat and add the chocolate. Stir the mixture constantly until the chocolate melts and no lumps remain. Allow the mixture to cool to room temperatue, then stir in the whiskey. Sift in the confectioners' sugar and add the dissolved coffee. Beat until well blended, then chill until the paste is firm enough to roll into balls.

Place the chopped walnuts on a plate. Using two forks, roll a little of the chocolate paste into a walnut-sized ball. *Do not* roll the mixture in your hands. Roll the truffles in the chocolate sprinkles or walnuts to cover completely. Place in paper cases. These truffles will keep up to 2 days in the refrigerator.

INGREDIENTS

⅔ cup heavy cream

8 oz semi-sweet chocolate, broken into small pieces

3 tablespoons whiskey

¾ cup confectioners' sugar

1 teaspoon instant coffee, dissolved in 1 tablespoon hot water and left to cool

chocolate sprinkles or ⅔ cup finely chopped walnuts

FRUITS DIPPED IN FONDANT

These exquisite confections are perfect to serve after dinner with coffee.
Other fruits ideal for dipping are kiwi fruit, tangerines, cherries and grapes.
Apricot or cherry brandy or a rose or orange flower water may be used instead
of Grand Marnier.

Makes about 1 lb

INGREDIENTS
1 cup sugar
1½ teaspoons corn syrup
6 tablespoons water
¾ lb strawberries, not hulled,
   washed and completely dry
1 teaspoon Grand Marnier
¼ cup superfine sugar

Heat the sugar, corn syrup and water together in a heavy-bottomed saucepan over gentle heat. Stir until the sugar dissolves. Use a brush dipped in water and brush any sugar crystals down from the sides of the pan.

Bring to the boil and boil without stirring until the temperature reaches 240° on a candy thermometer, or to the soft ball stage. Immediately dip the bottom of the pan into cold water and pour the syrup onto a dampened cookie sheet or marble slab.

Leave the syrup to cool for 5 minutes. Using a damp metal scraper, keep scraping the syrup in from the edges, until it cools slightly and becomes tinged with yellow. Work the fondant in a figure 8 pattern with a wooden spatula until it thickens. When very stiff, white and cold, knead it with damp hands. This process takes about 15 minutes.

Place the fondant in a rinsed-out bowl, cover with a damp cloth and leave in the refrigerator overnight.

Place the bowl of fondant in the top of a double boiler over simmering water. Stir as it begins to melt, add the Grand Marnier and place a candy thermometer in the fondant. The fondant only takes about 4 minutes to reach the correct temperature for dipping and should not be allowed to reach 150° or it will crack. Holding the strawberries by the stalk, dip two-thirds of it into the fondant. Allow the excess fondant to drip off, then roll the strawberry in the sugar. Place on a cookie sheet lined with wax paper. Leave to dry.

NOUGAT

To make this nougat, the syrup is first boiled to 280° on a candy
thermometer before adding the honey, because lengthy boiling at a high
temperature impairs the delicate flavor of the honey.

Makes 1¾ lb

INGREDIENTS
2 cups toasted blanched almonds
1 cup coarsely chopped pistachio
   nuts
⅓ cup candied cherries, rinsed, dried
   and coarsely chopped
1 cup granulated sugar
1½ tablespoons corn syrup
½ cup water
⅔ cup honey, warmed
2 egg whites, stiffly beaten
1 teaspoon vanilla extract
2 sheets wax paper

Mix the almonds, pistachios and candied cherries together and reserve. Place the sugar, corn syrup and water in a heavy-bottomed saucepan and heat gently, stirring until the sugar dissolves. Dip a brush in water and brush any sugar crystals down from the sides of the pan. Stir until the sugar dissolves. Bring to the boil and boil without stirring until the temperature reaches 280° on a candy thermometer, or to the soft crack stage. Stir in the warmed honey and continue to boil, until a temperature of 290° is reached.

Immediately pour the syrup in a thin stream onto the egg whites, beating constantly. Stir in the vanilla, nuts and cherries. Beat the mixture for 5 minutes or until the nougat begins to thicken. Pour into 9-inch square cake pan lined with wax paper. Spread the nougat into the pan and place a second sheet of wax paper on the top. Place a weight on top to knock out the air bubbles and leave to set overnight. Remove the weight and cut the nougat into bars or squares. Wrap in wax paper and store in an airtight container for 10 days.

FRUITS DIPPED IN FONDANT

GRAND MARNIER TRUFFLES

*These deliciously rich truffles are made by beating melted chocolate and cream together.
Many variations are possible, using different flavorings, nuts and liqueurs.
These will keep in the refrigerator for up to 2 days.*

Makes 35

INGREDIENTS
⅔ cup heavy cream
*10 oz semi-sweet chocolate, broken
    into small pieces*
6 tablespoons Grand Marnier
*⅔ cup finely chopped blanched
    almonds*
finely grated zest of 1 orange
2 tablespoons cocoa powder, sifted

Rinse out a saucepan with cold water. Pour in the cream and bring to the boiling point over moderate heat. Remove from the heat and add the chocolate. Stir the mixture constantly until the chocolate melts and no lumps remain. Allow the mixture to cool to room temperature, then stir in the Grand Marnier, almonds and orange zest. Beat the mixture until well blended, then chill until the paste is firm enough to roll into balls.

Using two forks, roll a little of the chocolate paste into a walnut-sized ball. Do *not* roll the mixture in your hands. Lightly roll the truffles in the cocoa powder – do not press them into the powder as this gives too thick a coating, and will make the truffles bitter.

Place the truffles in paper cases and arrange on a serving dish.

MARZIPAN SWEETMEATS

*Marzipan is delicious made with walnuts instead of almonds. Many
flavorings can be used – Grand Marnier, vanilla extract, orange
flower water, rum and brandy are just a few.*

Makes about 1½ lb

INGREDIENTS
1 lb dried whole dates
1⅓ cups ground walnuts
1 cup superfine sugar
1 small egg, beaten
1 teaspoon brandy
2 tablespoons slivered almonds

Cut the dates lengthwise on one side only and remove the pits. Mix the walnuts with the superfine sugar. Gradually mix in the egg and brandy, then stir until the mixture is well blended. Stuff the dates with some of the marzipan mixture. Place in paper cases and arrange on a serving dish.

Shape the remaining marzipan into small pear-shaped candies. Press a small piece of almond into the wide end of the sweet, to form a stem. Roll in superfine sugar and place on a serving dish. These pear-shaped candies may also be made with almond marzipan, colored a pale green with a few drops of green food coloring, and a sliver of pistachio nut to form the stem.

EVERTON TOFFEE

Everton toffee is made with molasses and has a rich buttery flavor.

Makes 1¾ lb

INGREDIENTS
8 tablespoons butter
1½ cups light brown sugar
1¼ cups molasses

Melt the butter over gentle heat, then stir in the sugar and molasses. Place a warmed thermometer into the toffee, and cook over moderately low heat, stirring frequently, until the temperature reaches 266° or the hard ball stage.

Immediately plunge the bottom of the pan into a bowl of cold water. Pour the toffee into a greased 8-inch square pan. As the toffee begins to set, cut it into 1-inch squares.

Store in an airtight container, individually wrapped, if desired.

MARSHMALLOWS

Marshmallows should be delicately flavored and colored. Rose or orange flower water are ideal as they lend a subtle fragrance as well as flavor.

Makes about 1¼ lb

Sift the confectioners' sugar and cornstarch together and use to coat the sides of a greased 9-inch square cake pan. Shake out any excess.

Place the sugar, corn syrup and 1 cup of the water in a heavy-bottomed pan. Stir over gentle heat until the sugar dissolves. Using a brush dipped in water, brush any sugar crystals down from the sides of the pan. Bring to the boil and boil, without stirring, until the temperature reaches 260° on a candy thermometer.

Meanwhile, place the remaining water and the rose water in a bowl. Sprinkle the gelatin over the liquid. Leave to soften for 5 minutes, then place the bowl over a pan of hot water and stir until the gelatin dissolves. Add the coloring then stir the gelatin into the syrup. Immediately remove the pan from the heat. Be very careful at this stage as the syrup bubbles. Pour the syrup in a thin stream onto the egg whites, beating constantly. Beat for 3 minutes or until thickened. Pour the mixture into the prepared pan and leave to set for 4 hours.

Ease the mixture away from the sides of the pan with a greased knife, then gradually ease it away from the bottom. Sift the remaining confectioners' sugar and cornstarch onto a baking tray and turn the marshmallow slab onto it. Turn over and coat the other side. Cut into 1-inch squares and store in an airtight, paper-lined container for 10 days.

INGREDIENTS

3 tablespoons confectioners' sugar
3 tablespoons cornstarch
few drops sunflower oil
2⅓ cups sugar
1¼ tablespoons corn syrup
1¼ cups water
3 tablespoons rose water
2½ tablespoons unflavored gelatin
1 drop of red food coloring
2 egg whites, stiffly beaten

MARSHMALLOWS

PRESERVES

PEACHES IN BRANDY

*This is an economical way of preserving fruit in brandy, by mixing a
thick sugar syrup with the alcohol. Buy the peaches in August and
bottle them for Christmas. They are delicious served in their syrup
with a rich velvety vanilla ice-cream.*

Fills a 2-quart jar

INGREDIENTS
12 large ripe peaches
water
5 cups sugar
2½ cups water
about 2½ cups brandy

Half-fill a large saucepan or preserving pan with water, and bring to the boil. Immerse the peaches in the water and poach for 4 minutes. Drain and peel, leaving the fruit whole.

Make a thin syrup by placing 1 cup of the sugar in a saucepan with the water. Stir over gentle heat until the sugar dissolves, then bring to the boil. Boil for 2 minutes. Add the peeled peaches and simmer for 1 minute. Remove the peaches, drain and cool.

Measure 2½ cups of the syrup and place it in a saucepan. Add the remaining sugar, and heat gently, stirring until the sugar dissolves. Using a pastry brush dipped in warm water, wash down any sugar crystals which have formed on the side of the pan; this prevents the syrup from crystallizing. Bring to the boil and boil steadily for 2 minutes, until the syrup reaches 216° on a candy thermometer. Immediately plunge the bottom of the pan in cold water to prevent the syrup from cooking any further. Cool. Pack the peaches into a large 2-quart jar. Pour an equal quantity of syrup and brandy over them to cover. Seal and store in a cool, dry place for 4–6 months.

APRICOT AND DATE CHUTNEY

*This delicious fruity chutney makes an excellent accompaniment to
cheese, cold meat, poultry and curry.*

Makes about 3 quarts

INGREDIENTS
*1 lb dried apricots or 2 lb fresh
  apricots*
2 lb dates
½ lb candied ginger, chopped
4 garlic cloves, crushed
1 lb light brown sugar
1 lb seedless raisins
5 tablespoons sea salt
about 5 cups white wine vinegar

If using dried apricots, cover them with cold water, and soak overnight. If using fresh apricots, remove the pits.

Pit the dates. Drain the apricots and place all of the ingredients in a preserving pan with only sufficient vinegar to cover, and bring to the boil. Reduce the heat, and simmer for about 2 hours, or until the fruit is soft and the chutney is thick. Pour into hot, dry, sterilized jars and seal with non-metallic lids. Store in a dark, cool, dry place.

PRESERVES

PRESERVES

—◆—

Preserves are ideal to give as gifts, to serve at breakfast, for an English tea, and on special occasions such as Christmas. The Pantry stocks a wide variety of preserves, but making your own – such as Apricot and Date Chutney and Peaches in Brandy – when the produce is in season, is a delightful way to pass an afternoon.

ORANGE AND WHISKY MARMALADE

Marmalade replaces jam or jelly on the English breakfast table. Seville oranges are imported from Spain and make the best marmalade. They have a very brief season but other bitter-flavored oranges can be used.

Makes about 10 cups

INGREDIENTS
1½ lb Seville oranges
juice of 1 lemon
7½ cups water
6 cups sugar
3 tablespoons Scotch whisky

Thoroughly wash and dry the oranges. With a sharp knife, remove the peel, leaving all of the white pith behind. Cut the peel into ¼-inch strips.

Squeeze the juice from the oranges and reserve the seeds. Roughly chop the squeezed flesh and pith and place it, with the seeds, in a large piece of cheesecloth and tie into a bundle.

Put the cut peel, orange and lemon juice, the cheesecloth bag of pith and seeds and the water into a large preserving pan. Bring to the boil and simmer for 2 hours or until the contents of the pan are reduced by half.

Remove the cheesecloth bag, add the sugar, and stir over gentle heat, until the sugar dissolves. Bring to the boil and boil rapidly for 15–20 minutes, until the setting point is reached (see below).

Remove the pan from the heat and add the whisky. Return to the heat and boil for 1 minute. Skim the marmalade and leave to cool for 30 minutes.

Stir the marmalade, then pour it into hot, dry, sterilized jars. When cold, cover with melted paraffin and seal. Store in a cool, dry place.
Note
To test for setting point, spoon a little of the conserve onto a saucer. Leave for a few minutes, then push with your finger. If the surface wrinkles, setting point has been reached.

QUINCE AND GERANIUM JELLY

*The golden, down-covered quince changes color when it is cooked to
give a pinkish-amber jelly. This autumnal fruit is high in pectin and is
therefore ideal for jams, jellies and preserves.
For an English touch to a meal, serve with meat or poultry. It is also
delicious spread on bread and butter.*

Makes about 10 cups

Wash and chop the quinces. Put them into a preserving pan with sufficient
water to just cover. Bring to the boil, reduce the heat and simmer for 25 minutes,
until soft and pulpy. As the fruit softens, mash it slightly from time to time.

Pour the fruit and juice into a jelly bag, or strain through a piece of
cheesecloth over a colander and leave to drip into a container overnight. Do *not*
squeeze the jelly bag or the result will be a cloudy, murky jelly.

Measure the juice and pour it into a preserving pan with the correct amount
of sugar. Heat gently, stirring, until the sugar dissolves, then bring to the boil.
Add the geranium leaves, and boil for 10 minutes or until setting point is
reached (see page 216). Remove the leaves and pour the jelly into hot, dry,
sterilized jars. Cover with melted paraffin, seal, store in a cool, dry place.

INGREDIENTS
5 lb quinces
water, to cover
*2 cups sugar to every 2½ cups juice
    (see method)*
*3–4 rose or lemon geranium
    leaves, tied together*

217

LIME MARMALADE

Limes have a refreshing tangy flavor and make a refreshing marmalade.

Makes about 8 cups

INGREDIENTS
1½ lb fresh limes, washed and dried
1¾ quarts water
6 cups sugar

With a sharp knife or swivel-bladed potato peeler, remove the lime zest, leaving all of the white pith on the fruit. Cut the zest into ¼-inch strips.

Place the zest and half the water in a preserving pan. Bring to the boil, cover, reduce the heat and simmer very gently for 2 hours or until the zest is tender. Meanwhile, roughly chop the peeled limes on a plate, so that none of the juice is lost. Place in a pan with the remaining water. Bring to the boil, cover, reduce the heat, and simmer gently for 1½ hours.

Strain the limes and liquid, through a piece of cheesecloth into the pan with the lime zest. Add the sugar and heat gently, stirring, until the sugar dissolves. Boil rapidly for 15–20 minutes or until setting point is reached (see page 216). Allow the marmalade to cool for 30 minutes. Stir gently and pour into hot, dry, sterilized jars. When cold, cover with melted paraffin and seal. Store in a cool, dry place.

TANGERINE AND ALMOND JAM

The addition of orange flower water makes this a fragrant and delicate jam.

Makes about 6 cups

INGREDIENTS
2 lb tangerines
4 cups sugar
¼ cup orange flower water
½ cup slivered almonds

Halve the tangerines. Squeeze out all the juice and reserve in a covered jar. Scrape the flesh and white pith from inside the peel and discard. Simmer the peel in water for 10 minutes, then drain. Cover the peel with cold water and leave to soak for 12 hours.

Drain the peel and roughly chop. Pour the reserved tangerine juice, sugar and chopped peel into a preserving pan. Heat gently until the sugar dissolves, then bring to the boil. Boil for 15–20 minutes or until setting point is reached (see page 221). Remove from the heat and stir in the orange flower water and almonds. Stir and boil again for 2 minutes.

Pour into hot, dry, sterilized jars. Cover with melted paraffin and seal. Store in a cool, dry place.

KIWIS IN COGNAC

This recipe demonstrates the simplest method of preserving fruits in Cognac or brandy. Other fruits suitable for preserving in this way are plums, peaches, cherries and apricots.

Fills a 2-pint jar

INGREDIENTS
6 kiwi fruits
3 tablespoons sugar
about 2½ cups Cognac or brandy

Do not peel the kiwi fruits. Prick each fruit with a toothpick in several places. Pack the fruit into clean, dry jars and sprinkle with sugar. Pour the Cognac or brandy over the fruit to cover completely.

Seal the jar and store for 4–6 months in a cool, dry place.

STRAWBERRY, PINEAPPLE AND KIRSCH CONSERVE

Rich in flavor and color, this conserve is easy and quick to prepare.
It can be made in summer when fruit is plentiful and stored until winter.

Makes about 4 cups

Place the pineapple, strawberries and sugar into a preserving pan. Heat gently, stirring until the sugar dissolves, then bring to the boil. Boil the conserve for 15–20 minutes or until setting point is reached (see page 216). Remove from the heat and stir in the kirsch. Return the pan to the heat and boil for 1 minute more.

Pour the conserve into hot, dry, sterilized jars. When cold, cover with melted paraffin and seal. Store in a cool, dry place.

INGREDIENTS
½ lb finely chopped fresh pineapple
(1 cup)
1½ lb strawberries, hulled
3 cups sugar
½ cup kirsch

ROSEMARY AND APPLE JELLY

This is a delicious accompaniment to serve with roast lamb.

Makes about six 1 lb jars

INGREDIENTS
5 lb tart apples
5 cups water
2 tablespoons chopped fresh
*   rosemary leaves or 1 tablespoon*
*   dried rosemary*
5 cups malt vinegar
sugar (see method for quantity)
sprigs of fresh rosemary

Remove any bruised or damaged portions from the apples and chop roughly into thick chunks without peeling or coring. Put the apples in a preserving pan with the water and the rosemary. Bring to the boil, then simmer for about 45 minutes, until soft and pulpy. Stir from time to time to prevent sticking. Add the vinegar and boil for 5 minutes.

Spoon the apple pulp into a jelly bag or piece of cheesecloth attached to the legs of an upturned stool. Allow the juice to strain into a large bowl for at least 12 hours. Do *not* squeeze the bag or the jelly will be cloudy. Discard the pulp.

Measure the extract and return to the pan with 1 lb sugar for every 2½ cups extract. Stir until the sugar dissolves. Bring to the boil and boil rapidly, without stirring, for about 10 minutes, until setting point is reached, or when a temperature of 221° is reached on a candy thermometer. (If you do not have a candy thermometer, see page 216 for the setting point test.) When setting point has been reached remove the pan from the heat. Skim the surface with a slotted spoon to remove any scum.

Pour into hot, dry, sterilized jars and add a sprig of rosemary to each. Place melted paraffin across the surface of the jelly. Label and store in a cool, dry place.

CHERRY AND APPLE JAM

This jam preserves two of summer's freshest flavors.

Makes about five 1 lb jars

INGREDIENTS
2 lb tart apples
3¾ cups water
4 lb Morello cherries
juice of 1 lemon
7 cups sugar
a knob of butter

Slice the apples without peeling or coring. Put them into a large saucepan with the water and simmer for 30–40 minutes, until they are well pulped. Spoon into a jelly bag and leave to strain for several hours. Do *not* squeeze the bag.

Put the apple extract, which should measure about 1¼ cups, into a preserving pan with the cherries and lemon juice. Simmer gently for about 30 minutes, until most of the moisture from the cherries has evaporated. Remove from the heat and stir in the sugar. Add the butter, bring to the boil and boil 10 minutes.

Test for a set (see page 216) and, when setting point is reached, take the pan off the heat and remove any scum from the surface with a slotted spoon. Pour into hot, dry, sterilized jars. When the jars are cold, cover with melted paraffin and seal. Store in a cool, dry place.

APRICOT AND AMARETTO CONSERVE

This luscious, glowing conserve makes an ideal gift. It is delicious eaten with warm buttered bread.

Makes about 2 lb

Halve the apricots and remove the pits. Place the pits in boiling water for a few minutes, then drain. Wrap the pits in a cloth, then crack them with a hammer or a rolling pin. Remove the kernels from their shells and blanch in boiling water. Split the kernels and reserve.

Place the apricots, sugar and water in a preserving pan, and heat gently, stirring until the sugar dissolves. Add the kernels and bring to the boil.

Boil for 15–20 minutes, or until setting point is reached (see below). Remove from the heat, stir in the Amaretto, and return to the boil for 1 minute. Pour the conserve into hot, dry, sterilized jars. Cover with melted paraffin and seal. Store in a cool, dry place.

INGREDIENTS
1½ lb fresh apricots
3 cups sugar
⅔ cup water
3 tablespoons Amaretto liqueur

MINT SAUCE

Mint sauce is traditionally served with roast lamb in England.

Makes about 1¼ cups

Put the chopped mint into dry, a wide-necked jar.

Dissolve the sugar in the vinegar in a saucepan, stirring with a wooden spoon, and bring to the boil. Remove from the heat and set aside until cold. Pour over the mint and seal to make the jars airtight.

To serve, lift out sufficient mint with a wooden spoon, together with a little of the liquid. Put into a pitcher or gravy boat and add a little fresh vinegar.

INGREDIENTS
¼ lb fresh mint, finely chopped
*   (1 cup)*
1 cup sugar
1¼ cups vinegar

PICCALILLI

*This bright golden relish is quite delicious served with a variety of cold
meat and cheese. Use only the freshest, undamaged vegetables and a
good quality vinegar, such as distilled white malt or a white
wine vinegar.*

Makes about 2½ quarts

Place the prepared vegetables into a large bowl, sprinkle with salt, cover and
leave for 12 hours or overnight.

Rinse the vegetables under cold water and drain. Pour 3¾ cups of the vinegar
into a large heavy-bottomed saucepan with the pickling spice. Bring to the boil
and boil for 5 minutes. Strain and return the vinegar to the pan.

Mix the remaining pickling sauce ingredients with the remaining vinegar,
then add to the vinegar in the pan. Bring to the boil and add the vegetables.
Simmer for 10 minutes.

Cool and pour into hot, sterilized jars, leaving about ⅛-inch headspace.
Cover with a non-metallic, air-tight lid and store in a cool, dark, dry place.

This recipe makes an ideal gift. It keeps for up to 6 months and makes a
special meal with crusty bread and cold sliced ham and pork.

INGREDIENTS
½ lb French-style green beans, cut
    into 1-inch pieces
2 cups roughly chopped shallots or
    onions
1½ lb zucchini, sliced crosswise
1 cucumber, peeled and diced
2 cauliflowers, divided into
    flowerets
6 tablespoons salt
Pickling sauce
5 cups distilled white malt, or
    white wine vinegar
2 tablespoons pickling spice
1 tablespoon ground turmeric
1 tablespoon dry mustard
1 tablespoon ground ginger
1 tablespoon cornstarch
1 cup light brown sugar

LIME CURD

*Curds are usually made in small quantities because they contain butter
and eggs, and are more perishable than jam. When cooled, the curd
should be stored in the refrigerator, where it will keep for
about 2 months.
Fruit curds may also be used as a filling for a sponge cake or a pastry
tart, or mixed with some whipped cream.*

Makes about 2 cups

Place the lime zest and juice, sugar and butter in the top of a double boiler. Grate
the limes directly into the top so that none of the zest is wasted. Stir over
simmering water until the butter melts and the sugar dissolves. Beat the eggs in
a small bowl, then strain them through a sieve into the lime mixture. Stir the
mixture constantly, for 15 minutes, or until the curd thickens and coats the back
of a spoon. Pour into a hot, dry, sterilized jar, cover with melted paraffin and
seal. Store in the refrigerator.

Tangerine curd
Use the finely grated zest and juice of 3 tangerines instead of the limes.

INGREDIENTS
freshly grated zest and juice of
    4 limes
¾ cup sugar
8 tablespoons unsalted butter
3 eggs

PICCALILLI

PEACHES IN BRANDY

This is an economical way of preserving fruit in brandy, by mixing a thick sugar syrup with the alcohol. Buy the peaches in August and bottle them for Christmas. They are delicious served in their syrup with a rich velvety vanilla ice-cream.

Fills a 2-quart jar

INGREDIENTS
12 large ripe peaches
water
5 cups sugar
2½ cups water
about 2½ cups brandy

Half-fill a large saucepan or preserving pan with water, and bring to the boil. Immerse the peaches in the water and poach for 4 minutes. Drain and peel, leaving the fruit whole.

Make a thin syrup by placing 1 cup of the sugar in a saucepan with the water. Stir over gentle heat until the sugar dissolves, then bring to the boil. Boil for 2 minutes. Add the peeled peaches and simmer for 1 minute. Remove the peaches, drain and cool.

Measure 2½ cups of the syrup and place it in a saucepan. Add the remaining sugar, and heat gently, stirring until the sugar dissolves. Using a pastry brush dipped in warm water, wash down any sugar crystals which have formed on the side of the pan; this prevents the syrup from crystallizing. Bring to the boil and boil steadily for 2 minutes, until the syrup reaches 216° on a candy thermometer. Immediately plunge the bottom of the pan in cold water to prevent the syrup from cooking any further. Cool. Pack the peaches into a large 2-quart jar. Pour an equal quantity of syrup and brandy over them to cover. Seal and store in a cool, dry place for 4–6 months.

APRICOT AND DATE CHUTNEY

This delicious fruity chutney makes an excellent accompaniment to cheese, cold meat, poultry and curry.

Makes about 3 quarts

INGREDIENTS
1 lb dried apricots or 2 lb fresh apricots
2 lb dates
½ lb candied ginger, chopped
4 garlic cloves, crushed
1 lb light brown sugar
1 lb seedless raisins
5 tablespoons sea salt
about 5 cups white wine vinegar

If using dried apricots, cover them with cold water, and soak overnight. If using fresh apricots, remove the pits.

Pit the dates. Drain the apricots and place all of the ingredients in a preserving pan with only sufficient vinegar to cover, and bring to the boil. Reduce the heat, and simmer for about 2 hours, or until the fruit is soft and the chutney is thick. Pour into hot, dry, sterilized jars and seal with non-metallic lids. Store in a dark, cool, dry place.

SPECIAL
OCCASIONS

TRADITIONAL CHRISTMAS DAY MENU

*Make merry with this traditional family Christmas feast
and all its trimmings.*

Serves 6–8

Chestnut and Apple Soup
***
Roast Goose with Fruit and Nut Stuffing
Spiced Cranberries with Port and Orange
***
Roast Potatoes and Parsnips
Brussels Sprouts with Almonds
Glazed Carrots
***
Polly Basset's Plum Pudding with Hard Sauce
***
Christmas Cake
Mince Pies

CHESTNUT AND APPLE SOUP

*All the flavors in this recipe combine beautifully to create a delicate but
tasty soup which is ideal to serve before a large meal.*

Serves 6–8

INGREDIENTS

4 tablespoons butter

6 tablespoons chopped shallots

2 bacon slices, finely chopped

½ cup chopped celery

*1 large tart apple, peeled and
roughly chopped*

*1½ lb canned unsweetened
chestnuts, drained*

*1¾ quarts chicken stock (see page
247)*

pinch of grated nutmeg

½ teaspoon sugar

salt and pepper

3 tablespoons medium dry sherry

Garnish

3 tablespoons butter

1½ tart apples, peeled and sliced

1½ teaspoons sugar

3 tablespoons light cream

Melt the butter in a large saucepan and sauté the shallots and bacon for 5 minutes. Add the celery and apple, and cover with a piece of buttered wax paper. Cover the pan and sweat the vegetables over gentle heat for 10 minutes. Remove the paper and stir in the chestnuts. Pour in the stock, add the nutmeg and sugar, and bring to a gentle boil. Cover and cook for 30 minutes.

Season with salt and pepper. Purée the soup, then stir in the sherry.

For the garnish, melt the butter, add the apple slices, sprinkle over the sugar and sauté until golden.

To serve, either pour the soup into a tureen or individual bowls, swirl in the cream, and garnish with the apples.

ROAST GOOSE WITH FRUIT AND NUT STUFFING

*Goose is at its best around Christmas time. A 10 lb goose will feed only
about 8 people due to the high percentage of bone and fat. Goose is
virtually self-basting and an excellent bird for roasting.*

Serves 6–8

To make the giblet stock, place the giblets, onion, carrot, bay leaf, parsley
sprigs, peppercorns and water in a saucepan, then bring to the boil. Skim the
scum from the surface, reduce the heat, partially cover the pan and simmer
gently for about 4 hours. Strain the stock and skim any fat from the surface.
Measure 2½ cups and reserve.

Meanwhile, soak the prunes and apricots in the red wine for 3–4 hours.
Preheat the oven to 400°.

Wipe the goose inside and out, remove any fat from the cavity and season.
Melt the butter and sauté the onion until soft. Add the liver and sauté for 2
minutes, or until it changes color. Cool slightly and place in a large bowl. Add
the remaining stuffing ingredients together with the prunes, apricots and the
wine in which they were soaking.

Mix and season well, then stuff the neck end of the goose loosely with the
mixture.

Truss the goose neatly and place it on a rack in a roasting pan. Prick the lower
legs, breast and sides of the bird, and roast breast side up for 20 minutes.

Remove from the oven and turn over onto the breast. Reduce the oven
temperature to 325° and roast for 1 hour. Turn the goose onto its back and roast,
breast side up, for a further 1–1¼ hours. The bird is cooked sufficiently if the
juices run clear when a skewer or fork is inserted into the leg. During cooking,
pour off excess fat from the roasting pan several times.

When the goose is cooked, leave in a warm oven with the door open for about
15 minutes before carving.

Meanwhile, to make the gravy, skim off most of the fat from the juices in the
roasting pan, then, over gentle heat, stir in the flour. Add the measured stock
gradually, then add the wine. Simmer, stirring, for about 10 minutes. Season
and strain into a gravy boat. Serve with the goose and stuffing.

INGREDIENTS
6 oz chopped prunes (1 cup)
4 oz chopped dried apricots (⅔ cup)
1 cup dry red wine
8–10 lb goose, dressed weight
salt and pepper
3 tablespoons butter
½ cup chopped onion
the goose liver, finely chopped
3 cups fresh bread crumbs
*2 large tart apples, peeled and
    roughly chopped*
1 cup chopped walnuts
3 tablespoons chopped parsley
1 teaspoon dried oregano
Giblet gravy
goose giblets, minus the liver
1 onion, quartered
½ cup chopped carrot
1 bay leaf
few parsley sprigs
4 black peppercorns
1½ quarts water
¼ cup unbleached flour
1¼ cups dry red wine
salt and pepper

SPICED CRANBERRIES WITH PORT AND ORANGE

An excellent accompaniment to poultry, game and cold meats.

Serves 6−8

INGREDIENTS

3 cups fresh cranberries
1 cup sugar
⅔ cup orange juice
finely grated zest of 1 orange
½ cup water
3 tablespoons port
3-inch cinnamon stick

Place all the ingredients in a saucepan over moderate heat. Stir until the sugar dissolves, then bring to the boil. Reduce the heat and simmer for 20 minutes. Remove the cinnamon stick and serve.

This dish can be served hot or made in advance and served chilled.

ROAST POTATOES AND PARSNIPS

Roast potatoes are traditionally served with the Christmas bird and trimmings in England. The sweet parsnip is also particularly good cooked in this way.

Serves 6−8

INGREDIENTS

2 lb potatoes, peeled and halved
2 lb parsnips, peeled and halved
salt
8 tablespoons butter

Cook the potatoes and parsnips in a large saucepan of lightly salted boiling water for 10 minutes. Drain.

Preheat the oven to 400°.

Place the butter in a baking dish, and put into the oven to melt. Scratch the surface of the potatoes only with a fork, to give them a crunchy skin when cooked.

When the butter is hot and sizzling, add the potatoes and parsnips and toss in the butter. Roast for about 1 hour, or until crunchy and golden.

BRUSSELS SPROUTS WITH ALMONDS

Few things could taste worse than soggy "sprouts" but, when served slightly crunchy with a lemon and almond butter, they are delicious.

Serves 6−8

INGREDIENTS

1½ lb Brussels sprouts, trimmed
with a cross cut in the bottom
6 tablespoons butter
½ cup slivered almonds
finely grated zest and juice of ½ a
lemon
salt and pepper

Steam or boil the sprouts until tender. Drain well.

Melt the butter, add the almonds and cook until slightly golden. Add the lemon zest and juice and remove from the heat.

Place the sprouts in a serving dish and pour the hot butter over. Season to taste.

From Left to Right: CHESTNUT AND APPLE SOUP, POLLY BASSET'S PLUM PUDDING, CHRISTMAS CAKE, MINCE PIES, HARD SAUCE, ROAST PARSNIPS, GLAZED CARROTS, ROAST GOOSE WITH FRUIT AND NUT STUFFING, ROAST POTATOES, BRUSSELS SPROUTS WITH ALMONDS, SPICED CRANBERRIES WITH PORT AND ORANGE.

GLAZED CARROTS

For this recipe the carrots may be peeled and cut into even "barrel" shapes, sliced into quarters lengthwise or left whole, depending on their size.
Serves 6–8

INGREDIENTS
1 lb carrots
⅔ cup water
2 teaspoons sugar
¼ teaspoon salt
4 tablespoons butter
chopped fresh herbs – thyme,
  parsley, sage, etc (optional)

Place the carrots, water, ½ teaspoon sugar, salt and 1 tablespoon butter in a saucepan and bring to the boil. Boil slowly, uncovered, until the water evaporates. Reduce the heat and add the remaining sugar and butter. Cook the carrots until glazed, shaking the pan from time to time. Sprinkle with a few chopped herbs and serve.

POLLY BASSET'S PLUM PUDDING

This dates back to the late 19th century. Although plum puddings, known as Christmas puddings in England, should be made well in advance, it is possible to make this pudding on Christmas Eve with very successful results.

Serves 8–10

INGREDIENTS
1⅓ cups dried currants
1⅓ cups dried sultanas
1⅓ cups raisins
1 cup firmly packed dark brown
  sugar
½ cup shredded beef suet
2 cups fresh bread crumbs
1 cup ground almonds
⅔ cup chopped blanched almonds
⅔ cup candied mixed peel
1 large tart apple, peeled and finely
  chopped
2 cups unbleached flour
finely grated zest of 1 lemon
finely grated zest of 1 orange
2 tablespoons lemon juice
½ cup stout or beer
4 eggs, beaten
pinch each ground cloves and ginger
¼ teaspoon grated nutmeg
½ teaspoon cinnamon
pinch of salt
5 tablespoons brandy

Mix all the ingredients together in a large bowl with 2 tablespoons of the brandy. Pour the mixture into a greased 2¼-quart heatproof pudding mold or bowl and cover with a double layer of greased wax paper or aluminum foil, pleated in the middle to allow for expansion. Tie a string under the rim and across the top to make a handle.

Place a trivet in the bottom of a large saucepan. Lower the pudding into the saucepan and fill with enough boiling water to come two thirds of the way up the sides of the mold. Cover and cook in simmering water for 8 hours. Pour in more boiling water as necessary.

When the pudding is cooked, pour the remaining brandy over the surface and re-cover. To reheat, boil gently for 3–4 hours.

To serve, decorate with a sprig of holly and flambé at the table with additional warmed brandy, if wished.

HARD SAUCE

Hard sauce may be made up to 3 weeks before Christmas, sealed in a jar and stored in the refrigerator. Serve with hot plum pudding or mince pies.

Makes about 1 cup

Cream the butter until pale, light and fluffy. Beat in the sugar and lemon zest until well mixed. Gradually add the brandy, beating constantly until well blended. Serve slightly chilled.

Rum butter

Use soft brown sugar instead of white, orange zest instead of lemon and replace the brandy with rum.

INGREDIENTS
8 tablespoons unsalted butter
½ cup superfine or confectioners' sugar
finely grated zest of 1 lemon
about ¼ cup brandy

MINCE PIES

Hot mince pies served on Christmas Eve in England herald the beginning of the holiday. Serve warm rather than hot, with hard sauce or rum butter. For the mincemeat flavors to blend, make the mixture at least 2 weeks in advance.

Makes 12

To make the mincemeat, mix all the ingredients together in a large bowl. Spoon into clean, dry screw-top jars, seal and store in a cool dry place for at least 2 weeks until required.

Roll out the dough on a lightly floured board.

With a 2¾-inch plain round cookie cutter, cut out 24 circles, re-rolling the trimmings until you have the required number.

Place half the dough circles on cookie sheets. Put a teaspoon of mincemeat in the center of each circle, leaving a border. Brush the edges with water, then place the remaining dough circle on top to cover the mincemeat. Press the dough edges together to seal. Fork the edges to decorate.

Preheat the oven to 350°.

Make a small hole in the top of each and bake for 15–20 minutes.

Place the pies on a wire rack and sprinkle with superfine sugar. Serve warm.

Note

The recipe for mincemeat will make 3 lb. You will need approximately 1 lb for the mince pies. Any left over mincemeat can be stored in an airtight container and kept for a maximum of 1 year.

INGREDIENTS
1 quantity rich pie crust dough (see page 248)
superfine sugar for dusting
Mincemeat
1⅓ cups dried currants
1⅓ cups golden raisins
1⅓ cups dark raisins
1 cup dark soft brown sugar
2 tart apples, peeled and finely chopped
⅔ cup candied mixed peel
1 cup shredded beef suet
½ cup chopped walnuts
½ cup dark rum
finely grated zest of 1 orange
finely grated zest of 1 lemon
2 tablespoons lemon juice
pinch each cinnamon, cloves, ginger and nutmeg

CHRISTMAS CAKE

This is a traditional spicy and rich fruit cake, which should be made during October or early November.

To decorate the Christmas cake, cover it first with marzipan, then with icing. The icing may be piped through a pastry bag fitted with a decorative tip or roughly done with a spatula. A most effective alternative decoration is to cover the top of the cake with only marzipan and arrange an assortment of nuts and candied fruits on the top. Cover the marzipan with a little apricot glaze, and make a pattern with brazil nuts, almonds and walnuts, candied cherries, candied pineapple and angelica. Brush the top with more apricot glaze and tie a wide satin ribbon around the cake.

Makes one 9-inch-round cake

INGREDIENTS

⅔ cup candied cherries, washed, dried and quartered

⅔ cup candied mixed peel

1⅓ cups golden raisins

1⅓ cups dried currants

1⅓ cups chopped seedless raisins

1⅔ cups unbleached flour

½ teaspoon salt

½ teaspoon cinnamon

¼ teaspoon grated nutmeg

¼ teaspoon ground cloves

16 tablespoons butter

1 cup dark brown sugar

finely grated zest of 1 lemon

finely grated zest of 1 orange

4 eggs

½ teaspoon vanilla extract

1 tablespoon molasses

½ cup ground almonds

⅔ cup chopped blanched almonds

3 tablespoons brandy

Preheat the oven to 300°. Lightly grease a 9-inch springform pan and line with aluminum foil, then grease again.

Place the cherries, candied peel, golden raisins, currants and raisins in a bowl. Sift the flour, salt and spices together. Stir ½ cup of the spiced flour into the fruits, making sure they are completely coated in the flour; this prevents the fruit from sinking to the bottom of the cake during baking.

Cream the butter until pale and fluffy. Gradually add the sugar and beat well. Add the lemon and orange zests.

In a small bowl, lightly beat the eggs, then add the vanilla extract and molasses. Gradually add the egg mixture to the butter and sugar, beating well between each addition to prevent it separating. (A little flour added with the last of the egg mixture will also prevent this.)

Gradually add the remaining flour to the egg mixture, then the fruit, together with any flour left in the bowl.

Add the ground and chopped almonds and the brandy. Mix thoroughly, then pour the mixture into the cake pan. Make a slight indentation in the center of the cake so that it will have an even surface when cooked.

Place the cake in the center of the oven and bake for 1½ hours. Reduce the temperature to 275° and continue baking for another 2½ hours. If the cake is browning too much, place a piece of lightly greased aluminum foil over the top. To test if the cake is cooked, insert a skewer or toothpick into the center of the cake. If it comes out clean, the cake is ready, but if any mixture clings to the skewer, bake for up to 30 minutes more.

Leave the cake in the pan for 30 minutes, then turn it out onto a wire rack and leave until cold. Wrap in aluminum foil and store in an airtight container.

To "feed" the cake during storage, make a few holes with a small fork or toothpick and pour a little brandy over the cake from time to time.

MARZIPAN

You will need 1½ lb for a 9-inch cake.

Makes about 1½ lb

INGREDIENTS

3 cups ground almonds

¾ cup superfine sugar

1¼ cups confectioners' sugar, sifted

2 tablespoons lemon juice

½ teaspoon orange flower water

½ teaspoon vanilla extract

1 whole egg

1 egg yolk

Place the almonds and sugars into a bowl. Mix well and add the remaining ingredients. Knead the mixture lightly with your hands until it forms a smooth paste. Do not knead the paste for too long because the almonds will become very oily. Wrap in plastic wrap until needed.

To decorate

Measure the circumference of the cake with a piece of string. Take two-thirds of the marzipan and roll it into a long strip, trim to the height and circumference of the cake. Brush the marzipan with a little egg white, then apply to the cake.

To cover the top of the cake with marzipan, use the baking pan as a guide. Roll the remaining marzipan into a circle and cut it slightly larger than the diameter of the cake.

Brush the marzipan with more egg white, then press the marzipan circle into place. Trim the edges and press into place. Leave for 1–2 days before icing.

ICING

FRESH EGG WHITE ICING

Makes about 2 cups

Sift the confectioners' sugar into a bowl.

Beat the egg whites until frothy, then gradually add the confectioners' sugar, a little at a time, beating well between each addition. Stir in the lemon juice and beat for 20 minutes.

If glycerin is available add 1 teaspoon to the icing to make it softer. Use it for covering a cake, but not for piping. Add the glycerin at the same time as the lemon juice, if using. Lastly, a few drops of blue coloring can be added to whiten the icing. Place the icing in a tightly sealed plastic container and leave overnight before using.

INGREDIENTS
6 cups confectioners' sugar
2 egg whites
1 tablespoon lemon juice
few drops of blue food coloring
   (optional)

SMOOTH ICING

With a pastry brush, remove any crumbs or sugar from the top of the marzipan. Pour sufficient icing to give a good coat on the top of the cake, then work it across the top and sides with a spatula. Use a metal ruler and place it on the top of the cake at a slight slant. Push it away from yourself across the top of the cake. Press the farthest edge of the ruler onto the cake, and draw it back across the top toward you. Once again, press the ruler edge nearest to you down onto the surface of the cake. Lift the ruler up – the top surface should be completely smooth.

To smooth the sides of the cake, place the cake on an icing turntable. Hold a scraper or metal ruler against the side of the cake, with your right hand. With your left hand, grasp the turntable and rotate counter-clockwise, to complete a full circle.

Leave the cake to dry in a cool airy place for 24 hours. Scrape away any rough edges. Repeat this process twice more, before decorating with piped icing.
Note
When icing a cake, *never* place icing on the center of the cake board to secure the cake, because it turns the cake moldy.

PICNIC
HAMPER

*Savour the long, lazy days of summer with this portable banquet
for a special occasion.*

Serves 8–10

Yogurt Cheese Balls (see page 100)
Smoked Eel Pâté (see page 47)

***

Granny Smith's Salad (see page 154)
Fennel and Salami with Black Olives (see page 125)
Raised Pork and Apple Pie (see page 31)
Sesame Bread Sticks (see page 196)

***

Grape Tarts (see page 164)
Melon and Strawberries with Champagne (see page 161)
Rum and Raisin Fudge (see page 208)

AFTERNOON TEA—
VICTORIAN STYLE

*Recapture the elegance of an English afternoon with
this classic Victorian tea.*

Serves 8–10

Cucumber Sandwiches
Meringues (see page 194)
Chocolate Eclairs (see page 193)
Irish Apple Cake (see page 191)
Scones with Jam and Whipped Cream (see page 196)
Dundee Cake (see page 182)

IRISH APPLE CAKE AND SCONES

GARDEN
PARTY MENU

—— • ——

*Celebrate a special birthday, an engagement or anniversary with this
splendid buffet served in the garden. The combined dishes in
this menu have been made to serve 50 people, although the
portions per recipe vary.*

Serves 50

Prosciutto and Figs with Caper Dressing
Black and Red Caviar served with Blinis
Satay Sticks with Peanut Sauce

***

Poached Salmon
New Potatoes with Mint Dressing
Avocado, Mozzarella and Tomato Salad
Chicken and Mandarin Rice
Endive, Watercress and Orange Salad
Green Bean and Lobster Tail Salad

***

Celebration Trifle
Strawberry Tarts with Praline Cream
Vanilla Soufflé with Pistachio Nuts

PROSCIUTTO AND FIGS WITH CAPER DRESSING

*These figs look attractive as part of a buffet. They are cut into a water
lily shape, then filled with fine strips of prosciutto.*

INGREDIENTS
50 fresh figs
*1 lb prosciutto cut into fine julienne
    strips*
lettuce to garnish
Caper dressing
2 cups sour cream
juice of 1½ lemons
1½ tablespoons Dijon mustard
salt and pepper
*3 tablespoons capers, drained and
    chopped*

Very carefully peel the figs, then cut through each one, from the top almost to
the bottom, to divide the fig into four. Open out the figs and fill them with the
prosciutto.

Mix all the dressing ingredients together and pour them into a serving bowl.

Place the bowl of dressing in the center of a large serving platter, then arrange
the lettuce leaves around the bowl. Place the figs on the lettuce. Cover with
plastic wrap and chill for at least 1 hour before serving.

From Left to Right: AVOCADO, MOZZARELLA AND TOMATO SALAD, POACHED
SALMON AND ENDIVE, WATERCRESS AND ORANGE SALAD.

BLACK AND RED CAVIAR SERVED WITH BLINIS

The blinis may be made ahead of time and reheated in a warm oven, wrapped in aluminum foil. Alternatively, reheat for a few seconds in a microwave oven.

For the blinis, mix the buckwheat flour and yeast together in a large mixing bowl, then gradually stir in the lukewarm milk and water to make a thick batter. Cover with plastic wrap and leave in a warm place for about 30 minutes or until risen.

Meanwhile, sift the unbleached flour and salt into a mixing bowl, make a well in the center and add the egg yolks and butter. Gradually beat into the flour, adding the milk as the mixture thickens.

Add the batter to the buckwheat mixture and beat together well. Cover with plastic wrap and leave in a warm place for 1 hour or until risen.

Beat the egg whites until stiff, then gently fold them into the risen batter.

Heat a griddle or a very large heavy-bottomed skillet, and grease lightly with butter. To make blinis about 2½-inches in diameter, drop the batter in tablespoonsful on to the hot griddle. Cook for about 1 minute or until golden brown underneath and bubbles appear on the surface. Turn over and cook the other side for 1 minute. Remove from the griddle and keep warm. Continue to make more blinis until all of the batter has been used or you have about 100.

For the dill butter, beat the butter until soft, then beat in the dill, seasoning and lemon juice to taste. Spoon into a serving dish.

To serve, spoon the caviars into separate serving bowls and set them on a bed of crushed ice. Serve the blinis hot in a napkin-lined basket with the dill butter.

INGREDIENTS
¾ lb black caviar, well chilled
¾ lb red caviar, well chilled
crushed ice, to serve
Blinis
1 cup buckwheat flour
¼ oz package active dry yeast
1 cup lukewarm milk mixed with
    ¼ cup water
2 cups unbleached flour
1 teaspoon salt
2 eggs, separated
4 tablespoons butter, melted
2 cups milk
Dill butter
½ lb butter
2 tablespoons chopped fresh dill or
    parsley
salt and pepper
lemon juice

SATAY STICKS WITH PEANUT SAUCE

*The rich, nutty flavor of the peanut sauce and the tender meat form a
perfect partnership for this unusual party dish.*

INGREDIENTS

3 lb sirloin, cut into ½-inch cubes

Marinade

2 oz tamarind pulp (¼ cup)

⅔ cup boiling water

2 oz fresh ginger root,
   chopped (¼ cup)

1½ cups finely chopped onion

2 garlic cloves, crushed

2 teaspoons ground cumin

2 teaspoons ground turmeric

2 teaspoons finely ground dried
   lemon grass

1 teaspoon ground coriander

salt and pepper

¼ cup soy sauce

Peanut sauce

2 tablespoons peanut oil

1½ cups finely chopped onion

2 garlic cloves, crushed

2 teaspoons finely ground dried
   lemon grass

¼ teaspoon ground cinnamon

1 teaspoon chili powder

juice of 1 lemon

1½ tablespoons dark brown sugar

12 oz unsalted peanuts, skinned and
   ground (3 cups)

2½ cups canned coconut milk

To serve

1 cucumber, cut into 2-inch pieces

3 large onions, thinly sliced

To make the marinade, put the tamarind pulp into a small bowl with the boiling water and leave to stand for 30 minutes. Strain the tamarind liquid through a sieve into a mixing bowl, pressing down on the tamarind to extract all the juices. Add all the remaining marinade ingredients and mix together well. Pour it over the steak, mix well, cover and leave to marinate for at least 2 hours.

Meanwhile, make the peanut sauce. Heat the oil in a saucepan and sauté the onion until soft. Add the garlic and spices and cook for a further 2–3 minutes, then stir in all of the remaining ingredients. Slowly bring the sauce to the boil, stirring constantly, then reduce the heat and simmer for 20 minutes, stirring frequently. Keep the sauce hot until ready to serve.

Thread the marinated steak onto bamboo skewers, about five pieces to each skewer. Brush with peanut oil and cook under a very hot broiler for 5–6 minutes, turning frequently.

Spoon the sauce into a hot serving bowl and place it on a very large hot serving platter. Arrange the cucumber and onions in another bowl and place them on the same platter. Arrange the hot satay sticks around the bowls and serve immediately.

NEW POTATOES WITH MINT DRESSING

*New potatoes and fresh mint is a traditional combination for summer.
If the mint is unavailable, substitute parsley, tarragon or chives.*

INGREDIENTS

10 lb new potatoes

⅔ cup hot chicken stock (see page
   247)

sprigs of fresh mint, to garnish

Dressing

3 cups mayonnaise

2½ cups sour cream

3 tablespoons chopped fresh mint

salt and pepper

Cook the potatoes in boiling salted water until they are just cooked. Drain well.

Put the potatoes into two large bowls and spoon the stock over them while they are still hot. Allow to cool.

Mix all the dressing ingredients together. Pour the dressing over the potatoes and toss gently but thoroughly together. Spoon into serving dishes and garnish with fresh mint. Cover with plastic wrap and chill until ready to serve.

POACHED SALMON

This recipe gives instructions for cooking and decorating one salmon,
which will serve 20–25 people. To serve 50 people, you will need to
cook at least two salmons. Make sure the fish kettle is large enough to
accommodate the salmon; it will need to be about 30-inches long.

To make the poaching stock put all the ingredients, except the wine, into a large saucepan. Bring to the boil, then reduce the heat and simmer gently for 30 minutes. Add the wine and simmer for a further 20 minutes. Allow to cool.

To prepare the salmon cut off the fins with sharp scissors. Scrape the fish with the back of a small knife, to remove as many of the loose scales as possible. Prick or remove the eyes and remove the gills, then remove the entrails of the fish through the gills; this means that the fish does not have to be slit along the belly, and will keep a better shape. Wash the salmon thoroughly under cold running water.

Place the salmon on the trivet inside the fish kettle. Strain the poaching stock into the fish kettle until it covers the salmon completely. Add a little cold water, if necessary.

Bring almost to the boil, until the water just begins to move. Reduce the heat and simmer for 10 minutes. Very carefully remove the fish kettle from the heat and put it in a cool place. Allow the salmon to cool in the poaching stock, preferably overnight, until it is completely cold.

Lift the salmon from the fish kettle, on the trivet, and drain well. Carefully remove the skin from one side, then turn the salmon over onto a large serving platter, or a board, and remove the skin from the other side. Neaten up the fish by removing any small bones from the fin areas.

Chop the set aspic jelly on a sheet of wet wax paper with a wet knife (this will make it sparkle). Arrange the jelly around the salmon. Decorate with the cucumber skin, dill, lemon or lime wedges and whole shrimp. Glaze or brush the salmon with the remaining aspic.

Keep the salmon in a cool place until ready to serve. Serve with mayonnaise.

INGREDIENTS
9 lb fresh salmon
mayonnaise, to serve
Poaching stock
1 cup sliced onion
2 cups sliced carrots
¾ cup sliced celery
4 bay leaves
large parsley sprig
small bunch fresh dill
1 tablespoon salt
12 black peppercorns
4½ quarts cold water
4½ cups dry white wine
Garnish
2 cups set aspic
3 tablespoons mayonnaise
cucumber skin strips
fresh dill
lime or lemon wedges
whole shrimp
⅔ cup liquid aspic

AVOCADO, MOZZARELLA AND TOMATO SALAD

Colorful and tasty, this salad is ideal as a side salad as well as a light
luncheon dish. Substitute the dried herbs with any of your favorite fresh herbs.

Mix all the dressing ingredients together. Cut the avocados in half lengthwise, remove the seeds and peel off the skin. Cut each avocado in half again, lengthwise, then cut across into thin slices. Put into a large bowl and pour the dressing over.

Arrange the tomatoes in neat rows on two large flat oval serving platters. Season well and sprinkle with the herbs. Sprinkle two-thirds of the cheese over the tomatoes, then arrange the avocados, in neat lines, on top of the cheese. Sprinkle the remaining cheese over the avocados.

INGREDIENTS
4 large ripe avocados
3 lb tomatoes, seeded and sliced
large pinch each dried basil,
    oregano and marjoram
1 lb mozzarella cheese, grated
Dressing
¼ cup white wine vinegar
⅔ cup olive oil
1 teaspoon Dijon mustard
salt and pepper
2 garlic cloves, crushed

CHICKEN AND MANDARIN RICE

*Mandarin orange segments add a zesty citrus taste to the rice and chicken.
Because it is prepared in advance, this dish is perfect to serve for a
lunch party as well as when catering for large numbers.*

INGREDIENTS

4 vegetable bouillon cubes

salt and pepper

3 cups long-grain rice

*1½ lb cooked chicken, off the bone;
    cut into thin strips*

1 head celery, thinly sliced

4 tablespoons chopped parsley

1 bunch scallions, sliced

1 cup mayonnaise

*1¼ lb canned mandarin orange
    segments, drained*

celery leaves, to garnish

Bring a large saucepan of 1½-quarts water to the boil, add the bouillon cubes and salt. Add the rice and cook gently for 20–25 minutes or until the rice is just cooked. Drain, rinse under cold running water, then drain again.

Put the rice, chicken, celery, parsley and scallions into a large bowl. Add the mayonnaise, season well, and mix gently together. Carefully stir in the orange segments. Cover and leave for at least 1 hour before serving, to allow the flavors to develop.

Spoon the rice into one large, or two small, serving bowls and garnish with celery leaves.

ENDIVE, WATERCRESS AND ORANGE SALAD

*This salad combines the sharp taste of the endive and watercress with
the refreshing flavor of the orange.*

INGREDIENTS

4 large oranges

6 large endive, trimmed

*4–6 bunches watercress, trimmed
    and washed*

Dressing

¼ cup red wine vinegar

salt and pepper

2 garlic cloves, crushed

2 teaspoons Dijon mustard

finely grated zest of 4 oranges

⅔ cup olive oil

Mix all the dressing ingredients together.

Remove the zest and all of the white pith from the orange. Using a sharp knife, carefully remove the segments from the oranges, cutting between the connecting membrane. Squeeze the juice from the remaining tissue into the dressing.

Cut the orange segments into small pieces and put them into a large salad bowl. Cut the endive into fine slices, cutting across the heads, and add them to the salad bowl. Add the watercress. Cover the salad bowl and chill for at least 1 hour.

Just before serving, pour the dressing over the salad and toss lightly together.

GREEN BEAN AND LOBSTER TAIL SALAD

*The addition of lobster tail meat transforms this salad into a dish suitable for any
special occasion. Prepare with smaller portions and serve as an elegant appetizer.*

INGREDIENTS

3 lb green beans, trimmed

*1 lb frozen lobster tail meat,
    defrosted and chopped*

Dressing

6 tablespoons lemon juice

6 tablespoons olive oil

*3 tablespoons chopped fresh dill or
    parsley*

salt and pepper

Cook the beans in a large saucepan of boiling salted water for 3–4 minutes or until they are only just cooked. Drain, rinse under cold running water and drain again. Spread them out on dish towels to dry thoroughly.

Cut the beans into 1-inch pieces and put into a large salad bowl. Add the lobster meat, then cover the bowl and chill for at least 1 hour.

Mix all the dressing ingredients together. Just before serving, pour the dressing over the beans and lobster, then toss well together.

CELEBRATION TRIFLE

From Left to Right: VANILLA
SOUFFLES WITH PISTACHIO
NUTS, CELEBRATION TRIFLE
AND STRAWBERRY TART
WITH PRALINE CREAM

*This delicious trifle will serve 8–10 guests, so you will need to make
two or more trifles, depending on the other desserts being served.
Make the day before to allow the flavors to develop.*

Put the raspberries into a large bowl and sprinkle with ½ cup of the superfine sugar. Cover and leave for about 1 hour or until the raspberries start to create juice.

Slice the cake slices in half horizontally, then sandwich together with the raspberry jam. Place in a large glass serving bowl and spread with more jam. Spoon 3 tablespoons of the sherry over the cake slices.

Spoon the raspberries and their juice over the pound cakes, then place the macaroons in a single layer on top and spoon the remaining sherry over. Arrange the sliced peach halves on top of the cakes. Cover and leave to stand while making the custard.

Very lightly beat the egg yolks with the remaining superfine sugar until thick. Heat the milk until it is almost boiling, then beat it into the egg yolks. Return the mixture to a heavy-bottomed saucepan and stir over a low heat until the custard thickens, but do not allow it to boil, or it may curdle. As soon as the custard thickens, remove from the heat immediately and strain it through a nylon sieve onto the peaches. Allow to cool, then cover and chill overnight.

Whip the cream with the confectioners' sugar and kirsch until it just holds soft peaks. Carefully spread the cream over the custard, mark into swirls and decorate with chocolate curls. Chill until ready to serve.

INGREDIENTS

1 lb fresh raspberries, hulled
¾ cup superfine sugar
*4 ¾-inch slices pound cake, sliced
    in half vertically to make 8 slices*
1 cup raspberry jam
6 tablespoons medium-dry sherry
4 oz macaroons
4 canned peach halves, sliced
12 egg yolks
3¾ cups milk
1¼ cups heavy cream
1 tablespoon confectioners' sugar
2 tablespoons kirsch
chocolate curls, to decorate

243

STRAWBERRY TARTS WITH PRALINE CREAM

*The quantities given are for two tarts, each one serving 8–10 guests.
The pastry bottoms may be made and frozen uncooked ahead of time,
then baked frozen. The tarts are decorated with spun sugar,
but if preferred they may be decorated with
piped whipped cream instead.*

INGREDIENTS

*1 quantity choux pastry (see page
    249)*

2 lb fresh strawberries, hulled

Sweet pastry

2½ cups unbleached flour

pinch of salt

¼ cup superfine sugar

12 tablespoons butter

4 egg yolks

Praline cream

¼ lb blanched almonds

½ cup superfine sugar

2½ cups heavy cream

Spun sugar

1 cup granulated sugar

6 tablespoons water

1 tablespoon corn syrup

For the sweet pastry, sift the flour and salt into a mixing bowl. Stir in the sugar, then cut in the butter until the mixture looks like fine bread crumbs. Mix to a dough with the egg yolks. Wrap in plastic wrap and chill for 30 minutes.

Divide the dough into two equal pieces, and roll out each one on an up-turned cookie sheet to a 11-inch circle. Prick the dough circle well with a fork. Chill.

Preheat the oven to 400°.

Put the choux pastry into a pastry bag fitted with a ½-inch plain tip. Pipe a single ring of choux pastry around the edge of each pastry bottom, piping it ¼-inch in from the edge. Bake for 25–30 minutes or until the choux pastry is well risen and golden brown. Remove from the oven and pierce the choux pastry, at intervals, to allow the steam to escape. Return to the oven for 2–3 minutes to dry. Carefully transfer the pastry cases from the cookie sheets to wire racks to cool.

For the praline cream, put the almonds and sugar into a small, heavy-bottomed saucepan and heat gently until the sugar dissolves and turns a rich caramel color. Immediately pour on to an oiled baking sheet and allow to cool and set hard. Grind the nut mixture in an electric grinder or crush finely with a rolling pin. Beat the cream until it just holds soft peaks, then gently fold in the praline.

Place the pastry cases on two large flat serving plates and fill them with the praline cream. Cut the strawberries into halves, or slices, and arrange them neatly on top of the cream.

To make the spun sugar, lightly oil a rolling pin. Cover the work surface with newspaper and also cover the floor immediately below. Cover the newspaper on the work surface with wax paper.

Put the sugar, water and corn syrup into a saucepan and heat gently until every granule of sugar dissolves, brushing down the sides of the pan with a little hot water. Boil the sugar syrup to a temperature of 320°. *Immediately* plunge the bottom of the pan into cold water to prevent further cooking. Dip two forks, held together, into the syrup, then hold them up high until a fine thread starts to fall. Gently throw, or spin, the sugar threads around the rolling pin until a good quantity of threads accumulate. Remove from the rolling pin and set aside. Repeat until all the syrup has been used.

Pile the sugar nests on top of the strawberry tarts and keep up to 2 hours until required.

VANILLA SOUFFLE WITH PISTACHIO NUTS

This very light creamy soufflé, decorated with pistachio nuts, will serve about 8 guests.
Make two or more soufflés, as required. They can be made the day before.

Make a paper collar for a 6½-inch soufflé dish by cutting a double strip of wax paper long enough to fit around the dish and wide enough to stand 2-inches above the rim. Secure the collar firmly and place the dish on a flat plate.

Sprinkle the gelatin over the water and leave for 2 minutes to soften. Stand the bowl in a saucepan of hot water and heat gently until the gelatin dissolves.

Beat the egg yolks with the superfine sugar and vanilla until they are very thick and will hold the trail of the beaters when lifted.

Whip 1¼ cups of the cream until it just holds soft peaks. Beat the egg whites until they are very stiff.

Beat the hot gelatin into the egg yolks, then fold in the cream. Very carefully, and quickly, fold in the egg whites. Pour the soufflé mixture into the prepared dish and chill for at least 2 hours or until set.

When set, carefully remove the paper collar. Coat the sides of the soufflé with the chopped nuts.

Whip the remaining cream until thick. Spoon into a small pastry bag fitted with a small star tip and pipe rosettes around the top edge of the soufflé. Decorate with pistachio nuts. Chill until ready to serve.

INGREDIENTS

4 teaspoons unflavored gelatin

¼ cup cold water

6 eggs, separated

¾ cup superfine sugar

2 teaspoons vanilla extract

2 cups heavy cream

2 tablespoons peeled and chopped pistachio nuts

whole pistachio nuts, to decorate

BASIC RECIPES

BEEF STOCK

Makes about 3½ quarts

INGREDIENTS

2 lb shin of veal, on the bone
2 tablespoons shortening
1 lb marrow bones, cut up
3 large carrots, roughly chopped
2 celery stalks, roughly chopped
2 onions, quartered
2 large garlic cloves, crushed
5 quarts water
1 bay leaf
8 black peppercorns
¼ teaspoon thyme
2 lb shin of beef, sliced 1½-inches
   thick

Preheat the oven to 425°.

Bone the veal and reserve the meat.

Place the veal bone, shortening, marrow bones, carrots, celery, onions and garlic in a roasting pan. Roast for 45 minutes, basting and turning occasionally.

Transfer the bones and vegetables to a large saucepan or stockpot, scraping any brown residue from the roasting pan. Add the water, bay leaf, peppercorns and thyme and bring to the boil. Do *not* add any salt.

Skim and wipe the edge of the pan. Partially cover and simmer for 4 hours. Strain the stock and cool slightly. *This is bone stock.*

For beef stock, skim 4 tablespoons of the fat from the surface of the bone stock and reserve. Return the stock to the pan. Brown the veal meat and the shin of beef in the reserved fat, turning occasionally, for about 10 minutes. Pour the strained stock over the meat and bring to the boil. Skim the surface and wipe the sides of the pan. Lower the heat and partially cover. Simmer for 3½–4 hours. Strain and cool. Remove the surface fat when ready to use.

Store in the refrigerator, boiling for 2 minutes every 3 days. Freeze in an ice cube tray (see fish stock, below) in freezerproof containers.

FISH STOCK

Makes about 1¼ cups

INGREDIENTS

1 fish, head and bones
1 carrot, roughly sliced
1 onion, quartered
bouquet garni
a few peppercorns
2 cups cold water

Place all the ingredients in a large saucepan or stockpot. Pour in the water and bring to the boil. Skim the surface, reduce the heat, and simmer for 20–30 minutes. Strain the stock, cool, cover and refrigerate until required.

To freeze, allow the stock to cool, then strain and freeze in an ice cube tray. Place the cubes in a freezerproof bag and freeze for up to 6 months. Defrost 1–2 hours at room temperature, or in a heavy-bottomed saucepan over high heat.

COURT BOUILLON

Makes about 1½ quarts

Place all the ingredients in a heavy-bottomed saucepan or stockpot and bring to the boil. Cover, reduce the heat and simmer for 30 minutes. Cool before using.

To freeze, rapidly boil the court bouillon until reduced to one-quarter its original amount. Allow to cool, then strain and freeze in an ice cube tray. Place the cubes in a freezerproof bag and store for up to 6 months. Defrost overnight at room temperature or defrost over moderate heat and cool before using.

INGREDIENTS
1¼ quarts water
1 carrot, sliced
1 onion, sliced
1 celery stalk, sliced
bouquet garni
1 slice fennel (optional)
2 cups dry white wine
6 peppercorns
salt

CHICKEN STOCK

Makes about 3 quarts

Place all the ingredients in a large saucepan or stockpot. Bring to the boil, slowly skimming off any scum that rises. Reduce the heat and partially cover the pan. Simmer for 3½ hours. Skim the surface, strain through a fine sieve, discard the flavoring vegetables and adjust the seasoning. Cool and refrigerate until required.

If not using immediately, the stock should be refrigerated and boiled every 2–3 days. Freeze as for fish stock (see left).

The leftover chicken meat is excellent to use in pot pies and curries, salads or sandwiches.

INGREDIENTS
3 lb broiler
2 chicken wings
1 veal knuckle
3¾ cups water
2 medium onions, quartered
2 celery stalks, roughly chopped
2 garlic cloves, crushed
1 leek, roughly sliced
4 carrots, roughly sliced
bouquet garni
6 peppercorns
salt

BASIC PIE CRUST DOUGH

Makes 1½ lb

Sift the flour with the salt into a bowl. Cut in the butter and shortening until the mixture resembles fine bread crumbs. Gradually add the water and mix lightly until the mixture begins to collect together. Form the dough into a ball, wrap in plastic wrap and leave to rest in the refrigerator for at least 30 minutes before rolling.

The uncooked dough will keep in the refrigerator for up to 4 days wrapped in aluminum foil or plastic wrap. It can be frozen for up to 3 months and left to defrost overnight at room temperature.

INGREDIENTS
3 cups unbleached flour
pinch of salt
8 tablespoons chilled butter, cubed
½ cup shortening, cubed
6 tablespoons ice water

RICH PIE CRUST DOUGH

Makes 1 lb

INGREDIENTS
2 cups unbleached flour
pinch of salt
12 tablespoons butter
1 tablespoon superfine sugar
1 egg yolk
about 3 tablespoons ice water

Sift the flour and salt into a bowl. Cut in the butter until the mixture resembles bread crumbs. Stir in the sugar, add the egg yolk and sufficient water to bind the dough. Mix lightly, form into a ball, wrap in plastic wrap and rest in the refrigerator for 30 minutes before rolling.

Store and freeze as for basic pie crust dough (see page 247).

TART PASTRY DOUGH

Makes ½ lb

INGREDIENTS
1 cup unbleached flour
pinch of salt
¼ cup superfine sugar
4 tablespoons butter
2 egg yolks
2 drops vanilla extract

Sift the flour with the salt onto a marble slab and make a well in the center. Place the remaining ingredients in the well. Using one hand, mix the sugar, butter, egg yolks and vanilla into a paste with your fingertips. Quickly draw in the surrounding flour and knead the dough lightly. Wrap in plastic wrap and leave to rest in the refrigerator for 45 minutes – 1 hour, before rolling.

Store and freeze as for basic pie crust dough (see page 247).

PUFF PASTRY DOUGH

Makes about 1 lb

INGREDIENTS
2 cups unbleached flour
pinch of salt
10 oz butter
¾ cup ice water

Sift the flour and salt into a bowl. Lightly cut in 2 tablespoons of the butter. Add sufficient water to make a firm dough. Turn out onto a floured surface and knead until smooth. Wrap the dough in plastic wrap and rest in the refrigerator for 30 minutes.

Lightly beat the remaining butter into a 5- × 4-inch block. Roll out the dough on a lightly floured surface into a 6- × 12-inch rectangle.

Place the butter in the middle of the dough and fold each end of the dough over the butter to form a neat package. Press the sides together and turn it over. Roll out the dough into an oblong shape, fold it over into three, and give the package a 90° counter-clockwise turn. Repeat once more, wrap and rest in the refrigerator for 30 minutes. Repeat the rolling, folding and resting process 6 more times, resting the dough for 15 minutes between rollings.

If the dough appears streaky after the final turn, roll it out just once more, and only once, because it will not rise properly if handled too much. Puff pastry is usually baked in a hot oven at 425° on a wet cookie sheet; the resulting steam helps the pastry to rise.

CHOUX PASTRY

Makes about 1 lb

Sift the flour and salt onto a sheet of wax paper. Place the water and butter in a saucepan and heat, melting the butter before boiling point is reached. Bring to a rolling boil, and *immediately* pour in the flour. Remove the pan from the heat. Beat the mixture until it is smooth and leaves the sides of the pan. Cool, then gradually beat in enough eggs to make the mixture glossy and smooth, and of a dropping consistency. You may not need to add all the eggs. Do not add the eggs while the mixture is warm or the eggs may scramble.

INGREDIENTS
¾ cup unbleached flour
a pinch of salt
¾ cup plus 3 tablespoons water
6 tablespoons butter
3 eggs, beaten

WHOLE WHEAT DOUGH

Makes 1 lb

Sift the flour with the baking powder and salt into a bowl. Tip in the bran left in the sieve and mix well. Cut in the butter until the mixture resembles bread crumbs. Gradually add the cold water and mix lightly until the dough forms a ball. Knead lightly, form into a ball and cover with plastic wrap. Rest in the refrigerator for 1 hour before rolling.

For a less crumbly dough, use half whole wheat flour and half unbleached white flour.

INGREDIENTS
2 cups whole wheat flour
1½ teaspoons baking powder
pinch of salt
10 tablespoons butter
4–5 tablespoons ice water

SUETCRUST DOUGH

Makes about 1 lb

Sift the flour, baking powder and salt into a large mixing bowl and mix in the pepper. Stir in the suet and add sufficient water to mix to a soft dough. Knead lightly until smooth. Form into a ball, cover and leave to rest 5 minutes. To use, roll out to ¼-inch thick.

Suetcrust dough can be used with both sweet and savory dishes and is best boiled or steamed.

INGREDIENTS
2½ cups unbleached flour
1½ teaspoons baking powder
good pinch of salt
freshly ground black pepper
1½ cups shredded beef suet
water

HOT-WATER PASTRY DOUGH

Makes enough to line a 1½-quart pudding mold or bowl

Warm a mixing bowl and sift the flour and salt into it. Make a well in the center and add the egg yolk. Cover the egg yolk with flour.

Melt the butter and water in a saucepan and bring it to the boil. (Make sure that the butter melts before boiling point is reached.) When the mixture is boiling, pour it onto the flour and mix vigorously with a knife.

When the mixture is cool, turn it out onto a lightly floured surface, and knead until the pastry is smooth. Rest in a cool place for 20 minutes.

INGREDIENTS
3 cups unbleached flour
1 teaspoon salt
1 egg yolk
8 tablespoons chilled butter, or
½ cup shortening
¾ cup water

MAYONNAISE

Makes about 1½ cups

INGREDIENTS

2 egg yolks, at room temperature

1 teaspoon Dijon mustard

salt and pepper

1½ tablespoons white wine vinegar

1¼ cups best olive oil, at room
*   temperature*

Place the egg yolks in a bowl, with the mustard, salt and pepper and 1 tablespoon of the vinegar. Beat the mixture until smooth.

Gradually add the oil, literally drop by drop, beating vigorously.

If the oil is added too quickly, the mayonnaise will separate. If this happens, place another egg yolk in a clean bowl and gradually add the separated mixture to the fresh egg yolk. If the mayonnaise is thickening too quickly, and there is still some oil to add, pour in a little more of the vinegar, and then continue to add oil. Adjust seasoning, adding a little more vinegar if necessary. Store 2–3 weeks in the refrigerator in a screw-top jar.

HOLLANDAISE SAUCE

Makes about 1¼ cups

INGREDIENTS

3 tablespoons white wine vinegar

5 peppercorns

1 bay leaf

8 tablespoons butter, cut into small
*   pieces*

2 egg yolks

a pinch of salt

Place the vinegar, peppercorns and bay leaf in a saucepan. Bring to the boil and reduce to 1 tablespoon. Reserve.

Place a small piece of butter, the size of a hazelnut, in a bowl, then add the egg yolks and salt and cream them together. Strain the vinegar into the yolk mixture and place in the top of a double boiler over simmering heat. Do not overheat the sauce or it will curdle.

Beat the mixture constantly until thick, adding the butter piece by piece. Do *not* boil the water in the bottom of the boiler.

Remove from the heat when sauce has thickened. Adjust the seasoning.

The sauce can be stored 1–2 days in the refrigerator, then warmed in the top of a double boiler, beating constantly. If the sauce curdles, beat in a teaspoon of boiling water, drop by drop. If still curdled, place an egg yolk in a clean bowl and slowly beat in the sauce.

RAGU (MEAT SAUCE)

Makes enough sauce for 1½ lb pasta

INGREDIENTS

4 tablespoons butter

1 tablespoon olive oil

1 garlic clove, crushed

½ cup chopped onion

6 bacon slices, chopped

½ cup chopped carrot

¼ cup chopped celery

½ lb lean ground beef

½ lb lean ground pork

2 oz chicken livers, chopped (¼ cup)

3 tablespoons tomato paste

¾ cup dry white wine

1 cup water

1 bay leaf

½ teaspoon oregano

salt and pepper

Melt the butter with the oil in a large saucepan and sauté the garlic, onion and bacon for 5 minutes. Add the carrot and celery and cook until softened.

Add the meat and liver and cook gently, stirring occasionally, until they begin to brown. Stir in the tomato paste and cook for 2 minutes before adding any liquid – this reduces the "raw" flavor of the tomato paste.

Add the wine, water, herbs and seasoning and bring to the boil. Cover and simmer for 1¼ hours, stirring occasionally and checking the amount of liquid from time to time. Add a little water if necessary.

Simmer for a few minutes. Serve with freshly cooked pasta.

Store for up to 2 days in the refrigerator. To freeze, place in a freezerproof container with ½-inch headspace and freeze for up to 3 months. Defrost overnight at room temperature or in a saucepan over gentle heat.

Variation

Melt 3 tablespoons butter and sauté 1 crushed garlic clove for 1 minute. Add 1 cup sliced mushrooms and cook gently for 5 minutes. Sprinkle with 1 tablespoon chopped parsley and add to the sauce at the end of the cooking time.

TOMATO SAUCE

Makes about 1¼ quarts

Heat the oil and sauté the garlic for 1 minute, stirring. Add the tomatoes and bring to the boil. Reduce the heat, cover and simmer for 15 minutes. Strain the tomatoes, using a soup ladle to push all the pulp through.

Return the pulp to the pan and simmer for 10 minutes, or until the sauce has reduced to the required consistency. Store for up to 2 weeks in the refrigerator or freeze for up to 3 months.

INGREDIENTS
5 tablespoons olive oil
3 garlic cloves, crushed
3 lb ripe tomatoes, quartered
2 teaspoons sugar
½ teaspoon salt

WALNUT SAUCE

Makes about 1½ cups

Place the pine nuts, garlic, parsley and salt in a mortar. Pound the ingredients with a pestle for 2 minutes, then add the walnuts. Pound until well blended, then add the cheese and water, incorporating these into the mixture. Gradually pour in the oil, and continue to pound the sauce until it is smooth and creamy.

Alternatively, place the pine nuts, garlic, parsley and salt in a blender or food processor. Mix until well blended, then add the cheese and water as above.

To store, cover and refrigerate for up to 2 days.

INGREDIENTS
3 tablespoons pine nuts
1 garlic clove, crushed
2 tablespoons chopped parsley
pinch of salt
1 cup ground walnuts
½ cup ricotta
1 teaspoon water
¼ cup olive oil
8 tablespoons butter (optional)
⅔ cup finely grated Parmesan cheese (optional)

PASTA DOUGH

Makes about 1½ lb

Sift the flour and salt onto a counter top or marble slab and make a well in the center. Pour the eggs into the well with the oil. Gradually incorporate the flour with the eggs and oil, until a dough has formed. Knead for 10 minutes. Wrap the dough in plastic wrap and rest for 1 hour.

If rolling the pasta in a machine, it is unnecessary to knead the dough for more than a minute or two, or to rest it. Lightly flour the pasta dough before passing it through the rollers. Use a ball of dough the size of an orange, set the adjustable rollers to the widest setting and gradually feed the dough through, until the desired thickness is reached. Cut into shapes (see below).

If making pasta by hand, take one ball of dough, the size of an orange, and cover the remainder until needed. On a lightly floured surface, roll out the dough until paper thin, then cut it into the desired shape (see below). Allow the pasta to dry for 30 minutes, by hanging it over a floured rack or chair back.

To cook the pasta, drop it into plenty of boiling salted water with a little vegetable oil, and cook until al dente, 2–3 minutes, depending on the shape.
Tagliatelle: Cut into ½-inch wide strips.
Lasagne: Cut into 4–6-inch wide strips.

INGREDIENTS
3 cups unbleached flour
1 teaspoon salt
4 eggs, lightly beaten
2 tablespoons olive oil

INDEX

ACKNOWLEDGEMENTS

The publishers would like to thank R. J. Brimacombe, R. B. Jakeman, M. H. Macrae,
J. R. A. Walker, A. P. Guyatt, Jenny O'Donoghue, Spencer Jacobs, Tim Dale,
Margaret Baber and the staff at Harrods for their invaluable assistance
and cooperation in the making of this book.

The publishers would also like to thank Beth Cox, Vera and Alfred
Chaney and Phaedra and Roxana Aslani.

Thanks also to Osborne and Little for wallpaper and fabrics for photography;
Range Rover courtesy of H. R. Owen.